2 SAMUEL

2 SAMUEL

2 SAMUEL

by
John M Riddle

JOHN RITCHIE LTD
CHRISTIAN PUBLICATIONS

40 Beansburn, Kilmarnock, Scotland

ISBN-13: 978 1 907731 92 1

Copyright © 2012 by John Ritchie Ltd.
40 Beansburn, Kilmarnock, Scotland

www.ritchiechristianmedia.co.uk

All rights reserved. No part of this publication may be reproduced, stored in a retrievable system, or transmitted in any form or by any other means – electronic, mechanical, photocopy, recording or otherwise – without prior permission of the copyright owner.

Typeset by John Ritchie Ltd., Kilmarnock
Printed by Bell & Bain Ltd., Glasgow

Contents

Preface	....	7
Introduction	....	9
Chapter 1	....	13
Chapter 2	....	22
Chapter 3	....	30
Chapter 4	....	39
Chapter 5	....	46
Chapter 6	....	56
Chapter 7	....	65
Chapter 8	....	74
Chapter 9	....	83
Chapter 10	....	91
Chapter 11	....	99
Chapter 12	....	108
Chapter 13	....	116
Chapter 14	....	126
Chapter 15	....	134
Chapter 16	....	144
Chapter 17	....	153
Chapter 18	....	162

2 Samuel

Chapter 19A	170
Chapter 19B	178
Chapter 20	186
Chapter 21	195
Chapter 22A	204
Chapter 22B	213
Chapter 23A	221
Chapter 23B	227
Chapter 24	234

Preface

This book represents the substance of Bible Class discussions on Friday evenings between August 2003 and September 2004 at Mill Lane Chapel, Cheshunt. As in the case of previous publications in this series, it does not purport to be a commentary in the usual sense of the word. In fact, as before, the original notes were written without any thought of publication.

It should be said that, like its predecessors, this book represents the contributions and observations of more than one person. A case could be made for adding a string of names to the name given on the front cover! At the same time, the named author gladly acknowledges that in all probability he has benefited more than any from these studies, not only in preparing for them, but from the considerable help received from fellow-members of the Bible Class. Let it be said again that there is great joy and satisfaction in working through a passage together.

We are advised that good physical health demands a wide range of different vitamins. For most people these are found in their ordinary meals, although some advocate 'additives' in one form or another. One thing is abundantly clear: the spiritual vitamins we need are all found in God's word, and 2 Samuel is a case in point. Put another way, we are to be "nourished up in the words of faith and good doctrine" (1 Tim 4.6). We certainly do not need 'additives' when it comes to spiritual health! We have "the faith which was once (once for all) delivered unto the saints" (Jude v.3).

The Bible Class at Cheshunt is indebted to John Ritchie Ltd for their willingness to publish its notes, and to Mr John Grant for kindly taking considerable time and trouble to edit the large quantities of material which appear on his computer, via a disc, from time to time. It was Mr Grant who first suggested that the Mill Lane Bible Studies should be circulated in book form.

2 Samuel

The man or woman who can say with the Psalmist, "O how I love thy law! It is my meditation all the day" will also say, with the same Psalmist, "I rejoice at thy word, as one that findeth great spoil" (Psalm 119.97, 162). There is certainly "great spoil" in 2 Samuel. Some of it was discovered at Cheshunt between August 2003 and September 2004, but keep looking. In the words of an old Sankey hymn, there is "always more to follow!"

John Riddle
Cheshunt, Hertfordshire
April 2013

Introduction

Read the whole book

We must commence our studies in 2 Samuel by repeating our introduction to 1 Samuel, where we reminded ourselves that "whatsoever things were written aforetime were written for our learning, that we through patience and comfort of the scriptures might have hope" (Rom 15.4). This puts Bible history into a class of its own. God has carefully selected and recorded those facts and events best suited to teach us valuable lessons. We can therefore expect to hear God speaking to us throughout 2 Samuel. We must say several things about the book in general.

1) The Name of the Book
Surprise, surprise! This is almost a word for word repetition of our introduction to 1 Samuel. In the Hebrew manuscripts, 1 & 2 Samuel form one book, and the same format applies to 1 & 2 Kings and 1 & 2 Chronicles. In the Septuagint translation of the Hebrew scriptures into Greek, made at Alexandria in the third century BC (the work actually commenced in BC280), 1 & 2 Samuel and 1 & 2 Kings are called the First, Second, Third, and Fourth Books of the Kingdoms. (It is called the "Septuagint" because, it is alleged, seventy scholars were involved in the translation). The word "Kingdoms" refers, of course, to the two kingdoms of Judah and Israel. The Latin Vulgate translation repeated the Septuagint division of Samuel and Kings into two books each, but called them the First, Second, Third, and Fourth Books of the Kings (not "Kingdoms"). This is the origin of the sub-titles to these four books in our Authorised Version. For example, under the title "The Second Book of Samuel", you will find, *"Otherwise called the Second Book of the Kings."*

2) The Authorship of the Book
The author of 2 Samuel is, of course, the Holy Spirit. After all, the Bible has only one author! We must bear this in mind when quoting J. Sidlow Baxter

here: "The authorship of Second Samuel is far from certain, though the likeliest indications still favour the older view that while Samuel himself is responsible for the first twenty-two chapters of the *first* of these two books which bear his name, the remaining chapters, to the end of Second Samuel are the work of the two prophets, Nathan and Gad." See 1 Chronicles 29.29-30, "Now the acts of David the king, first and last, behold they are written in the book of Samuel the seer, and in the book of Nathan the prophet, and in the book of Gad the seer, with all his reign and his might, and the times that went over him, and over Israel, and over all the kingdoms of the countries."

3) The Position of the Book
While 1 Samuel recounts "eventful history interwoven with the biographies of three colourful personalities, Samuel, Saul, and David" (J.Sidlow Baxter, *Explore the Book)*, 2 Samuel describes the period of David's reign over Israel. 1 Samuel therefore describes the **rejection** of God's anointed king, and 2 Samuel the **reign** of God's anointed king. The book commences with his reign over Judah, and concludes with his old age. This was approximately thirty-nine years. (BC 1056 - 1017). His actual death is recorded in 1 Kings. David reigned for forty years. See 2 Samuel 5.4-5, "And David was thirty years old when he began to reign, and he reigned forty years. In Hebron he reigned over Judah seven years and six months; and in Jerusalem he reigned thirty and three years over all Israel and Judah." See also 2 Kings 2.11. Under his leadership, Israel became a dominant world-power. "The fame of David went out into all lands; and the Lord brought the fear of him upon all nations" (1 Chron 14.17). This leads to:

4) The Promise of the Book
The covenant with David is recorded in chapter 7.8-17. "Thine house and thy kingdom shall be established for ever before thee: thy throne shall be established for ever" (v.16). The covenant was confirmed by an oath; see Psalm 89.34-37. As C. I. Scofield points out, there was one condition: "disobedience in the family would be visited with chastisement, but **not** to the abrogation of the covenant." The promise to David will be fulfilled by the Lord Jesus, of whom it was said, "for unto us a child is born, unto us a son is given: and the government shall be upon his shoulder: and his name shall be called Wonderful, Counsellor, The mighty God, The everlasting Father, The Prince of Peace. Of the increase of his government and peace there shall be no end, upon the throne of David, and upon his kingdom, to order it, and to establish it with judgment and

with justice from henceforth even for ever. The zeal of the Lord of hosts will perform this" (Is 9.6-7). Centuries later, in fulfilment of this prophecy, Mary was told: "Behold, thou shalt conceive in thy womb, and bring forth a son, and shalt call his name JESUS. He shall be great, and shall be called the Son of the Highest: and the Lord God shall give unto him the throne of his father David: and he shall reign over the house of Jacob for ever; and of his kingdom there shall be no end" (Lk 1.31-33). He is David's Lord, yet David's son (Mt 22.41-46): He is "the root and offspring of David" (Rev 22.16). He is at present rejected, but He will reign! He will reign as "King of kings, and Lord of lords."

5) The Plan of the Book

Once again, J. Sidlow Baxter sets out the plan of 2 Samuel with admirable clarity. "This second book of Samuel, as Matthew Henry is quick to observe, falls into two main parts. Alas, there is no mistaking it. David's great sin, recorded in Chapter 11, marks the sad divide, right in the middle of the book, and right in the middle of David's forty years' reign, for it falls about the end of his first twenty years. Up to this point all goes triumphantly for David; but after this there are ugly knots and tangles, grievous blows and tragic trials. In the first part we see David's triumphs. In the second part, we mourn David's troubles." Bearing this in mind, the general outline of the book can be set out as follows. We must remember, of course, that any general analysis does not cover **all** the subject matter!

A) David's Triumphs, Chapters 1-10

King over Judah only, at Hebron	Chapters 1-4	(Civil War Period: 7 years)
King over all Israel, at Jerusalem	Chapters 5-10	(Conquest period: 13 years)

B) David's Tragedy, Chapters 11-12

One verse says it all: "David did that which was right in the eyes of the Lord, and turned not aside from anything that he commanded him all the days of his life, **save only** in the matter of Uriah the Hittite" (1 Kings 15.5)

C) David's Troubles, Chapters 13-24

David's troubles in his family	Chapters 13-19	(Amnon's sin to Absolom's revolt)
David's troubles in the nation	Chapters 20-24	(Sheba's revolt to the Pestilence)

2 Samuel

The book ends with reference to an altar. "And David built there (the threshing floor of Araunah, or Ornan, the Jebusite) an altar unto the Lord, and offered burnt-offerings and peace-offerings. So the Lord was intreated for the land, and the plague was stayed from Israel" (24.25). The place was most significant. See 2 Chronicles 3.1, "Then Solomon began to build the house of the Lord at Jerusalem in **mount Moriah**, where the Lord appeared unto David his father, in the place that David had prepared in the threshingfloor of Ornan the Jebusite."

Doesn't this remind us that we have very good reason to thank God for the final sacrifice of the Lord Jesus, who has met God's claims against us, and delivered us from "the wages of sin?" (Rom 6.23).

CHAPTER 1.1-28

"How are the mighty fallen"

1 Samuel concludes with the death of Saul on Mount Gilboa, and 2 Samuel commences by repeating the sad story. There are, however, at least two important differences.

i) 1 Samuel 31 simply describes the defeat of Israel by the Philistines, with the death of Saul and his three sons. The writer gives us the bare facts. 2 Samuel 1 tells us how **David reacted** when the news reached him. It is impossible to tell whether the battle at Gilboa occurred before or after the return of David to Ziklag (quite possibly they took place at the same time), but God **does** want us to know how David received the report of Saul's death. When the Bible doesn't give precise information, or any relevant information at all, we can be sure that the lessons He wants us to learn lie somewhere else! So there's really no profit in speculating about something that God has withheld from us, but great profit in concentrating on what He **has** told us! "The secret things belong unto the Lord our God: but those things which are revealed belong unto us and to our children for ever" (Deut 29.29).

ii) 1 Samuel tells us how Saul died, and 2 Samuel 1 tells how the Amalekite **said** he died. The stories are quite different. When the Bible appears to give conflicting information, we must not assume that the differences arise from inaccuracy. God's word does not, and cannot, contradict itself. We will deal with the differences in the two reports later, but what was an Amalekite doing in the camp of Saul anyway? He identifies himself as "the son of a stranger, an Amalekite" (v.13), which means, according to Keil & Delitzsch, that he was the son of an Amalekite who had emigrated to Israel. Perhaps he was a foreign mercenary in Saul's army. If this was the case, and we cannot speak with certainty, then it is another indication of Saul's weakness, and also explains why he went straight to David with Saul's crown and bracelet. If he had served in Saul's army, or lived for any time in Israel for that matter, he would have certainly heard of David! It must be significant that the man who carried the news of Saul's death to David, belonged to a nation that he should have "utterly destroyed" (1 Sam 15.3).

Very clearly, the chapter can be divided into two main sections: **(1)** David learns of the death of Saul and Jonathan (vv.1-16). **(2)** David laments the death of Saul and Jonathan (vv.17-27).

1) David Learns of the Death of Saul and Jonathan (vv.1-16)
It must be significant that having "returned from the slaughter of the Amalekites" (v.1), David learns of the slaughter of Israel (v.4). David was victorious over **his** enemies, and Saul was defeated by **his** enemies. This brings us to the first of four matters for consideration in this section. They are **(A)** The defeat of Israel (vv.1-4); **(B)** The death of Saul (vv.5-10); **(C)** The desolation of David (vv.11-12); **(D)** The death of the Amalekite (vv.13-16).

A) The defeat of Israel, (vv.1-4)
"And David said unto him (the Amalekite), How went the matter? I pray thee, tell me. And he answered, That the people are fled from the battle, and many of the people also are fallen and dead; and Saul and Jonathan his son are dead also" (v.4). God's people had been defeated! They had not been defeated by an unknown foe, but by "the auld enemy." During our studies in 1 Samuel, we noticed that the Philistines never "waved the white flag", and surrendered. They were defeated time and time again, but they kept coming back, and now they inflict a devastating defeat on Israel. Whilst this is not the end of the story, for David ultimately "smote and subdued" them (2 Sam 8.1), we must not forget the lesson here. Our spiritual enemies do not "take time off". They are always there. The hymn-writer puts it like this:

> My foes are ever near me,
> Around me and within.

Israel's defeat was not "a quirk of fate", and it cannot be attributed to "the fortunes of war." Israel was defeated because of sin. This is always the case. Disobedience saps our spiritual strength, and makes us easy prey to our enemies. We must remember, too, that our personal conduct affects other people. One individual's immorality at Corinth brought disrepute on the whole assembly: "It is reported commonly that there is fornication among you" (1 Cor 5.1). Other people become involved in the affect of our personal disobedience.

This is particularly true in the case of spiritual leaders. The defeat of Israel was a solemn indictment of Saul's sin and misrule, which reminds us that "the nation never rose higher than its king, nor will assemblies rise higher than their leaders." A. McShane *(Lessons for Leaders)*. James makes it very clear that leaders amongst God's people carry great responsibility: "My brethren, be not many masters (teachers), knowing that we shall receive the greater condemnation" (Jas 3.1). If you aspire to leadership, remember that "unto whomsoever much is given, of him shall be much required" (Lk 12.48).

B) The death of Saul (vv.5-10)
We dealt with this in studying 1 Samuel 31.1-6. Here is the relevant part of the passage: "Then said Saul to his armour-bearer, Draw thy sword, and thrust me through...But his armour-bearer would not; for he was sore afraid. Therefore Saul took a sword and fell upon it, And when his armour-bearer saw that Saul was dead, he fell likewise upon his sword, and died with him" (vv.3-5). This is corroborated by another historian in 1 Chronicles 10.4-5, but the Amalekite had a different story. Here is the relevant part of **his** report to David: "And he said unto me again, Stand, I pray thee upon me, and slay me: for anguish is come upon me, because my life is yet whole in me. So I stood upon him, and slew him, because I was sure that he could not live after that he was fallen" (2 Sam 2.9-10). So which of the two reports do we believe? Without repeating our previous study in detail, it does seem more than likely that the Amalekite was somewhat "economical with the truth" in order to extract a reward from David. This is confirmed in 2 Samuel 4.10. The subject is treated more extensively in our notes on 1 Samuel 31. Perhaps a little revision will help here!

Leaving aside the details, Saul died in defeat. He could not say like his erstwhile namesake, "I am now ready to be offered, and the time of my departure is at hand. I have fought a good fight, I have finished my course, I have kept the faith: henceforth there is laid up for me a crown of righteousness" (2 Tim 4.6-8). Saul, the son of Kish, died in disgrace and lost his crown. Saul of Tarsus died in honour, and gained a crown! C.H. Spurgeon, who must have attended countless deathbeds, once said, "Our people die well." Solomon put it like this, "A good name is better than precious ointment; and the day of death than the day of one's birth" (Eccl 7.1).

2 Samuel

C) The desolation of David (vv.11-12)
"Then David took hold on his clothes, and rent them; and likewise all the men that were with him: And they mourned, and wept, and fasted until even, for Saul, and for Jonathan his son, and for the people of the LORD, and for the house of Israel; because they were fallen by the sword."

There was nothing cosmetic about David's sorrow. He certainly did not rejoice in the death of the man of whom he said, "the king of Israel is come out to seek a flea, as when one doth hunt a partridge in the mountains" (1 Sam 26.20). There was not even grim satisfaction that his own words had been fulfilled: "As the LORD liveth, the LORD shall smite him; or his day shall come to die; or he shall descend into battle, and perish" (1 Sam 26.10). This reminds us of Proverbs 24.17), "Rejoice not when thine enemy falleth, and let not thine heart be glad when he stumbleth". David's genuine sorrow arose:

i) From the death of Saul and Jonathan. He "mourned...**for Saul, and for Jonathan."** It was no comfort to him that he had been vindicated, and that the way was now clear for him to ascend the throne. When God's people get into trouble, it is all too easy to gleefully say (although we try to cover it up), "I told you so!". The decline and defeat of God's people should cause ***us*** distress.

ii) From the death of God's people. He "mourned...for the **people of the LORD."** This is how David saw them. Not as "followers of Saul", but as "the people of the LORD." These were not ordinary people. They were the **Lord's** people. They were precious to Him. How do ***we*** see our fellow-Christians?

iii) From the disgrace on the nation. He "mourned...for the **house of Israel."** Israel means "a prince with God", for it was said to Jacob, "Thy name shall be called no more Jacob, but Israel: for as a prince hast thou power with God and with men, and hast prevailed" (Gen 32.28). But it didn't look much like that now! How much are we concerned about the testimony of God's people in the eyes of the world?

D) The death of the Amalekite (vv.13-16)
The execution of the Amalekite, in the circumstances, is not without difficulty. F. Gardiner *(Ellicott's Commentary)* resolves the problem by saying, "It does not matter whether he (David) fully believed his story or not, the man must be judged by his own account of himself." Keil & Delitzsch quote another

writer: "If thou hast done it, thou receivest the just reward of thy deeds. If thou hast not done it, then throw the blame on thine own lying testimony, and be content with the wages of a wicked flatterer; for, according to thine own confession, thou art the murderer of a king, and that is quite enough to betray thine evil heart" As A. McShane observes, "On his own confession, he had slain the Lord's anointed, and had therefore done what David himself would not do, had he been in similar circumstances, for he had said, "Who can stretch forth his hand against the Lord's anointed, and be guiltless?" (1 Sam 26. 9). Like Doeg, who slew the priests (1 Sam 22.6-19), his confession demonstrated that he had no respect for the anointing oil." We must leave it there.

2) David Laments the Death of Saul and Jonathan (vv.17-27)

These verses contain David's elegy on the death of Saul and Jonathan. "It is an inspired natural song, and makes no reference to God, or to religious sentiment, but is purely a composition viewing the departed from a human standpoint...It is a pity when only natural, and not spiritual, virtues of those who are dead can be recalled." (A. McShane). What will people recall about **us?**

Notice, too, that David omits all reference to Saul's failures. He didn't want people to remember Saul's shortcomings, and in particular his animosity to him personally. When future generations read the "book of Jasher" (v.18), they would find nothing but good about their first king and his son. Now there's another lesson for us. Some people seem to delight in recalling the failures of others, even after their death David certainly didn't gloat over Saul's inglorious departure.

The elegy is introduced with the words, "And David lamented with this lamentation over Saul and over Jonathan his son: (Also he bade them teach the children of Judah *the use* of the bow: behold, it is written in the book of Jasher)" (vv.17-18). The italicised words should be omitted, and the sense of the verse is conveyed in the translation, "he bade them teach the children of Judah (the song of) the bow" (JND). The song was given the title, "the bow." Presumably, it was included in "the book of Jasher" under this title. Keil and Delitzsch suggest that it was called "the bow" *(kesheth)* "not only because the bow is referred to in v.22, but because it is a martial ode, and the bow was one of the principal weapons used by the warriors of that age, and one in the use of which the Benjaminites, the tribe-mates of Saul, were particularly skilful." See, for example, 1 Chronicles 8.40; 12.2; 2 Chronicles

2 Samuel

17.7. The "book of Jasher" (meaning "upright" or "righteous") is only mentioned here and in Joshua 10 v.13. It is usually regarded as a collection of national odes. It evidently chronicled outstanding events in Israel's military history, and is generally thought to be the same as "the book of the wars of the Lord" (Num 21.4).

The elegy, ode, or dirge (whatever you want to call it!) refers **(A)** To the death of Saul and Jonathan (vv.19-22), and **(B)** to the lives of Saul and Jonathan (vv.23-27). The words, "how are the mighty fallen" occur three times (vv.19,25,27), and introduce what Keil & Delizsch call "three strophes." (The word "strophe" comes from a Greek word meaning "turning", so three turns or divisions will do nicely!) The first "strophe" (vv.19-24) commemorates the virtues of Saul and Jonathan, the second (vv.25-26) commemorates the friendship between David and Jonathan, and the third (v.27) "simply utters the last sigh, with which the elegy becomes silent."

A) Their death (vv.19-22)
David begins: "The beauty of Israel is slain upon thy high places: how are the mighty fallen!" (v.19). The word rendered "beauty" *(tsebi)* also means "gazelle." (AV "roe" or "roebuck"). The gazelle is certainly a beautiful animal. Some commentators say that it is used here in the sense of "ornament," and quote Ezekiel 7.20 in support: "As for the beauty of his ornament, he set it in majesty." The "high places" refer to Gilboa. An ornament enhances appearance, and it does seem that David is referring to Saul and Jonathan in this way. They were "the ornament of Israel." How well do we represent the Lord's people? How well do we represent the Lord? Paul urged converted slaves to "adorn the doctrine of God our Saviour in all things" (Tit 2.10). Let's notice the following:

i) The disaster was not to be publicised. "Tell it not in Gath, publish it not in the streets of Askelon; lest the daughters of the Philistines rejoice, lest the daughters of the uncircumcised triumph" (v.20). The Philistines didn't need a news-flash from Israel anyway!

But this does remind us that we must be very careful what we say about each other, and about assembly matters, in the presence of unsaved people. Paul censured the assembly at Corinth for the way in which they were "washing their dirty linen in public". "Brother goeth to law with brother, and that before the **unbelievers**" (1 Cor 6.6). Abram's herdmen and Lot's herdmen didn't get on at all well. That was bad enough, but the Bible adds, "and the Canaanite and the Perizzite dwelled then in the land" (Gen 13.7). You can almost see them watching and listening!

However aggrieved you might be over some injustice or wrong, do not talk about it to non-Christians. In fact, don't talk about it to other Christians if non-Christians are present. (It is sometimes good policy not even to talk about it to other Christians!) There are plenty of people about who would love an opportunity to disparage our testimony, and we must not give them the necessary ammunition. Remember, too, that little ears flap at meal tables, and if something critical is said about another believer by the adults, you can be sure that the children will soak it up like blotting paper! If you can't say anything good about someone in ordinary conversation, it is best not to say anything at all. Do notice the contrast between the "daughters of the uncircumcised", and the "daughters of Israel" (v.24).

ii) The disaster was to be solemnly remembered. "Ye mountains of Gilboa, let there be no dew, neither let there be rain upon you, nor fields of offerings: for there the shield of the mighty is vilely (or, "as defiled") cast away, the shield of Saul, as though he had not been anointed with oil" (v.21). Gilboa was to be a place of perpetual mourning. It is, of course, strong poetical language. The barrenness of Gilboa was to be a kind of war memorial. On a technical note, the expression "fields of offerings" refers to the provision of the "first-fruits" as offerings to God. On another technical note, the words, "for there the shield of the mighty is vilely cast away, the shield of Saul, as though he had not been anointed with oil", are better rendered "for there the shield of the mighty was vilely cast away, The shield of Saul (as) not anointed with oil" (JND). According to F. Gardiner, "It was customary to oil metal shields, as well as those of wood and leather, for their preservation, and the idea here is that Saul's shield was thrown away uncared for." He had no further use for it: his fighting days were over.

Whilst David referred to the barrenness of mount Gilboa as a memorial to a fallen hero, we must make a practical application. We should not live in the past, but we ought to learn the lessons of the past. If we do not learn from our own mistakes, and the mistakes of other people, it is highly likely that we will repeat them! Our personal defeats should flash like warning lights. Remember, defeat brings barrenness. How glad we should be that God makes provision for restoration and recovery, but only on repentance and confession.

iii) The disaster was not to erase memory of past victories. "From the blood of the slain, from the fat of the mighty, the bow of Jonathan turned not back, and the sword of Saul returned not empty" (v.22). If this part of the elegy was to remind Israel that defeat at Gilboa must not make them forget the better days, then it has the same message for us. Sometimes we remember people's failures and blunders, and completely forget their virtues and successes. Sadly, we often remember the last thing that someone said or did! It is possible, however, that David is telling us here that Jonathan and Saul were valiant to the end, and that they died fighting.

B) Their lives (vv.23-27)
David speaks about Saul and Jonathan together (v.23), then about Saul alone (v.24), and then about Jonathan alone (vv.25-26).

i) Saul and Jonathan. "Saul and Jonathan were lovely (people to be loved, or amiable) and pleasant (agreeable, affectionate or kind) in their lives, and in their death they were not divided: they were swifter than eagles, they were stronger than lions." We would have said that Jonathan was "lovely and pleasant" in his life, and, perhaps, tactfully omitted all reference to Saul. But not David! He "forgets all the injury that Saul has inflicted upon him, so that he only brings out and celebrates the more amiable aspects of his character" (Keil & Delitzsch). He remembers the best about them personally, their loyalty to each other (it wasn't always like that: sometimes there was mutual hostility), and their prowess in battle. Only the grace of God could enable David to write like this! A. McShane understands that the words, "swifter than eagle...stronger than lions", refer to their agility and vigour. Could anything like this be truthfully said of ***us?*** Are ***we*** "lovely and pleasant" people? Can others see that ***we*** are "striving together for the faith of the gospel?" (Phil 1.27) Are ***we*** quick and vigorous in the Lord's service?

ii) Saul alone. "Ye daughters of Israel, weep over Saul, who clothed you in scarlet, with other delights, who put on ornaments of gold upon your apparel." This refers to the spoils of war which Saul brought to the nation. His victories are recorded in 1 Samuel 14.47-48. The "daughters of Israel" once rejoiced over the victories of Saul and David (1 Sam 18.6-7), but those days were over. It was time to "weep." Do people "weep" over ***us?*** Perhaps we once gave people cause for great joy, and they benefited from our fellowship and help, but now they look at our spiritual decline, and weep. Does it have to be said of us, "Ye did run well; who did hinder you that ye should not obey the truth?" (Gal 5.7).

iii) Jonathan alone. "I am distressed for thee, my brother Jonathan: very pleasant hast thou been unto me: thy love to me was wonderful, passing the love of women." David looked back, and remembered their first encounter: "And it came to pass, when he had made an end of speaking unto Saul, that the soul of Jonathan was knit with the soul of David, and Jonathan loved him as his own soul" (1 Sam 18.1). He expressed his love for David by giving him his "robe…and his garments, even to his sword, and to his bow, and to his girdle." He did this voluntarily. David did not put pressure on him. Jonathan did it because he loved David. Can we say to the Lord Jesus, like Peter, "Lord, thou knowest all things; thou knowest that I love thee" (Jn 20.17). Can He look, with pleasure, on our love for Him? Can He look with pleasure on our love for each other? (1 Jn 5.1).

CHAPTER 2.1-32

"They anointed David king over the house of Judah"

Approximately seven years lie between David's anointing by Samuel (1 Sam 16.13) and his anointing by the men of Judah (2 Sam 2.4). They were difficult years for David, to put it mildly! But God does not revoke his promises. "Fill thine horn with oil, and go, I will send thee to Jesse the Beth-lehemite: for I have provided me a king among his sons." His eldest brother, Eliab, didn't see it like that, and accused him of boyish curiosity when he arrived with supplies at the army headquarters (1 Sam 17.28). Saul didn't see it like that, and relentlessly pursued David so that he cried, "the king of Israel is come out to seek a flea, as when one doth hunt a partridge in the mountains." (1 Sam 26.20). Achish, king of Gath, didn't see it like that either. He thought David was mad on one occasion (1 Sam 21.14) and an asylum-seeker on another! (1 Sam 27.12). Jonathan was different. He did believe that David would be king. See 1 Samuel 23.17.

We now begin to see the fulfilment of God's promise, and this reminds us that God will fulfil His promise to Christ: "Sit thou at my right hand, until I make thine enemies thy footstool. The Lord shall send the rod of thy strength out of Zion: rule thou in the midst of thine enemies" (Ps 110.1-2). To the majority of people, this looks highly unlikely, and the very idea is greeted with unbelief and contempt. Thank God that we can be like Jonathan, and say, "Thou shalt be king!" In this chapter, David is anointed "king over the house of Judah", and in chapter 5, he is anointed "king over Israel" (v.4).

We can divide the chapter as follows: **(1)** The division in the nation (vv.1-11); **(2)** The defeat of Israel (vv.12-17); **(3)** The death of Asahel (vv.18-23); **(4)** The decision of Joab (vv.24-32).

1) The Division of the Nation (vv.1-11)
The north/south divide lasted for seven and a half years (2 Sam 5.5), and

Chapter 2

the difference between the two is painfully obvious. We must notice the reign of David in Hebron (vv.1-7) and the reign of Ish-bosheth, Saul's son, in Mahanaim (vv.8-11).

A) David's reign over Judah in Hebron (vv.1-7)
As we can expect, there are valuable lessons everywhere here! We must never forget that "whatsoever things were written aforetime were written for our learning, that we through patience and comfort of the scriptures might have hope" (Rom 15.4). Yes, we do keep on quoting this verse! It reminds us that there is no "baggage" in the Old Testament. So, "pay attention!" We mustn't miss the lessons God wants us to learn!

i) His arrival in Hebron (vv.1-3).
Let's start by saying that David did not assert his right to the throne. He was not an opportunist. He could have said, "I've been waiting all this time, and now it's quite obvious that the time has come. There's no point in delaying. After all, it is God's will that I should be king!" He didn't just "turn up" in Hebron. He waited God's time, and asked God for guidance. Not once, but twice. "Shall I go up to any of the cities of Judah?...Whither shall I go up?" As A. McShane observes, "Former days had taught him the value of the will of God, so he made enquiries as to his movements, and God graciously granted to him the light he sought." Let's remember that favourable circumstances are not in themselves a reliable guide. Everything seemed to be working out well for Jonah, but it wasn't God's will for him to flee to Tarshish! We must ask God for guidance, and wait for Him to show us His will.

When God answered, David raised no objection, and made no delay: "So David went up thither." Simple, isn't it? David acted as soon as he knew God's will for him. Perhaps **we** don't always find it quite so simple! We do like to "do our own thing!" But "to obey is better than sacrifice, and to hearken than the fat of rams" (1 Sam 15.22). Do remember that there can be no progress in the Christian life unless we obey God's word. We are to be "obedient children" (1 Pet 1.14).

Notice too that everybody was involved: "his two wives also...and his men that were with him did David bring up, every man with his household: and they dwelt in the cities of Hebron." During the difficult and dangerous years of exile, God had wonderfully preserved David and his men, together with their families, and they removed intact to Hebron. This also reminds us that we must act in fellowship with each other, and "stand fast in one spirit, with one mind striving together for the faith of the gospel" (Phil 1.27). Do notice that God told them to go to Hebron. According to Gesenius, Hebron means "joining". Scofield says it means "alliance". Most preachers say that it means "fellowship!" As you can see, there's not much difference in the three meanings! It's nice to be "in fellowship", isn't it? That means fellowship with God, and fellowship with each other (1 Jn 1.3). That's the place to be! Hebron is first mentioned in Genesis 13.8. "Then Abram removed his tent, and came and dwelt in the plain of Mamre, which is in Hebron, and built there an altar unto the Lord." He was certainly in fellowship with God!

ii) His anointing by Judah (v.4). This was not the complete fulfilment of God's word to Samuel, and it is sad to notice that he was not recognised by the remaining tribes. As we shall see, the enthronement of Ish-bosheth over Israel brought sad consequences. Let's say that our failure to recognise the undisputed and unrivalled reign of Christ in our lives will have the same result. However, it is at least encouraging to see that David enjoyed the confidence of his own tribe. Doesn't this remind us that we can hardly expect support from further afield if people on "our own patch" can't see anything worth recognising!

iii) His approval of Jabesh-Gilead (vv.5-7). While David took the opportunity to announce his reign over Judah (perhaps he was an opportunist here: it does appear that Ish-bosheth had not yet been proclaimed king over Israel), the men of Jabesh-Gilead must have been rather surprised to receive David's commendation! After all, he had been persecuted by Saul for years. A. McShane has a nice piece here: "The principle of conciliating former enemies appears in all David's dealings at this time. He has learned that there is no point in perpetuating opposition if by any means peace can be obtained. Perhaps it takes more wisdom than most think to know how to deal with those who have formerly been our persecutors and antagonists, for it often proves to be beneficial to all if the past can be forgotten and enemies made friends." These are wise words.

Notice that David's message was more than a common courtesy. "Blessed be ye of **the Lord**...now **the Lord** shew kindness and truth unto you: and I also will requite this kindness, because ye have done this thing." It was a prayer for their blessing. Compare Paul's prayer for Onesiphorus (2 Tim 1.16-18).

Chapter 2

B) Ish-bosheth's reign over Israel in Mahanaim (vv.8-11)
Mahaniam means "two hosts" (Gen 32.2), and Abner and Ish-bosheth soon fell out, with disastrous results (see 3.8-11). David and his men were "one host!"

The enthronement of Ish-bosheth was remarkably different to the enthronement of David. There's not a word about guidance from God. The interests of the "family" took precedence over God's will. Abner was Saul's cousin (1 Sam 14.50-51). He was the power behind the throne. It was a case of "keep it in the family." It's called "nepotism." A lot of people were killed as a result of this, including Abner himself, and a lot of damage has been done amongst God's people because "blood is thicker than water." Abner wanted to build a dynasty, and perpetuate the rule of the house of Saul, although he evidently knew about God's promise to David. (See 3.9 & 18). Let's remember that we are not here to make a name for ourselves, but to bring honour and pleasure to God.

> Not I, but Christ, be honoured, loved, exalted;
> Not I, but Christ, be seen, be known, be heard;
> Not I, but Christ, in every look and action;
> Not I , but Christ, in every thought and word.
> Frances E Bolton

Some people see a little technical problem in the words, "Ish-bosheth...reigned **two years**." Since David was recognised as king over all Israel after the death of Ishbosheth (5.1), that is, after reigning for seven and a half years over Judah, we can assume that he was not made king by Abner at the same time as David. Some five years elapsed before this took place. Mahanaim was on the eastern side of the Jordan. Incidentally, Ish-bosheth means "man of shame." He started life as Esh-baal (1 Chron 8.33, 9.39). Esh-baal means "fire of Baal." As Keil and Delitzsch observe, this is probably equivalent to "destroyer of Baal." We could say that anyone who rivals God's anointed King, is a "man of shame." Is it possible for us to be "men of shame?" Think about it!

It's significant that as soon as God's purpose for David begins to reach fulfilment, a rival appears. This reminds us that when spiritual progress is made, opposition is inevitable.

2) The Defeat of Israel (vv.12-17)
It gets worse! As you can see, Abner representing Ish-bosheth, and Joab,

representing David, sat on opposite sides of "the pool of Gibeon", some five or six miles north-west of Jerusalem. According to F. Gardiner (Ellicott's Commentary), "the pool of Gibeon" was "a large reservoir or tank, arranged to store the overflow from a subterranean reservoir fed by a spring in the rocky hill-side. Its ruins still remain (this was written a long time ago!), about 120 feet long by 100 broad." Instead of an all-out battle, twelve soldiers from each of the two sides fought each other to decide the issue. It certainly merited the name, Helkath-hazzurim, meaning "the field of sharp edges." All twenty four died in the combat! The AV calls it playing! The word means "to joke or play", and is used here to denote the war-play of single combat" (Keil and Delitzsch). The failure to decide the issue was followed by the all-out battle that Abner had tried to avoid, and Israel was defeated by David's men.

What a waste of young life! Twenty-four young men died, and two older men, who should have known better, let it happen. There is an important lesson for elders here.

Whilst there is such a thing as "friendly rivalry", the rivalry between Judah and Israel was far from friendly. Rivals like this inevitably fight, with disastrous results. It all happened because God's anointed king was not recognised throughout the nation. If only all Israel had bowed to the will of God! But then, if only **we** bowed at all times to the will of God and the word of God! We must learn from this. The church at Corinth sorely needed to learn the lesson. Just look at the internal strife there: "everyone of you saith, I am of Paul; and I of Apollos; and I of Cephas; and I of Christ" (1 Cor 1.12). Notice the big "I" here. John the Baptist said, "He must increase, but I must decrease" (Jn 3.30). Now the "I" is in the right place!

The churches in Galatia were also engaged in "civil war": "but if ye bite and devour one another, take heed that ye be not consumed one of another" (Gal 5.15). Once again, A. McShane has a telling comment. "It was sad enough to witness the Philistines destroying the nation, but sadder still to see the two parts of the kingdom devouring each other." It is equally sad when God's people do the same today. Needless to say, the Lord was not consulted in all this. David "enquired of the Lord", but neither Joab nor Abner followed his example.

3) The Death of Asahel (vv.18-23)
Asahel was one of three brothers: Joab, Abishai, and Asahel (v.18). Their

mother, Zeruiah, was David's sister. See 1 Chronicles 2.16. As we shall see, David was not impressed by his nephews: "these men the sons of Zeruiah be too hard for me" (3.39). Once again, there are some important lessons for us here. Speaking generally, when God's people are divided, someone gets hurt. In this case, a young man is lost to the nation. If you are spoiling for a fight with another Christian, do remember the effect on the assembly. The testimony will be weakened. We cannot afford loss of personnel in this way. Now notice the following:

i) Asahel did not consult the Lord. Unlike David, who faced Goliath with the assurance of divine help, Asahel pursued Abner in his own strength. Sadly, some people are so absorbed in achieving their objectives that they never stop to think about the will of God. If you are intent on pursuing something or somebody to the bitter end, please stop and pray. Do you really think that it is God's will for you to relentlessly hunt one of His people?

ii) Asahel did not use wisdom. He had plenty of youthful energy, and eventually overtook the older man, but that was as far as it went. His zeal was unquestionable, but it was "not according to knowledge" (Rom 10.2). Courage and enthusiasm are excellent qualities, and we all need more of them, but they must be combined with sound judgement. Asahel completely underestimated the strength and experience of Abner. This does not imply that we should never venture against superior odds. Israel was told that the seven nations of Canaan were "greater and mightier than thou", but they were also told that "the Lord thy God shall deliver them before thee" (Deut 7.1-2). We can rest with assurance that "greater is he that is in you, than he that is in the world" (1 Jn 4.4) but this does not mean that we can tackle anything without prayerful consideration and reflection. We must always "count the cost." See Luke 14.26-33.

iii) Asahel did not heed warnings. Let's be fair to Abner. He did try to spare Asahel, and eventually killed him in self-defence. It was not a cold-blooded murder. He even told Asahel to pick on someone else! See v.21. But to no avail. He was determined to seize the biggest prize of all, and lost his life as a result. Let's face it, God **does** warn us. Haven't you heard His voice when danger threatens, and you are tempted to disobey Him? A Bible verse flashes into your mind, or part of someone's sermon suddenly stirs in your memory. Asahel "refused to turn aside: wherefore Abner with the hinder end of the spear smote him under the fifth rib (we would say, 'in the abdomen'), that the spear came out behind him; and he fell down there,

2 Samuel

and died in the same place." On a technical note, the "hinder end of the spear" was sharpened so that it could be stuck in the ground. See 1 Samuel 26.7. As we shall see, Joab avenged his brother's death, to David's sorrow, by killing Abner in cold blood.

4) The Decision of Joab (vv.24-32)
The death of Asahel did not deter his two brothers. Joab and Abishai "pursued after Abner: and the sun went down when they came to the hill of Ammah, that lieth before Giah by the way of the wilderness of Gibeon." At long last, however, wisdom prevailed, but not until Abner and Joab had blamed each other for the conflict. That's still true to life, isn't it? Even amongst God's people. Sadly, it is not unknown for believers to blame each other for discord, with neither side admitting that they are wrong.

A) The wisdom of Abner (vv.25-26)
"Then Abner called to Joab, and said, Shall the sword devour for ever? Knowest thou not that it will be bitterness in the latter end? How long shall it be then, ere thou bid the people return from following their brethren?" As you can see, Abner placed responsibility firmly in Joab's court! Even so, he had a point. We do well to weigh Abner's question, "Shall the sword devour for ever?" As A. McShane observes, "Irrespective of who wins, the losses can never be replaced. Satan ever seeks to stir up strife in the assemblies of the saints, and where he succeeds there will always be bitter results." In this case, Judah lost twenty men, including Asahel, and Israel lost three hundred and sixty. If you are tempted to either commence or continue a row with a fellow-believer, sit down, count the cost, and leave the matter in the Lord's hands. If you have a just cause, He will vindicate you. If you haven't, He will make it clear to you. But, either way, commit it to Him.

2 Samuel chapters 1-3 each contain a crucial question, and it does seem that they are included to concentrate the mind on important issues. So: "How wast thou not afraid to stretch forth thine hand to destroy the Lord's anointed?" (1.14). "Shall the sword devour for ever" (2.26). "Died Abner as a fool dieth?" (3.33).

B) The wisdom of Joab (vv.27-29)
"And Joab said, As God liveth, unless thou hadst spoken, surely then in the morning the people had gone up every one from following his brother." Now it is Joab's turn, and he placed responsibility firmly in Abner's court! However, he appeared to take Abner's remarks on board: "So Joab blew a trumpet,

and all the people stood still, and pursued after Israel no more, neither fought they any more." So far so good. But Joab didn't let it rest there. He nursed a bitter grievance against Abner, and when the opportunity came, he killed him. Sometimes impressive words and actions hide a hard heart. On a technical note (yet again), Joab's charge, "unless thou hadst spoken, surely then in the morning the people had gone up every one from following his brother", probably refer to Abner's suggestion that the young men should engage in single combat.

Do notice that both Abner and Joab refer to Judah and Israel as "brethren" (vv.26-27). This highlights the great lesson of the chapter. "Brethren" should not act in this way. Compare 1 Corinthians 6.6, "**brother** goeth to law with **brother**, and that before the unbelievers." But why? We must repeat the earlier lesson. It all happened because God's people did not unitedly recognise God's anointed king. Things will go terribly wrong if we fail to crown the Lord Jesus as "Lord of all." We'll end up like "Abner and his men" and "Joab and his men." Both sides trudged wearily home "all night" (vv.29,32). Many of the men didn't get home. There were empty chairs in Mahanaim, and empty chairs in Hebron. Don't forget the lesson, will you?

CHAPTER 3.1-33

"Died Abner as a fool dieth"

Having been anointed "king over the house of Judah" (1 Sam 2.4) at Hebron, the historian now describes events leading to his anointing by "all the elders of Israel" (1 Sam 5.3). The story does not make good reading. It involved two murders, and a great deal of unpleasantness. Let's remember that it all stemmed from failure to recognise God's appointed king from the very outset. We cannot stress the lesson sufficiently. On a personal level, failure to recognise the undisputed and unrivalled reign of Christ in our lives can only lead to sorrow and confusion. It will also have a devastating effect on our united testimony. Just look at the first verse of this chapter: "Now there was long war between the house of Saul and the house of David: but David waxed stronger and stronger, and the house of Saul waxed weaker and weaker." (1 Chron 12.19-22 will help here). We are glad to see that God vindicated the "man after his own heart" (1 Sam 13.14), but it did involve a "long war" between God's people! Far better "for brethren to dwell together in unity!" (Ps 133.1). David calls that "good" and "pleasant."

The chapter can be divided into four main paragraphs as follows: **(1)** David's marriages and children" (vv.2-5); **(2)** Abner's moves towards unity (vv.6-21); **(3)** Abner's murder by Joab (vv.22-30); **(4)** David's mourning for Abner vv.31-39).

1) David's Marriages and Children (vv.2-5)
Keil & Delitzsch say that "proof of the advance of the house of David is furnished by the multitude of his family at Hebron...in harmony with the custom of beginning the reign of every king with certain notices concerning his family." That may be so, but there are serious lessons here.

At this stage, David had six wives, and it didn't end there! Now read 2 Samuel 5.13-16. We have to say that this is a long way from God's ideal.

This was stated at creation in Genesis 2.22-24, and quoted by the Lord Jesus in Mark 10, "But from the beginning of the creation God made them male and female. For this cause shall a man leave his father and mother, and cleave to his wife; and they twain shall be one flesh: so then they are no more twain, but one flesh" (Mk 10.6-8). The expression, "one flesh", cannot possibly accommodate one man and six wives.

We must notice that while David is nowhere censured for his polygamy, it did bring him untold sorrow, in the same way that it brought great sorrow to others. Just think about the bitterness between Sarah and Hagar, and between Leah and Rachel. David reaped a sad harvest. Look, for example, at his two sons, by different mothers, Amnon (v.2) and Absalom (v.3). Amnon raped his half-sister Tamar, and was subsequently murdered by her brother Absalom. We read the sad story in 2 Samuel 13. This in turn resulted in Absalom's rebellion against his father, and eventual death in "the thick boughs of a great oak" (2 Sam 18.9). Absalom's mother, Maacah, was the daughter of Talmai, king of Geshur, and David therefore entered what the New Testament calls "an unequal yoke" (2 Cor 6.14). Another son, Adonijah (v.4), was never corrected by his father, and plotted to seize the kingdom once David was dead. See 1 Kings 1.5-9. If, with all the difficulties, David had concentrated on his marriage to Michal, and therefore maintained God's original order for marriage, he would have been spared so much trouble. As A. McShane observes, "Had David been as exercised about God's guidance as to whom he should marry as he was about where he should live (2.1), the story might have been very different. Perhaps next in importance to one's conversion, is the choice of a partner." It is so important, not only to marry a Christian, but to marry the **right** Christian.

2) Abner's Moves towards Unity (vv.6-21)
Our attention is now diverted from David's domestic affairs, to affairs of state. But not entirely, as we shall see. Ish-bosheth, Saul's son was king of Israel only in name. The power behind the throne was Abner. "And it came to pass, while there was war between the house of Saul and the house of David, that Abner made himself strong for the house of Saul" (v.6). With Abner in charge, there seemed little possibility that the war would cease. After all, David's men had given his army a thorough thrashing at Gibeon, and reconciliation was not on the agenda. But suddenly things changed. To our ears, it is a strange story. Let's look at it like this:

A) Abner's decision (vv. 7-11)

We should notice the circumstances of his decision, and the conviction underlying his decision.

i) The circumstances (vv. 7-8). According to F. Gardiner (Ellicott's Commentary), "The harem of an Eastern monarch was considered to be the property of his successor, and therefore the taking of a woman belonging to it as the assertion of a claim to the throne." See 2 Samuel 12.8, 16.21 and 1 Kings 2.22. As F. Gardiner observes, it is improbable that Abner had any designs on the throne of Israel, but Ish-bosheth evidently regarded Abner's conduct as an act of treachery. This is the force of Abner's reply to Ish-bosheth, "Am I a dog's head that belongeth to Judah?" (RV). For further references to Rizpah, see 2 Samuel 21.8-11. Concubines are now called "common law wives." Once again, we are a long, long way from God's ideal. Do remember His creatorial intention that marriage, with all its sacred relationships, should be between one man and one woman. Over the centuries, society has endeavoured to "improve" on God's ideal, with tragic results.

ii) The conviction (vv. 9-11). We get the impression here that Abner was acting against his better judgement in supporting Ish-bosheth. "So do God to Abner, and more also, except as **the Lord hath sworn to David**, even so I do to him; to translate the kingdom of the house of Saul, and to set up the throne of David over Israel and over Judah, from Dan even to Beersheba." This certainly seems to be a confession by Abner that he had been wrong in opposing David. It has been pointed out that whilst there is no record of a divine oath to give the kingdom to David, the promises of God have the same force. See, again, 1 Samuel 15.28-29. At the same time, we do have to say that Abner was motivated by revenge for the insult of Ish-bosheth, rather than by deep conviction. But he was evidently aware that God had promised the kingdom to David.

This reminds us that it is sadly possible for us to support a wrong cause against our better judgement. In this case, family considerations weighed heavily with Abner. Remember that Abner was Saul's cousin, and therefore Ish-bosheth was his second cousin. While in some circumstances it is not easy, our loyalty to God and His word should override other loyalties, whether in the family, in business, or in the religious world.

B) David's demand (vv. 12-16)

"And Abner sent messengers to David on his behalf, saying, Whose is the land? Saying also, Make thy league with me, and, behold, my hand shall be with thee, to bring about all Israel unto thee." Commentators divide over the meaning of, "Whose is the land?" Some say that it means, "Is not the land thine by promise?", and others, "I'm the only one who can bring all Israel under your control". Since Abner proposes some kind of an agreement between himself and David ("make thy league with me, and...my hand shall be with thee"), the second suggestion is not outrageous! However, it does seem, in view of vv.9-10, that the first is more likely. Abner's words, "make thy league with me" suggest that he was looking for some recompense. At the very least, this could be the guarantee of his safety and security.

David then spelt out his terms: "I will make a league with thee: but one thing I require of thee, that is, Thou shalt not see my face, except thou first bring Michal Saul's daughter when thou comest to see my face." Michal was David's first wife. See 1 Samuel 18.20-28. But during David's exile, Saul totally disowned David by severing the family relationship. He gave "Michal his daughter, David's wife, to Phalti the son of Laish, which was of Gallim" (1 Sam 25.44). For the third time in this chapter, we encounter the sad results of overthrowing God's ideal in marriage. "And Ish-bosheth sent, and took her from her husband, even from Phaltiel the son of Laish. And her husband went with her along weeping behind her to Bahurim. Then said Abner unto him, Go, return, And he returned." The involvement of Ish-bosheth, the king, gave legality to the proceedings: David did not reclaim his wife by force.

What can we make of all this? Quite obviously, it was immeasurably distressing for Phaltiel and, presumably, for Michal. However, Michal had been unjustly taken from David by Saul, after he had rightfully acquired her for his wife by paying the dowry demanded (1 Sam 18.27), and in spite of her love for him (1 Sam 18.28; 19.11-12), and given to another man. David could therefore demand her back again with perfect justice. It is often pointed out that David may have had political grounds for claiming Michal. "The renewal of his marriage to the king's daughter would show all Israel that he cherished no hatred in his heart towards the fallen king", Keil & Delitzsch. There were certainly political reasons, although not on David's part, for the marriage in the first place. See 18.20-21

One thing is clear, Saul was quite wrong to give Michal to Phaltiel. His intervention in the marriage is totally unsupportable. He completely disregarded God's will in marriage, and this is yet another example of what can happen when God's word is flouted. But was David wise in reclaiming her? It certainly didn't do him any good. See 2 Samuel 6.16-23. Phaltiel and Michal were both obliged to live lonely and miserable lives. A. McShane has a valid point in saying, "it can be our wisdom to let pass our lawful claims, and be content to forget the wrongs done on us."

C) Abner's discussions (vv.17-19)

Abner now begins to "translate the kingdom from the house of Saul, and to set up the throne of David over Israel and over Judah" (v.10). We should notice the following:

i) They must not delay. "Ye sought for David in times past to be king over you: now then **do it.**" They were to act now. Abner evidently refers to 1 Samuel 18.5,7,16,30 here. Notice what Israel said to David at Hebron: "and moreover in time past, even when Saul was king, thou wast he that leddest out and broughtest in Israel: and the Lord thy God said unto thee, Thou shalt feed my people Israel, and thou shalt be ruler over my people Israel" (1 Chron 11.1-3). The time had now come to make David king over all Israel. There are times when God says to **us**, "now therefore perform the doing of it" (2 Cor 8.11). Perhaps you have been delaying an important decision about your spiritual life. Does it have to be said of us, "How long halt ye between two opinions?" (1 Kings 18.21). The reason for an immediate decision in favour of David follows:

ii) They needed deliverance. "Now then do it: for the Lord hath spoken of David, saying, By the hand of my servant David I will save my people Israel out of the hand of the Philistines, and out of the hand of all their enemies." The first thing that David did after he had been anointed king over Israel was to thrash the Philistines twice in quick succession. See 5.17-25. He did it again in 8.1, and followed this by dealing similarly with all the rest of Israel's enemies in 8.2-18 and 10.1-19. But Israel's victories were only possible when the right man reigned over them. We can only be victorious as we are "strong in the Lord, and in the power of his might" (Eph 6.10).

iii) They must not be disunited. "And Abner also spake in the ears of Benjamin." This was the tribe to which Saul belonged, and it was most important that they should recognise the new king. If anybody objected, it would be Benjamin. Abner wanted no dissenting voices, and took steps to ensure that Israel spoke with one voice. That's important, isn't it? Read 1 Corinthians 1.10, Ephesians 4.3, and Philippians 1.27. Happily, Abner was able to "speak in the ears of David in Hebron all that seemed good to Israel, and that seemed good to the whole house of Benjamin."

D) Abner's departure (vv.20-21)
It all looks promising. "And Abner said unto David, I will arise and go, and will gather all Israel unto my lord the king, that they may make a league with thee, and that thou mayest reign over all that thy heart desireth. And David sent Abner away; and he went in peace." Notice the expressions, "he went in peace" (v.21), "he was gone in peace" (v.22), and "he is gone in peace" (v.23). But not for long!

3) Abner's Murder by Joab (vv.22-27)
There is no need to recount the story. It is clear enough. Some of the details call for comment. We must notice **(A)** The conspiracy of Joab (vv.22-27), and **(B)** The consequences for Joab (vv.28-30).

A) The conspiracy of Joab, (vv.22-25)

i) He slandered Abner (vv.24-25) "Then Joab came to the king, and said, What hast thou done? Behold, Abner came unto thee; why is it that thou hast sent him away and he is quite gone? Thou knowest Abner the son of Ner, that he came to deceive thee, and to know thy going out and thy coming in, and to know all that thou doest."

Perhaps all this was a smoke-screen, and Joab's recriminations concealed his annoyance over a lost opportunity to avenge the death of his brother, Asahel. Having said that, the fact remains that Joab was guilty of what Paul calls "evil surmisings" (1 Tim 6.4). If we are not careful, we too can be guilty in this way. It is all too easy to become suspicious of people without good reason, and to reach very firm conclusions about their motives for doing and saying things. This does the victim a gross injustice, and sows the seeds of suspicion and discord in the minds of other people. We must be careful what we say about people behind their backs, and for that matter, we ought to be careful what we say to people when we are in their company!

ii) He slew Abner (vv.26-27). He did this "for the blood of Asahel his brother." Abishai was also involved (v.30). Keil & Delitzsch call this "a treacherous act of assassination, which could not even be defended as blood-revenge, since Abner had slain Asahel in battle after repeated warnings, and only for the purpose of saving his own life." They continue: "The principal motive for Joab's act was the most contemptible jealousy, or the fear lest Abner's reconciliation to David should diminish his own influence with the king, as was the case at a later period with the murder of Amasa (20.10)." Perhaps there is an element of speculation here, but history shows that Joab could brook no rival. Do notice that it all took place at Hebron, which was a city of refuge. See Joshua 20. Abner was "so near (in the gate), but so far."

B) The consequences for Joab (vv.28-30)
i) David proclaimed his innocence (v.29). "I and my kingdom are guiltless before the Lord for ever from the blood of Abner the son of Ner. See also 1 Kings 2.32. Unlike Pilate, who proclaimed his innocence (see Matthew 27.24) he was not a party to the crime. As we shall see, David wasn't even secretly relieved that Abner had been removed. He was innocent in thought as well as action. He had "no fellowship with the unfruitful works of darkness, but rather reproved them" (Eph 5.11).

ii) David pronounced against Joab (v.30). Joab's guilt would never be forgotten. "Let it rest upon the head of Joab, and on all his father's house." This included his brother Abishai (v.30). His family would also reap the consequences of his sin: "Let there not fail from the house of Joab one that hath an issue, or that is a leper, or that leaneth on a staff, or that falleth on the sword, or that lacketh bread." It would be quite inappropriate for us to use language like this-see Matthew 5.43-44, but we must remember that our actions do have consequences for other people. Sadly, the sins of parents often have a devastating effect on their families. There is an implied rebuke in the words, "So Joab and Abshai his brother slew Abner, because he had slain their brother Asahel at Gibeon in the battle" (v.30). This suggests that there was no comparison between the deaths of Asahel and Abner. One died in battle: the other in cold blood.

4) David's Mourning for Abner (vv.31-39)
We must notice some very interesting and important lessons in this paragraph, which records David oration at Abner's funeral.

A) The unity with David
"And David said unto Joab, and to **all** the people that were with him…and the king lifted up his voice, and wept at the grave of Abner; and **all** the people wept…And **all** the people wept again over him…And when **all** the people came to cause David to eat meat…And **all** the people took notice of it, and it pleased them: as whatsoever the king did pleased **all** the people. For **all** the people and **all** Israel understood that day that it was not of the

king to slay Abner the son of Ner." There is a first-class sermon here on the subject of unity! They were united in sorrow (v.31-34), in their concern for David (v.35), in their appreciation of David (v.37), and in understanding the innocence of David (v.37). It is a happy assembly when the saints are united in grief, in concern for each other, in appreciation of each other, and in understanding each other.

B) The example of David
He was an example of his instructions to other people. "And king David (the first reference to "king David") **himself** followed the bier" (v.31). He led the mourning. "And the king lifted up his voice, and wept at the grave of Abner, and all the people wept" (v.32). Elders are to be "ensamples to the flock" (1 Pet 5.3). See also 2 Thessalonians 3.7-8.

C) The lament of David
"Died Abner as a fool dieth? Thy hands were not bound, nor thy feet put in fetters: as a man falleth before wicked men, so fellest thou." David's question can be rendered, "Should Abner die as a fool dieth?" In other words, Abner should never have died in this way, but he did. "Anyone with a grain of common sense would have avoided giving Joab the private opportunity to avenge his brother...Also the lament makes it clear that his death was not a judicial killing, but a murder by someone of evil intent. He had not been bound or chained because of any wrongdoing...His death was like a death at the hands of a criminal, and everyone would know whom David meant" (H. Mowvley).

D) The tribute by David
"Know ye not that there is a prince and a great man fallen this day in Israel? David spoke well of Abner. As in the case of Saul (1.23-24), he did not mention Abner's past failings, particularly the way in which he had installed Ish-bosheth as king of Israel. There is nothing commendable in rehearsing the failures of fellow-believers, past or present. We should commend what we can, and leave the rest unsaid!

E) The limitations of David
"And I am this day weak, though anointed king; and these men the sons of Zeruiah be too hard for me: the Lord shall reward the doer of evil according to his wickedness." David evidently felt unable to deal with Joab, although he deserved to die for the murder of Abner. This may have been due to his comparative youth, and inexperience as king. David therefore felt obliged

to leave the matter with God, and in due course, after his death, Joab was executed by Benaiah on the instructions of Solomon, see 1 Kings 2.28-34. This reminds us that situations arise in our lives causing us to say, like David, "too hard for me." Sometimes we know what we ought to do, but feel unable or unqualified to carry it out, especially where other people are concerned. David committed his problem to God, and we should do the same. In due course, God executed judgment on Joab, and even his hold "on 'the horns of the altar' could not save him from the sword of justice" (A. McShane).

CHAPTER 4.1-12

"Behold the head of Ish-bosheth"

Events in this chapter make it clear that the eleven tribes which remained loyal to the house of Saul could no longer look to his family for effective leadership. By the end of the chapter Abner had been assassinated (v.1), Mephibosheth had been incapacitated (v.4), and Ish-bosheth had been assassinated (vv.5-12). The removal of all opposition in this way paved the way for David's recognition as king over all Israel. Chapter 5 therefore opens with the words, "Then came all the tribes of Israel to David unto Hebron...and they anointed David king over all Israel" (vv.1-3). It is noteworthy that David never dealt with the obstacles himself. He knew that he would be king, and left the mechanics to God. In His absolute sovereignty, God removed every barrier. It required a great deal of patience on David's part, but in this matter his character and conduct were exemplary. He did not assert his right to the throne, reminding us that "promotion cometh neither from the east, nor from the west, nor from the south. But God is the judge: he putteth down one, and setteth up another" (Ps 75.6-7).

The chapter can be divided as follows: **(1)** The apprehension over Abner's death (vv.1-3); **(2)** The accident to Mephibosheth (v.4); **(3)** The assassination of Ish-bosheth (vv.5-7); **(4)** The anger of David (vv.8-12).

1) The Apprehension over Abner's Death (vv.1-3)

"And when Saul's son heard that Abner was dead in Hebron, his hands were feeble, and all Israel were troubled" (v.1). We must notice the "cause and effect" here. A weak leader led to a disturbed and alarmed people. It all arose from the fact that Ish-bosheth was not God's choice. He had been installed by Abner (2.8-10). He had also been installed in the wrong place. Mahanaim was on the wrong side of Jordan!

A) The effect on Ish-bosheth

"His hands were feeble." The "strong man", Abner, was dead, and Ish-

2 Samuel

bosheth had no personal authority. We know that Ish-bosheth was afraid of Abner (3.11), but the death of his general left him without any support as the nominal king of Israel. Whilst we must not forget the immediate circumstances, this does raise an important issue. Do we need "propping up" all the time? Yes, we do need each other's fellowship and help. Paul makes this very clear in 1 Corinthians 12, where he uses the analogy of the human body to illustrate our inter-dependence. For example, "And the eye cannot say to the hand, I have no need of thee: nor again the head to the feet, I have no need of you" (v.21). But, at the same time, we must be "strong in the Lord, and in the power of his might" (Eph 6.10). Some believers are only strong as long as they have others to support them. Joash, one of the kings of Judah, is a case in point. He "did that which was right in the sight of the Lord all the days of Jehoida the priest." But after the death of Jehoida, it was a different story. Read all about it in 2 Chronicles ch.24. How deep is **our** spiritual life. How deep are **our** convictions? Do remember that the people you rely on just don't go on for ever! Remember too, that they can let you down! Be "strong in the Lord" **yourself!**

B) The effect on Israel

"All the Israelites were troubled." The eleven tribes knew that Ish-bosheth could not succeed. It doesn't take too much imagination to see the dismay written all over their faces! The future looked very uncertain. You see, God's people will suffer if the right men are not leading them. David was God's man. **"He** chose David also his servant, and took him from the sheepfolds: from following the ewes great with young **he** brought him to feed Jacob his people, and Israel his inheritance" (Ps 78.70-71). This is still true. Read Acts 20.28, "Take heed therefore unto yourselves, and to all the flock, over (among) the which the **Holy Ghost** hath made you overseers, to feed the church of God, which he hath purchased with his own blood." It is worth noticing that God places great value on shepherds. David was a shepherd in more ways than one (Israel knew this: read 2 Sam 5.2), and New Testament "overseers", or "elders", are also involved in shepherd work. Lack of spiritual leadership and care can only have a detrimental effect on "the flock of God" (1 Pet 5.2). We must pray that "the chief Shepherd" will continue to provide men who will feed and tend His "sheep."

The historian then notes that Ish-bosheth had "two men that were captains of bands: the name of the one was Baanah, and the name of the other Rechab, the sons of Rimmon a Beerothite, of the children of Benjamin" (v.2). As "captains of bands", they were evidently experienced leaders of guerrilla bands, and as Benjamites, they were trusted supporters of the house of Saul. Well, that's how it seemed at the time. They turned out to be the murderers of Ish-bosheth. The little explanatory note is interesting: "for Beeroth also was reckoned to Benjamin: and the Beerothites fled to Gittaim, and were sojourners there until this day" (vv.2-3). The original inhabitants of Beeroth fled to Gittaim, which is the plural of Gath, and was presumably in Philistine territory. Beeroth was part of the territory belonging to the Gibeonites (Josh 9.16-21), which accounts for the fact that they were not eliminated by Joshua. It would not have been surprising if two non-Israelite men had murdered Ish-bosheth, but this was not the case. The tribe of Benjamin had acquired Beeroth, and it was two Benjamites who rose against their own leader. But before the story unfolds, we have an apparent deviation.

2) The Accident to Mephibosheth (v.4)

"And Jonathan, Saul's son, had a son that was lame of his feet, He was five years old when the tidings came of Saul and Jonathan out of Jezreel, and his nurse took him up, and fled: and it came to pass, as she made haste to flee, that he fell, and became lame. And his name was Mephibosheth."

This incident took place about seven years previously, so why is this inserted here? It is not even in chronological order. Surely it would have been more appropriate in chapter 9! Let's remember that there is nothing out of place in God's word. This information is included at this point to emphasise the complete hopelessness of the house of Saul. The fact that he was handicapped, and therefore incapable of going to war, made him an unlikely contender for the throne.

It is interesting to notice that the names of uncle and nephew ended in the same way: Ish-bosheth and Mephibosheth, or, to give them their other names, Esh-baal and Merib-baal (1 Chron 8.33-34). As we have seen, Ish-bosheth means "man of shame." Mephibosheth means "destroying shame." Esh-baal means "fire of Baal", and Merib-baal means, possibly, "contender against Baal." There does seem to have been a man with the name "Baal" in the family tree (1 Chron 8.30), but don't try preaching a sermon on the subject! There is better subject-matter elsewhere!

The details of the accident are much more significant. Mephibosheth was evidently dropped by his nurse (probably because she acted on the "spur of the moment", and that can be dangerous), and this reminds us of the excellent nursing care bestowed on the young Christians at Thessalonica. Unlike Mephibosheth's nurse, who acted contrary to her calling, Paul and his colleagues did not drop them! "We were gentle among you, even as a nurse cherisheth her children" (1 Thess 2.7). In actual fact, their ministry was akin to a nursing-mother with her own children. A mother's deep love for her child permeated their care for them: "So being affectionately desirous of you, we were willing to have imparted unto you, not the gospel of God only, but also our own souls, because ye were dear unto us" (1 Thess 2.8). Perhaps we should remember that the care included a well-balanced spiritual diet. Just read through 1 and 2 Thessalonians again, and notice Paul's references to teaching given during his visit to the city. He covered a wide variety of subjects! The care also included recognition of their progress (e.g. 1 Thess 1.3), and encouragement to do even better (e.g. 1 Thess 4.10). A "night out at the amphitheatre" doesn't figure anywhere!

We will encounter Mephibosheth again in chapter 9. "And the king said unto him (Ziba), Is there not yet any of the house of Saul, that I may shew the kindness of God unto him." And Ziba said unto the king, "Jonathan hath yet a son, which is lame on his feet" (v.3). "So Mephibosheth dwelt in Jerusalem: for he did eat continually at the king's table; and was lame on both his feet" (v.13). The story makes a splendid gospel message, as we shall see.

3) The Assassination of Ish-Bosheth (vv.5-7)
The historian now returns to Rechab and Baanah, the sons of Rimmon. "And the sons of Rimmon the Beerothite, Rechab and Baanah, went, and came about the heat of the day to the house of Ish-bosheth, who lay on a bed at noon. And they came thither into the midst of the house, as though they would have fetched wheat; and they smote him under the fifth rib (just like Asahel, 2.23 and Abner, 3.27); and Rechab and his brother escaped" (vv.5-6). Further details of the murder follow: "For when they came into the house, he lay on his bed in his bed-chamber, and they smote him, and slew him, and beheaded him, and took his head, and gat them away through the plain all night." Let's notice some of the details.

i) "Ish-bosheth...**lay on a bed at noon**." So it was siesta time! It would be rather churlish to criticise Ish-bosheth for taking a nap at midday, but it is rather interesting to notice that Abraham "sat in the tent door in the heat of the day" (Gen 18.1). Abraham was alert. He "lift up his eyes and looked, and, lo, three men stood by him." Ish-bosheth was vulnerable. If he did see

Rechab and Baanah, it was too late. Doesn't this remind us that we need to "watch and pray?" Do remember what happened to Samson when he was asleep. Read Judges 16.18-19. Do notice what happened to a field when the owner took a nap. Read Proverbs 6.9-11 and 24.30-34. It was "while men slept" that the "enemy came and sowed tares among the wheat, and went his way" (Mt 13.25). Remember that "the drunkard and the glutton shall come to poverty: and drowsiness shall clothe a man with rags" (Prov 23.21). We are not "to sleep, as do others" but "watch and be sober" (1 Thess 5.6).

ii) Rechab and Baanah "came thither into **the midst of the house**." Their easy access does seem quite astonishing doesn't it? Surely the king's residence should have been well guarded. But nobody seems to have been security-conscious. This does remind us of Paul's warning to the Ephesian elders at Miletus: "For I know this, that after my departing shall grievous wolves enter in among you not sparing the flock...Therefore watch, and remember that by the space of three years I ceased not to warn every one of you night and day with tears" (Acts 20.29-31). But false teachers don't always look like wolves! They often act quietly and covertly. See Galatians 2.4, "false brethren unawares brought in, who came in privily to spy out our liberty which we have in Christ Jesus". Note 2 Peter 2.1, "there shall be false teachers among you, who privily shall bring in damnable heresies" and Jude 4, "there are certain men crept in unawares". This is why it is necessary to interview, courteously and graciously, unknown visitors to the assembly. John puts it like this, "try the spirits whether they are of God: because many false prophets are gone out into the world" (1 Jn 4.1). Notice how the assembly at Ephesus handled the problem. Read Revelation 2.2.

iii) Rechab and Baanah "came thither into the midst of the house, **as though they would have fetched wheat**." The assassins practised deception. They had a hidden agenda. We mustn't expect Satan to be straightforward. "For such are false apostles, deceitful workers, transforming themselves into the apostles of Christ. And no marvel; for Satan himself is transformed into an angel of light. Therefore it is no great thing if his ministers also be transformed as the ministers of righteousness" (2 Cor 11.13-15). We must not be "ignorant of his devices" (2 Cor 2.11).

Once they were in, the damage was soon done. It has been pointed out that although the text is repetitive, the Hebrew style does favour "such expansive additions" (J. Baldwin). Keil & Delitzsch quote J. P. F. Konigsfeldt

2 Samuel

here: "The Hebrews often repeat in this way, for the purpose of adding something fresh, as for example, in this instance, their carrying off the head." We can trace the route taken by the two murderers to David in Hebron. "They gat them away through the plain all night." They travelled south-east "by way of the Arabah, the dry rift valley of the Jordan and Dead Sea, to avoid meeting other travellers" (J. Baldwin). No doubt they thought that they had 'got away with it.' But they did not get the welcome they expected.

4) The Anger of David (vv.8-12)

Rechab and his brother put the best possible complexion on their crime. They presumed "to spread the name of God and his providence as a cloak and covering over their villainy, as the wicked are accustomed to do." (Quoted by Keil & Delitzsch). "Behold the head of Ish-bosheth the son of Saul thine enemy, which sought thy life; and the Lord hath avenged my lord this day of Saul and his seed" (v.8). It is not unknown for Christians to say, "the Lord led me to do this, or say that", when they are clearly in breach of God's word. Sadly, all kinds of wrong-doing are practised in God's name. We must now notice David's reply (vv.9-11), and David's reward (v.12).

A) David's reply (vv.9-11)

i) He calls on God to witness his reply. "As the Lord liveth, who hath redeemed my soul out of all adversity." Rechab and Baanah had implied that the Lord had authorised their evil deed. David can confidently call on God to witness his integrity. Paul did the same: "for neither at any time used we flattering words, as ye know, nor a cloke of covetousness; God is witness…Ye are witnesses, and God also, how holily and justly and unblameably we behaved ourselves among you that believe" (1 Thess 2.5 & 10).

ii) He reminds them that God had vindicated him. "As the Lord liveth, who hath **redeemed my soul out of all adversity.**" David had not taken the initiative to rid himself of Saul, and had not permitted others to do so on his behalf. He acted on the principle of Romans 12.19, "Dearly beloved, avenge not yourselves, but rather give place unto wrath: for it is written, Vengeance is mine; I will repay saith the Lord." See 1 Samuel 24.1-6 and 26.8-11. As A. McShane observes, "God's men must never stoop to the schemes of the wicked in order to reach their destined position." If we feel unjustly treated, we leave our case with God. David could testify that "he redeemed my soul out of all adversity." When the Lord Jesus was "reviled", he "reviled not again; when he suffered, he threatened not; but committed himself to him that judgeth righteously" (1 Pet 2.23).

iii) He recognised that they expected a reward. This does seem to be implied in his words, "When one told me, saying, Behold, Saul is dead, thinking to have brought good tidings, I took hold of him, and slew him in Ziklag, who thought that I would have given him a reward for his tidings."

iv) He emphasised the wickedness of their crime. The Amalekite had been executed for his attempt to make money out of bad news. Saul had been slain in battle by the Philistines on Mount Gilboa, but Rechab and Baanah had "slain a righteous person in his own house upon his bed." Their cold-blooded murder of Ish-bosheth deserved at least the same sentence. Let's remember too, that two Benjamites had murdered one of their own tribesmen, or, to put it differently, they had murdered one of God's people. Sadly, Paul was obliged to warn Christians, "But if ye bite and devour one another, take heed that ye be not consumed one of another" (Gal 5.15).

v) He acknowledged the integrity of Ish-bosheth. David calls him "a righteous person." Although "he was Saul's son, he was not personally involved in his father's guilt, and had done nothing to deserve death" (J. Baldwin).

B) David's reward (v.12)
David was consistent in dealing with evil. "And David commanded his young men, and they slew them, and cut off their hands and their feet, and hanged them up over the pool in Hebron." The two murderers got their reward! As A. McShane observes, "Their hands and feet were removed because the former had been used to do the smiting and the latter had run to shed innocent blood." Their bodies were hung over the pool in Hebron as "a stern warning to all who frequented the city that murder would not be tolerated by the king." The head of Ish-bosheth was given a decent burial in the tomb of Abner, to whom he was related. On reflection, Ish-bosheth's downfall was largely due to his own weakness, and this is a warning that **we** must not forget.

CHAPTER 5.1-25

"And David went on, and grew great"

This is a landmark chapter. "All the elders of Israel came to the king to Hebron; and king David made a league with them in Hebron before the Lord: and they anointed David king over Israel." He was king at last! But there was no arrogance on David's part. He could have said, "I told you so! The shepherd-boy had waited a long time or, more accurately, he had waited God's time, and now the hour had come for him to reign over all Israel. God had kept His word. He always does! This reminds us that the Lord Jesus will ultimately be recognised as "KING OF KINGS, AND LORD OF LORDS" (Rev 19.16). Like David, He waits for God's time: "The Lord said unto my Lord, Sit thou at my right hand, until I make thine enemies thy footstool" (Ps 110.1). Notice the certainty. Not "in case I make thine enemies thy footstool", or "it is possible that I will make thine enemies thy footstool", but "**until** I make thine enemies thy footstool."

The chapter can be divided into five paragraphs as follows: **(1)** The anointing of David (vv.1-5); **(2)** The city of David (vv.6-9); **(3)** The progress of David (vv.10-12); **(4)** The family of David (vv.13-16); **(5)** The victories of David (vv.17-25).

1) The Anointing of David (vv.1-5)

The chapter begins with national unity. "Then came **all** the tribes of Israel to David unto Hebron...so **all** the elders of Israel came to the king to Hebron" (vv.1-2). The nation was united around God's appointed king. Need we say more? Let's remember that believers in the Lord Jesus are already united. "There **is** one body, and one Spirit, even as ye are called in one hope of your calling; one Lord, one faith, one baptism, one God and Father of all, who is above all, and through all, and in you all" (Eph 4.4-6). We do not have to **make** unity. But we do have to **keep** it! The Ephesians were told to "walk worthy of the vocation wherewith ye are called, with all lowliness and meekness, with longsuffering, forbearing one another in love; endeavouring (using diligence, JND) to **keep** the unity of the Spirit in the bond of peace" (Eph 4.1-3). With this in mind, we should "all speak the same thing, and that there be no division among you; but that ye be perfectly joined together in the same mind and in the same judgment" (1 Cor 1.10), and "stand fast in one spirit, with one mind striving together for the faith of the gospel" (Phil 1.27). Now let's notice some of the details.

A) Their relationship with David (v.1)
"Behold, we are thy bone and thy flesh." He fulfilled the necessary qualification in Deuteronomy 17.15, "Thou shalt in any wise set him king over thee, whom the Lord thy God shall choose: one from among thy brethren shalt thou set king over thee: thou mayest not set a stranger over thee, which is not thy brother." The words "we are thy bone and thy flesh" recall an even more intimate relationship." Adam said of Eve, "This is now bone of my bones, and flesh of my flesh" (Gen 2.23), and his words are cited in Ephesians 5 where they are used to describe the relationship between Christ and the church: "For no man ever yet hated his own flesh; but nourisheth and cherisheth it, even as the Lord the church: for we are members of his body, of his flesh, and of his bones..." (vv.29-32). Israel was one with David, and the church is one with Christ.

B) Their recognition of David (v.2)
"Also in time past, when Saul was king over us, thou wast he that leddest out and broughtest in Israel: and the Lord said unto thee, Thou shalt feed my people Israel, and thou shalt be captain over Israel."

i) They recognised his work. "Thou wast he that leddest out and broughtest in Israel."

ii) They recognised his call. "The Lord said unto thee, Thou shalt feed my people Israel, and thou shalt be captain over them." Notice the expressions "thou shalt **feed**" and "thou shalt be **captain**."

Now read Psalm 78.70-72, "He chose David also his servant, and took him from the sheepfolds: from following the ewes great with young he brought him to feed Jacob his people, and Israel his inheritance. So he fed them according to the integrity of his heart; and guided them by the skilfulness of his hands." This is the pattern for New Testament leadership. See, for example 1 Thessalonians 5.12-13, "And we beseech you, brethren, to know them which **labour among you**, and are **over you** (take the lead among you, JND) in the Lord, and admonish you; and to esteem them very highly in love for their work's sake": 1 Peter 5.1-2, "The elders which are among you I exhort...Feed the flock of God which is among you, taking the oversight thereof..." The work is placed before the position in both cases. If an elder does not care for God's people, he cannot expect them to recognise his authority! Israel recognised that David had been called by God through the work that he did.

C) The reign of David (vv.3-5)
David is anointed for the third time. See 1 Samuel 16.13 and 2 Samuel 2.4. We must not overlook the details given here:

i) The commencement of his reign (v.3). "So all the elders of Israel came to the king to Hebron; and king David made a league with them in Hebron before the Lord: and they anointed David king over Israel." Notice the three references to "king." This emphasises the beginning of the new chapter in Israel's history. The word "league" means "covenant", and while we have no further details, it could include agreement on David's part to care for them and to lead them; in other words, to undertake the responsibilities of a king. However, the lack of further information on this point is unimportant. Otherwise, we would have had the details. What **is** important, since it **is** mentioned, is the fact that the "league with them" was made "before the Lord." Perhaps David was referring to this in his "last words." See 2 Samuel 23.3, "The God of Israel said, the Rock of Israel spake unto me, He that ruleth over men must be just, ruling in the fear of God." This does remind us that all work for God should be undertaken soberly and responsibly. Now read Ecclesiastes 5.2.

ii) The duration of his reign (v.4). "David was thirty years old when he began to reign, and he reigned forty years." Perhaps it comes as something of a surprise to be told that David was only thirty years old. "So much has happened, so many decisions made, so many victories won, so much maturity shown, such strong leadership given" (H. Mowvley). How are **you** shaping up for future responsibility? Compare 1 Timothy 4.12, "Let no man despise thy youth; **but** be thou an example of the believers, in word, in conversation, in charity, in spirit, in faith, in purity." Don't expect recognition if you haven't earned it! The **"but"** here is most important. Notice, too, that the Lord Jesus commenced His public ministry at thirty (Luke 3.23), that Joseph was thirty when he stood before Pharaoh and commenced his public service in Egypt (Gen 41.46), and that the Levites were thirty when they commenced their service (Num 4.3).

iii) The periods in his reign (v.5). "In Hebron he reigned over Judah seven years and six months: and in Jerusalem he reigned thirty and three years over all Israel and Judah." This brings us to another "landmark." Jerusalem now becomes the capital city.

2) The City of David (vv.6-9)
This isn't the first time that Jerusalem is mentioned in the Old Testament (see Josh 10.1-5, Judg 1.7-8, 1 Sam 17.54 etc), but it now takes centre stage in Israel's history. It will be "the joy of the whole earth...the city of the great King" (Ps 48.1-2) in the millennial reign of the Lord Jesus. This is the "place" referred to in Deuteronomy 12.10-11, "But when ye go over Jordan, and dwell in the land which the Lord your God giveth you to inherit...then there shall be a place which the Lord your God shall choose to cause his name to dwell there..." We read that "the Lord loveth the gates of Zion more than all the dwellings of Jacob. Glorious things are spoken of thee, O city of God. Selah" (Ps 87.2-3).

Whilst Jerusalem is mentioned previously in the Old Testament, this is the first mention of Zion. Both names are used of the city, but there is a difference. According to Gesenius *(Hebrew-Chaldee Lexicon to the Old Testament)*, Zion refers particularly to "the higher and southern hill on which the city of Jerusalem was built. It included the more ancient part of the city, with the citadel and temple (Mount Moriah, on which the temple was built, being reckoned to Zion, from which it was separated by a narrow valley)." Gesenius says that Zion means a "sunny place" or a "sunny mountain", although J. Baldwin *(Tyndale Old Testament Commentaries)* states that the meaning is uncertain, perhaps "eminence."

This raises two questions: ***(a)*** Why the move from Hebron? and ***(b)*** Why the move to Jerusalem? We are not told how David was directed to Jerusalem, but subsequent events proved that this was certainly the will of God. The following may help:

a) Hebron was a Judean city, and the remaining tribes may not have looked favourably on it as the capital of the united kingdom. In any case, it was too far south to be serviceable in this way.

b) Jerusalem was actually in the territory of Benjamin (the tribe of Saul), but it was right on the border with Judah as well. That was good thinking! It was easily defended. "It was built on one of the hills in the hill country of Judea. To the east was the Kidron valley, which was deeper in those days than it is now. To the south was the Valley of Hinnom. At this time, the city was built on the south-eastern slope and not on the top of the hill. There was a city wall well down the slope, but not at the very bottom. This made it difficult for an attacker to breach the wall. The water supply was from a spring, Gihon, outside the wall, but there was a vertical shaft leading down to it from inside in case of a siege. All this made it an excellent site for a capital" (H. Mowvley).

Jerusalem therefore seemed impregnable, but it became "the city of David" (vv.7,9). We should notice:

i) The attackers (v.6). "And the king and his men went to Jerusalem unto the Jebusites, the inhabitants of the land." The expression, "the king and his men" suggests that "David took the relatively small army which had supported him in his fugitive days; loyal and resourceful, they could be depended upon to vie with each other in achieving the impossible" (J. Baldwin). John describes the Lord's disciples as "his own" (Jn 13.1), and said, "ye are they which have continued with me in my temptations (trials)" (Lk 22.28). How about **our** commitment to the Lord Jesus? Have we proved **our** loyalty to Him?

ii) The defenders (v.6). They were very sure of themselves! "Except thou take away the blind and the lame, thou shalt not come in hither: thinking, David cannot come in hither." The New Translation (JND) reads "'Thou shalt not come in hither, but the blind and the lame will drive thee back: as much as to say, David will not come in hither." Bearing in mind that stones could easily be rained down on attackers, this rendering certainly seems viable! Even the blind and the lame could defend the city. But "let him that thinketh he standeth take heed lest he fall" (1 Cor 10.12). "Pride goeth before destruction, and an haughty spirit before a fall" (Prov 16.18). Many Christians have made the same mistake as the Jebusites!

iii) The assault (vv.7-8). "Nevertheless David took the stronghold of Zion: the same is the city of David." The details follow: "Whosoever getteth up to the gutter, and smiteth the Jebusites, and the lame and the blind, that are hated of David's soul, *he shall be chief and captain.*" There has been considerable debate over the precise means by which

David and his men entered Zion. It is commonly held that "the gutter" refers to a water channel or "water shaft" (RSV), and this certainly makes good sense. The Hebrew word *(sinnor)* is translated "waterspouts" in Psalm 42.7. The verb "getteth up" is usually translated "to touch", but it does have the idea of "assault" in 2 Samuel 14.10. According to H. Shanks *(The City of David, A Guide to Biblical Jerusalem)* one of two shafts beginning at the same opening into the hill (on which Jerusalem is built) became "a stair-case leading to a platform, which led into a horizontal semi-circular tunnel at a level about half-way down to the spring (Gihon). At the end of the tunnel is another shaft (about forty-nine feet deep) going further down the mountain. The bottom of this shaft ends in what was then a water-filled channel which leads to the spring Gihon...by lowering a bucket down the last shaft, the Jebusites could reach the water." The archaeologist Kathleen Kenyon *(Royal Cities of the Old Testament)* reached the conclusion that "there is every reason to suppose that this is the method by which the Jebusites had access to the spring in time of war, and that it was the means whereby the capture of the town by David was achieved. The position of the head of the shaft would be inside the town, while the spring would be outside the walls." David's men would have had to scale this forty-nine foot shaft, and although extremely difficult, "it was the kind of exploit that would appeal to David's mighty men, and like commando troops today, they needed to have opportunity to achieve the impossible", J.Baldwin. Interesting, isn't it?!

Do notice the italicised words, *"he shall be chief and captain."* This means that they were not in the original text, but have been supplied by the translators to give better sense. We know from the parallel passage in 1 Chronicles 11.6, that this is certainly what David actually said: "And David said, Whosover smiteth the Jebusites first shall be chief and captain. So Joab the son of Zeruiah went first up, and was chief." Very clearly, Jerusalem was not taken without considerable effort and difficulty. But then, victory over the enemy is always difficult, isn't it? But we mustn't give up:

> Got any valleys you think are uncrossable?
> Got any mountains you can't tunnel through?
> God specialises in things thought impossible:
> He can do what no other can do!

This leaves the words, "the lame and the blind, that are hated of David's soul... Wherefore they said, The blind and the lame shall not come into the house." Very clearly, it would be quite wrong to conclude that David hated incapacitated people! Mephibosheth was lame, and David certainly didn't hate him! Quite clearly, David is using the language of the Jebusites themselves, "except thou take away the blind and the lame, thou shalt not come in hither." He uses their language to describe **all** the defenders of Jerusalem. As Keil & Delitzsch explain, this gave rise to the proverb, "The blind and the lame shall not come into the house." Since we do not know how the proverb was applied, it is unwise to speculate. The "house" could refer to the temple (built at a later date), or it could simply mean that God's people were not to compromise with aliens.

iv) The occupation (v.9). "So David dwelt in the fort, and called it the city of David. And David built around from Millo and inward." "The name Millo (meaning "the filling") probably originated in the fact that through this tower or castle, the fortification of the city, or the surrounding wall, was filled or completed" (Keil & Delitzsch).

3) The Progress of David (vv.10-12)
This is a delightful paragraph. "And David went on, and grew great, and the Lord of hosts was with him." The title, "the Lord of hosts", has its roots in Genesis 2.1, "Thus the heavens and the earth were finished, and all the **host** of them." Keil and Delitzsch explain as follows: "It is simply applied to Jehovah as the God of the universe, who governs all the powers of heaven, both visible and invisible, as He rules in heaven and on earth." No wonder David "went on, and grew great!" Let's remember that we have His presence too: "he hath said, I will never leave thee, nor forsake thee. So that we may boldly say, The Lord is my helper, and I will not fear what man shall do unto me" (Heb 13.5-6). Here is a little trilogy for development: ***(a)*** David ***"went out"*** (1 Sam 19.8). This refers to his conflict. ***(b)*** David ***"went on"*** (2 Sam 5.10). This refers to his continuance. ***(c)*** David ***"went in"*** (2 Sam 7.18). This refers to his communion. Are ***you*** "going on?" Are ***you*** growing? See 2 Peter 3.18.

David's progress and exploits were recognised by Hiram, the king Tyre. As we shall see, the Philistines took another view entirely (vv.17-18). It is said that "Hiram was ever a lover of David" (1 Kings 5.1). How much encouragement and help are ***we*** giving to servants of God? But do notice that this didn't go to David's head. He "perceived that the Lord had established him king over Israel, and that he had exalted his kingdom for his people Israel's sake." This is most important:

*i) **He recognised that his position was God-given**.* He "perceived that the Lord had established him king over Israel", just as he recognised that the Lord had preserved him in difficult times. See 4.9. There's no need to develop this. Just read Acts 20.28, "over the which the **Holy Ghost** hath made you overseers"; Romans 12.3, "think soberly, according as **God** hath dealt to every man the measure of faith"; 1 Corinthians 3.5, "Who then is Paul, and who is Apollos, but ministers by whom ye believed, even as the **Lord** gave to every man?"; 1 Corinthians 12.18, "but now hath **God** set the members every one of them in the body, as it hath pleased him"; 1 Timothy 1.12, "I thank Christ Jesus our Lord, **who hath enabled me**, for that he counted me faithful, putting me into the ministry".

*ii) **He recognised that his purpose was God-given**.* He "perceived…that he had exalted his kingdom for his people Israel's sake." God had chosen David for the benefit of His people. He had not chosen David purely for David's benefit. Now that's worth thinking about. Let's remember that "the manifestation of the Spirit is given to every man to profit withal" or "for the common good" (1 Cor 12.7 RSV). Our divinely-given gifts are intended to benefit other believers. We are part of His provision for our brothers and sisters in Christ, and vice versa. God intended to bless Israel through David, and He intends to bless other Christians through us.

4) The Family of David (vv.13-16)
We'll say nothing much about this paragraph, except to say that a king was not "to multiply wives to himself" (Deut 17.17), and that the paragraph is located immediately after some very encouraging verses. David recognised what **God** had done for him (v.12), and then **he** "took him more concubines and wives." It all seems rather disappointing, doesn't it? Our comments on 1 Samuel 3.2-4 are equally appropriate here. Solomon is mentioned, which means that the list refers to children born at various times during David's tenure of Jerusalem. But the mention of Solomon does remind us that he followed his father when it came to wives. See 1 Kings 1.1-8. He certainly exceeded his father here, and unlike his father, became idolatrous as a result, but he does seem to have followed his father's bad example. There is a warning for us here. We must be careful about our behaviour: we just don't know who will follow our example, either for good or bad.

5) The Victories of David (vv.17-25)
Re-enter the Philistines! We hardly need comment on the introduction "But when the Philistines heard that they had anointed David king over Israel, all

the Philistines came up to seek David...The Philistines also came and spread themselves in the valley of Rephaim" (vv.17-18). Things were going well in Israel, and the enemy leapt into action! There's nothing unusual about this. There are examples everywhere in the Bible. Do remember that your spiritual progress, or the progress of the assembly, will attract enemy attention. We've heard nothing from the Philistines for seven and a half years. They weren't particularly worried when God's people were divided and devouring each other. But now things had changed, and alarm bells were ringing in the five royal Philistine cities. Do notice that the Philistines wanted David particularly. If the leadership can be eliminated, then the rest becomes much easier. Do pray for the elders in your assembly. According to J. Baldwin, the "valley of Rephaim" is "within sight of Jerusalem, among the precipitous hills to the south-west of the city." Some commentators believe that the Philistine threat took place immediately after David's anointing at Hebron and before he had conquered Jerusalem, but we will stay with the Bible chronology. David evidently launched his attack from more familiar ground. He "went down to the hold." Perhaps this was the cave of Adullam (1 Sam 22.1-2). Two battles followed. Do notice that in both cases, David had no strategy of his own. He asked for God's guidance.

i) The first battle (vv.18-21). Having "enquired of the Lord" (undoubtedly through the priest using the "Urim and Thummim", Ex 28.30, Num 7.21 etc), and gained the assurance of victory, "David came to Baal-perazim, and David smote them there, and said, The Lord hath broken forth upon mine enemies before me, as the breach of waters. Therefore he called the name of the place Baal-perazim", meaning "the possessor of breaches" (Keil & Delitzsch), or "Lord of the break-through", (J. Baldwin). David gave credit for the victory to the Lord: "The **Lord** hath broken forth upon mine enemies before me." When the Philistines captured the ark of the covenant (1 Samuel 4), they discovered, to their total discomfort, that God could look after his own interests perfectly well! But the Philistine idols were taken away and burnt! That was a wise move. It took temptation out of the way! See also 1 Chronicles 14.12. Compare Deuteronomy 7.5 & 25. Now we know what we have got to do with *our* idols!

ii) The second battle (vv.22-25). David asked God for guidance again. He did not trust in his previous experience against the Philistines, but asked for fresh instructions. He did not take it for granted that the previous strategy would succeed again, and he was right: "Thou shalt not go up; but fetch a compass behind them, and come upon them over against the mulberry trees (in all probability, the Hebrew word refers to the balsam trees) And let it be, when thou hearest the sound of a going in the tops of the mulberry trees, that then thou shalt bestir thyself: for then shall the Lord go out before thee, and smite the host of the Philistines." The second attack was in two phases:

a) Waiting. David was required to wait until he heard "the sound of a going in the tops of the mulberry trees." As J. Baldwin observes, "the wind which would cause a sound like the rushing of feet was in this case the wind of the Spirit of God, "for then shall the Lord go out before thee." Keil & Delitzsch put it like this: "The sound of a going", i.e. of the advance of an army, was a significant sign of the approach of an army of God, which would smite the enemies of Jehovah and of His servant David." The Lord Jesus instructed His disciples to remain in Jerusalem and "wait for the promise of the Father" (Acts 1.4). Once the Holy Spirit had come, they became active for God (Acts 2.14).

b) Acting. "Then thou shalt bestir thyself: for then shall the Lord go out before thee, and smite the host of the Philistines." There was a time for waiting, and a time for acting. David was required to "move quickly" (AV "bestir thyself") once it became evident that the Spirit of God was actively engaged in the battle. He had to move with the Spirit of God in order to defeat the enemy. Notice the connection: "Then shall the Lord go out before thee, and **smite** the host of the Philistines. And David did so, as the Lord had commanded him: and **smote** the Philistines from Geba until thou come to Gazer." It was a case of "Not by might, nor by power, but by my spirit, saith the Lord of hosts" (Zech 4.6)

The key to victory lay in the words, "And David did so, as the Lord commanded him." He proved that "to obey is better than sacrifice, and to hearken than the fat of rams" (1 Sam 15.22). Sadly it was a lesson that Saul did not learn. Have **you** learnt the lesson?

CHAPTER 6.1-23

"They brought in the ark of the Lord"

There is no doubt about the subject of this chapter. It is all about the "ark of the covenant." The ark is often called by this name (see, for example, Joshua 4.9) because it contained, amongst other things, the two tables of the law (Heb 9.4). Read through the chapter, and you will see that it is called "the ark of God" *(Elohim* plural) seven times (vv.2,3,4,6,7 and v.12 twice), "the ark of the Lord" *(Jehovah)* seven times (vv.9,10,11,13,15,16,17), and "the ark" once (v.4). In fact, the Scriptures assign seventeen different titles to the ark, of which sixteen are found in the Old Testament. The importance of the ark is clear from the fact that when God gave instructions to Moses, He began with the ark. This should not surprise us. The ark is a most beautiful picture, the highest figure, of the Lord Jesus, and it is therefore most fitting, not only that it should be placed first, but that it should receive so much attention in the Scriptures. Unlike the other tabernacle furniture, the ark was never replaced, and its central place in the tabernacle, and in the national life of Israel, sometimes quite apart from the tabernacle (e.g.1 Samuel 7.1 and 2 Samuel 6.1-19), reminds us that God has ordained "that in all things **He** might have the pre-eminence" (Col 1.18).

The "ark of the covenant" foreshadowed the mystery of the incarnation, in which the Lord Jesus, being God (pictured by the gold), became man (pictured by the wood), not as a dual personality, but as one unique Person. He is very God and very Man. In Bible language, "Unto us a **child is born** (the 'shittim wood'), unto us a **son is given** (the 'pure gold')" (Is 9.6); "And the **Word** (the 'pure gold') was made **flesh** ('became flesh', the 'shittim wood'), and dwelt among us" (Jn 1.14); "For in Him dwelleth **all the fulness of the Godhead** (the "pure gold") **bodily** (the 'shittim wood')" (Col 2.9). This should give you an appetite to study the ark in more detail!

The chapter can be divided into three paragraphs **(1)** The carriage of the ark (vv.1-11); **(2)** The enthusiasm of David (vv.12-19); **(3)** The contempt of Michal (vv.20-27).

1) The Carriage of the Ark (vv.1-11)

"David gathered together all the chosen men of Israel, thirty thousand. And David arose, and went with all the people that were with him from Baale of Judah, to bring up from thence the ark of God." We last saw the ark at Kirjath-jearim. "And the men of Kirjath-jearim came, and fetched up the ark of the Lord, and brought it into the house of Abinadab in the hill" (1 Sam 7.1). It remained there for something like ninety years until David arranged for its removal to Jerusalem. His deep concern for the ark is recorded in Psalm 132, "Surely I will not come into the tabernacle of my house, nor go up into my bed; I will not give sleep to mine eyes, or slumber to mine eyelids, until I find out a place for the Lord, an habitation for the mighty God of Jacob. Lo, we heard of it at Ephratah, we found it in the fields of the wood" (vv.3-6). There is no contradiction here. Kirjath-jearim means "city of the woods." Baale of Judah is the same place as Kirjath-jearim (Josh 15.60; 18.40).

The transfer of the ark from the obscurity of Kirjath-jearim to Jerusalem, the capital city, arose from David's desire for the Lord to be at the centre of national life. He was "the Lord of hosts that dwelleth between the cherubims", and the fact that the ark had been 'stored in the hillside home of a simple Israelite in no way detracted from its sacredness, as the sequel will show' (A. McShane). This reminds us that the Lord Jesus, the true ark, should be central to every part of **our** lives. We should say to Him, like the two disciples at Emmaus, "Abide with us" (Lk 24.29).

The nation was with David to a man. This is clear from the parallel passage in 1 Chronicles 13.1-14. "And David said unto all the congregation of Israel, If it seem good unto you, and that it be of the Lord our God, let us send abroad unto our brethren every where...And all the congregation said that they would do so: for the thing was right in the sight of the people: So David gathered all Israel together, from Shihor of Egypt even unto the entering of Hemath, to bring the ark of God from Kirjath-jearim." The "thirty thousand" chosen men were not fighting men, but picked men. They were evidently the representatives of the entire nation. This reminds us that the Lord Jesus should be at the centre of our assembly life. It is a happy assembly that can sing in sincerity and truth:

2 Samuel

> With Jesus in our midst,
> We gather round the board;
> Though many, we are one in Christ,
> One body in the Lord.

The journey from Kirjath-jearim to Jerusalem was interrupted by disaster, and we must now consider **(A)** the results of the improper carriage of the ark (vv.3-9) and **(B)** the results of the proper carriage of the ark (vv.10-11). It's worth remembering that David had just inflicted two crushing defeats on the Philistines (5.18-25). Perhaps his great success in battle had made him careless in other ways. There's a lesson here!

A) The improper carriage of the ark (vv.3-9)
This resulted in the death of Uzzah at Nachon's threshingfloor. There are some important lessons here:

i) They copied the world (vv.3-4). "And they set the ark of God upon a new cart, and brought it out of the house of Abinadab that was in Gibeah (meaning "hill", see 1 Sam 6.1).and Uzzah and Ahio, the sons of Abinadab, drave the new cart." This contravened God's instructions for the transportation of the ark. It was to be carried by the Kohathites, one of the three Levitical families. See Numbers 4.4-15. Whilst wagons were provided for the transportation of other parts of the tabernacle (Num 7.1-8), the Kohathites were to carry the ark, the table of shewbread, the candlestick, the altar of incense, and the brasen altar. They felt the weight of these holy things. Their responsibilities demanded strength and dignity, and this reminds us that we must never treat "the things concerning Himself" (Lk 24.27) lightly or carelessly.

But Israel copied the Philistines, who returned the ark to Beth-shemesh on "a new cart" (1 Sam 6.7-8). It seemed a very good idea! After all, it was much more convenient and efficient to transport the ark in this way, so why bother about those stuffy old instructions given by Moses about three hundred and fifty years ago! Let's "get with it!". Israel was about to discover that God expected His people to obey His word, and nothing has changed. See 1 Corinthians 14.37, "If any man think himself to be a prophet, or spiritual, let him acknowledge that the things that I write unto you are the commandments of the Lord." As C I. Scofield *(The Scofield Bible)* observes, "The church is full of Philistine ways of doing service for Christ." Above all people, the priests and Levites present (see 1 Chronicles 13.2) should have known better, and it is always tragic when things go wrong, and responsible men stay silent.

ii) They made plenty of noise (v.5). "And David and all the house of Israel played before the Lord on all manner of instruments made of fir wood, even on harps, and psalteries, and on timbrels, and on cymbals." There was nothing wrong with that! It was all part of their praise to God, and it's worth remembering that the temple choirs were not involved in public entertainment either. See 1 Chronicles 6.31; 9.33. The New Testament epistles have nothing to say about musical instruments or musical accompaniment, but they have a lot to say about praise! See, for example (Eph 5.19; Col 3.16). But Israel's rejoicing was not accompanied by obedience to God's word. Let's remember that "to obey is better than sacrifice, and to hearken than the fat of rams" (1 Sam 15.22).

iii) They encountered disaster (vv.6-8). "Uzzah put forth his hand to the ark of God, and took hold of it; for the oxen shook it. And the anger of the Lord was kindled against Uzzah; and God smote him there for his error; and there he died by the ark of God." Uzzah paid with his life for his perilous disregard for the holiness of God. He failed 'to observe the regulations laid down to safeguard respect for God's holiness' (J Baldwin). As H. Mowvley says, "The difference between God and humanity must always be maintained, and there was need for reverence and awe in God's presence." We must never forget that "holiness becometh thine house, O Lord, for ever" (Ps 93.5), and "holy and reverend is his name" (Ps 111.9). The Lord Jesus taught His disciples to call God "our Father", but also to say, "Hallowed be thy name" (Mt 6.9).

The Philistines were not struck dead when they handled the ark, for the simple reason that they knew nothing at all about the instructions in Numbers 4. Privilege determines responsibility. The Lord Jesus taught that "unto whomsoever much is given, of him shall much be required" (Lk 12.48). See also James 3.1, "My brethren, be not many masters (teachers), knowing that we shall receive the greater condemnation."

iv) They felt intense disappointment (v.9). "And David was afraid of the Lord that day, and said, How shall the ark of God come to me?" The answer should have been clear to him. "To this man will I look, even to him that is poor and of a contrite spirit, and trembleth at my word" (Is 66.2). The Lord Jesus said, "If a man love me, he will keep my words: and my Father will love him, and we will come unto him, and make our abode with him" (Jn 14.23).

B) The proper carriage of the ark (vv.10-11)
"So David would not remove the ark of the Lord unto him into the city of David.but David carried it aside into the house of Obed-edom the Gittite." "Obed-edom (see 1 Chron 26.4,8) was a Levite of the family of the Korahites, who sprang from Kohath, and belonged to a class of Levitical doorkeepers, whose duty it was, in connection with other Levites, to watch over the ark in the sacred tent (1 Chron 15.18, 24). Obed-edom is called the Gittite, or Gathite, from his birthplace, the Levitical city of Gath-rimmon in the tribe of Dan (Josh 21.24; 19.45)" (Keil & Delitzsch).

It is important to notice that David **"carried"** (not personally, of course) the ark into the house of Obed-edom. This was the scriptural way to transport the ark. The "new cart" had been abandoned! If the improper carriage of the ark resulted in disaster (v.7), then its proper carriage resulted in blessing. "And the ark of the Lord continued in the house of Obed-edom the Gittite three months: and the Lord blessed Obed-edom, and all his household." So the ark was "carried", and "continued", and brought blessing. How much more when the Lord Jesus Himself is present amongst His people! The Lord Jesus said, "If ye love me, keep my commandments" (Jn 15.15), and when we do this we can also expect His richest blessing.

2) The Enthusiasm of David (vv.12-19)
David saw that it **was** possible to live in close proximity to the ark, and made arrangements for the resumption of the journey to Jerusalem. "And it was told king David, saying, the Lord hath blessed the household of Obed-edom, and all that pertaineth to him because of the ark of God. So David went and brought up the ark of God from the house of Obed-edom into the city of David with gladness." He had learned from his mistake. "And it was so, that when they that **bare** the ark of the Lord had gone six **paces**...." David now realised that obedience to God's word brought joy and blessing, and that enthusiasm and sincerity were not enough. This is clear from the parallel passage in 1 Chronicles 15.1–16.3, which is followed by a psalm of praise (1 Chronicles 16.4-36). "None ought to carry the ark of God but the Levites: for them hath the Lord chosen to carry the ark of God, and to minister unto him for ever… sanctify yourselves, both ye and your brethren, that ye may bring up the ark of the Lord God of Israel unto the place that I have prepared for it. For because ye did it not at the first, the Lord our God

made a breach upon us, for that we sought him not after the due order....And the children of the Levites bare the ark of God upon their shoulders with the staves thereon, as Moses commanded according to the word of the Lord" (1 Chron 15.2,11-15).

If we do not learn from our mistakes, we will certainly repeat them. Jehoshaphat made alliances with three successive generations of wicked kings in Israel. Read 2 Chronicles 18.3, 20.35; 2 Kings 3.7. We must now notice:

A) David's joy (vv.12-15)
"And David danced before the Lord with all his might: and David was girded with a linen ephod." A. McShane observes that "possibly at no other time in his life did he attempt priestly manners as on this occasion. He put off his kingly robes and dressing in the priestly attire of linen, he girded himself with a linen girdle: he even went as far as to bless the people. In all this he is a shadow of the King Priest Who will sit in David's throne." See Zecheriah 6.13. All believers are priests: see, for example Revelation 1.6.

Whilst David's exuberance cannot be taken as a precedent for modern practices, where people dance in the aisles, and are carried along on the crest of emotional waves, his enthusiasm does remind us that we should have a holy joy in divine things. There is no New Testament teaching or exhortation about 'dancing before the Lord', but a miserable Christian is not a good advertisement for the gospel of Christ! Obedience brings joy. "If ye keep my commandments, ye shall abide in my love; even as I have kept my Father's commandments, and abide in his love. These things have I spoken unto you, that my joy might remain in you, and that your joy might be full" (Jn 15.10-11). "His commandments are not grievous 'burdensome'" (1 Jn 5.3).

It is quite possible that Psalm 47 recalls the procession of the ark here. The words, "God is gone up with a shout, the Lord with the sound of a trumpet" (v.5) certainly seem to echo 2 Samuel 6.15, "So David and all the house of Israel brought up the ark of the Lord with shouting, and with the sound of a trumpet."

B) Michal's disdain (v.16)
But David's enthusiasm and devotion to the Lord were not shared by his wife, Michal. "And as the ark of the Lord came into the city of David, Michal

Saul's daughter looked through a window, and saw king David leaping and dancing before the Lord; and she despised him in her heart." She despised "the man after God's own heart" (1 Sam 13.14). Sadly, she had no conception of the spiritual values which were so precious to her husband.

Don't be too surprised if you discover that your love and devotion to the Lord Jesus isn't appreciated by everybody. Sadly, even fellow-Christians can be critical at times. The Lord's own family thought He was "beside himself" (Mk 3.21). Oh, by the way, do **you** think that some Christians are a bit "over the top" at times? Perhaps their enthusiasm puts us to shame.

C) David's devotion (v.17)
"And they brought in the ark of the Lord, and set it in his place, in the midst of the tabernacle (tent) that David had pitched for it: and David offered burnt-offerings and peace offerings before the Lord." Notice that it was only the ark that David brought to Jerusalem. The tabernacle itself, with all its furniture and fittings, was not brought up to Jerusalem until the days of Solomon. See 1 Kings 8.4.

The burnt-offerings and peace-offerings were voluntary offerings. Both were offerings "made by fire, of a sweet savour unto the Lord" (Lev 1.17; 3.16). Perhaps this is a good opportunity to remind ourselves of the significance of these offerings. They were offerings made in worship, rather than because of sin.

i) "The burnt-offerings." In this case, the whole of the victim was burnt (the word means to burn as incense), reminding us of the Lord Jesus who said, "I delight to do thy will, O my God", Psalm 40.8, quoted (but not completely) in Hebrews 10.7,9. In the burnt offering, the excellence of the offering was imputed to the offerer, reminding us that we are "accepted in the beloved" (Eph 1.6). (In the case of the sin offering, the sin of the offerer was imputed to the offering). Just think about that! We can draw near to God in worship because we are accepted in all the fragrance of Christ Himself!

ii) "The peace-offerings." In this case, part of the offering was burnt on the altar (God's portion); part was eaten by the priest, and part was eaten by the offerer. In other words, the peace-offering beautifully depicts men and women enjoying fellowship and communion with God. We enjoy what God enjoys! F. B. Meyer puts it nicely. "We feed on the peace-offering when we meditate on the love and death of our blessed Lord, and enter into some of the Father's thoughts of satisfaction at the work He did, and the spirit in which He did it."

D) David's distribution (vv.18-19)
"And as soon as David had made an end of offering burnt-offerings and peace-offerings, he blessed the people in the name of the Lord of hosts. And he dealt among all the people, even among the whole multitude of Israel, as well to the women as men, to every one a cake of bread, and a good piece of flesh, and a flagon of wine. So all the people departed every one to his house." The close connection between the presentation of the offerings and the blessing of the people reminds us that all our blessings flow from the work of the Lord Jesus. The people went home with provision for a good family meal. It doesn't take much imagination to arrive at the subject of the table-talk that night. They were eating a celebratory meal. The sacred ark was now resident in Jerusalem. God was amongst them! (Don't think that the wine went to their heads, will you? It seems that "a flagon of wine" could mean "a raisin cake!").

David, the chosen leader of the people, gave his subjects something to eat, and spiritual leaders should do the same. God's people should be well-nourished by good Bible teaching. God censured Israel's shepherds: "Woe to the shepherds of Israel that do feed themselves! Should not the shepherds feed the flocks?" (Ezek 34.2). See also Acts 20.28 and 1 Peter 5.2. (In both cases, the word "feed" means "tend").

3) The Contempt of Michal (vv.20-23)
David got a rude shock when he went home. Having "blessed the people" (v.18), he returned to "bless his household, and was greeted with contempt. Listen to her sarcasm: "How glorious was the king of Israel today!" Her hopes had been dashed. This was the man who had killed two hundred Philistines for the privilege of marrying her. As J. Baldwin observes, "She preferred the brave warrior image to that of the humble, worshipping king, stripped of all his royal regalia, and as she saw it, uncovering himself, or maybe showing off. Michal did not share her husband's enthusiasm. Like her father, she had no interest in the ark. See 1 Chronicles 13.3.

David's reply shows very clearly that he was more concerned with honouring the Lord than boosting his own ego. He had "rejoiced before Jehovah" and "played before Jehovah" (JND). Notice his willingness to abase himself. "I will be base in my own sight." This gives rise to two very interesting observations.

i) That his place in God's purposes did not go to his head. He did not have a high opinion of himself. He gave all honour to God. "It was before the Lord, which chose me before thy father, and before all his house, to appoint me ruler over the people of the Lord, over Israel: therefore will I play before the Lord" (v.21).

ii) That he would be honoured by the very people that Michal thought would scoff and jeer at him. "And of the maidservants which thou hast spoken of, of them shall I be had in honour" (v.22). They appreciated David's devotion to God, even if his wife didn't!

The closing words of the chapter probably imply that "from this point on the marital relations between her and David came to an end. The relationship between them had irrevocably broken down" (J. Baldwin). She would never provide a successor to the throne.

CHAPTER 7.1-29

"Thy throne shall be established for ever"

The promises made to David in this chapter are clear and unambiguous. In the first place, they provide for the **future of Israel:** "I will appoint a place for my people Israel, and I will plant them, that they may dwell in a place of their own, and move no more; neither shall the children of wickedness afflict them any more…" (v.10). David understood this perfectly: "Thou hast confirmed to thyself thy people Israel to be a people unto thee for ever: and thou, Lord, art become their God" (v.24). In the second place, they provide for the **future of David's throne**: "Thine house and thy kingdom shall be established for ever before thee: thy throne shall be established for ever" (v.16). David understood this perfectly as well: "And now, O Lord God, the word that thou hast spoken concerning thy servant, and concerning his house, establish it for ever, and do as thou hast said. And let thy name be magnified for ever, saying, The Lord of hosts is the God of Israel: and let the house of David thy servant be established before thee" (vv.25-26).

These promises, which form the covenant with David, will be fulfilled by the Lord Jesus. He will sit "upon the throne of David, and upon his kingdom, to order it, and to establish it with judgment and with justice from henceforth even for ever. The zeal of the Lord of hosts will perform this" (Is 9.7). At His birth, the angel said, "He shall be great, and shall be called the Son of the Highest: and the Lord God shall give unto him the throne of his father David: and he shall reign over the house of Jacob for ever; and of his kingdom there shall be no end" (Lk 1.32-33). These promises are called "the sure mercies of David" (Is 55.3; Acts 13.34).

The covenant with Abraham secured the land for Israel: "For all the land which thou seest, to thee will I give it, and to thy seed for ever" (Gen 13.15). The covenant with David secured the throne for Israel.

2 Samuel

This important chapter comprises three clear paragraphs: **(1)** The proposal by David (vv.1-3); **(2)** The promises to David (vv.4-17); **(3)** The prayer of David (vv.18-29).

1) The Proposal by David (vv.1-3)
In this paragraph we should notice **(A)** David's rest (v.1); **(B)** David's reflection (v.2); **(C)** Nathan's reply (v.3).

A) David's rest (v.1)
The chapter begins with David sitting in his house, and ends with David sitting in the presence of God (v.18). "And it came to pass, when the king sat in his house, and the Lord had given him rest round about from all his enemies..." (See also v.11). This does not mean that David retired on pension from military service! In the very next chapter, he secures his kingdom by completely subduing his neighbours. He obviously believed that the best means of defence was attack! But there are no clouds on the horizon at the beginning of Chapter 7. Nobody dared to raise an army against David, not even the Philistines! "The Lord had given him rest...from all his enemies." God had fulfilled his promise in Deuteronomy 12.10.

Our spiritual enemies are not likely to give us rest! The conflict is ongoing. The Christian life is a battle-field, not a playing-field! But God does give encouragement and strength. Listen to Paul on the subject: "When we were come into Macedonia, our flesh had no rest, but we were troubled on every side; without were fightings, within were fears. Nevertheless God, that comforteth those that are cast down, comforted us by the coming of Titus...so that I rejoiced the more" (2 Cor 7.5-7).

David didn't just sit there and enjoy the view. He sat and thought about the goodness of God, and asked himself if he was honouring God as he should. This brings us to:

B) David's reflection (v.2)
"The king said unto Nathan the prophet, See now, I dwell in an house of cedar, but the ark of God dwelleth within curtains." David's house had been built by courtesy of Hiram, king of Tyre: see 2 Samuel 5.11. The ark of the covenant had been "set in his place, in the midst of the tabernacle that David had placed for it" (1 Sam 6.17). The word translated "curtains" is used to describe the two inner coverings of the tabernacle (see Exodus

26.1-13) and, presumably it refers here to the "tabernacle" (or "tent") that David had erected for the ark in Jerusalem. There seemed to be no comparison between the place where David dwelt ("in an house of cedar"), and the place where God dwelt ("within curtains"). "He realised how inconsistent it was for him to be living in a cedar palace, while the ark, with all its glory, rested in a mere tent" (A. McShane).

Perhaps we ought to sit down more often and ask ourselves if we have become so occupied with our blessings that we have forgotten to give the Lord the place of highest honour in our lives. "Honour the Lord with thy substance, and with the firstfruits of all thine increase" (Prov 3.9).

C) Nathan's reply (v.3)

We now meet Nathan for the first time. We shall see more of him in due course. Nathan and Gad were evidently David's biographers. See 1 Chronicles 29.29-30. David had obviously discussed the matter with Nathan in some detail. "And Nathan said to the king, Go, do all that is in thine heart; for the Lord is with thee." David seems to be getting into bad habits. On previous occasions, he asked for God's guidance. See 2.1; 5.19; 5.21. But he didn't seek divine guidance in connection with the removal of the ark from Kirjath-jearim to Zion, or in connection with his desire to build a "house" Like us, both Nathan and David made the same mistake, and David got wrong advice as a result! Nathan could see that it was an excellent idea, and he knew that it flowed from pure motives. There seemed no reason why he should not give the project his blessing, but events proved that it wasn't God's will at the time! As A. McShane observes, it "teaches most clearly the distinction between exercise and guidance!" A good idea isn't necessarily God's will. In chapter 6, David learnt that God's service must be undertaken in the right *way*: in chapter 7, he learnt that it must be undertaken by the right *man.*

However, God did reveal His will to David, and we can be sure that if our hearts and motives are right, He will graciously correct our thinking and set us on the right path.

2) The Promises to David (vv.4-17)

"And it came to pass that night, that the word of the Lord came unto Nathan, saying, Go and tell my servant David, Thus saith the Lord…" The details of the covenant made with David follow, but we mustn't miss two lessons in the preamble:

2 Samuel

i) The description of David. He is called, "my servant David." He was a great servant of God: so was Moses ("my servant Moses...who is faithful in all mine house", Num 12.7), and so was Job ("Hast thou considered my servant Job", Job 1. 8). But while all three failed in one way or another, there was no failure in the Perfect Servant: "Behold my servant, whom I uphold; mine elect in whom my soul delighteth" (Is 42.1).

ii) The directions to Nathan. Nathan faithfully related God's message to David, even though it was contrary to David's desire, and contrary to his own initial advice. It isn't always easy to stop people in their tracks once they start to nurture a good idea, and even more difficult to go back on previous advice! We sometimes forget that whilst a project can be right in itself, it may not be God's immediate will. In fact, it might not be His will at all. Our motives, objectives and methods may be right, but this does not mean that we should go ahead. This is why we must constantly pray for His guidance. After all, His will is perfect, and so is His timing! So be careful about putting your good ideas into practice. Ask the Lord to guide you, and don't think that He has written you off if He squashes your cherished ambitions! He wants the best for you, and your ideas could turn out to be the worst thing possible! Neither Nathan nor David resented the alteration in their plans. Notice what follows:

A) David would not build a house for God, (vv.4-7)
The question, "Shalt thou build me an house for me to dwell in?" (v.5) implies a negative answer, and this is confirmed by the parallel passage in 1 Chronicles 17.4, "Go and tell David my servant, Thus saith the Lord, Thou shalt not build me an house to dwell in..." God does not dismiss the suggestion, but makes it clear that it would not be built by David: "**Thou** shalt not build me a house to dwell in." It would be built by "thy seed after thee, which shall proceed out of thy bowels" (vv.12-13). However, God did tell David why he would not have the privilege of building "an house of rest for the ark of the covenant of the Lord." Read 1 Chronicles 28.2-3.

In these verses, the Lord allays David's fear that he had dishonoured Him by leaving the ark in a tent whilst he dwelt in "an house of cedar" (v.1). A "house to dwell in" was neither necessary nor appropriate in the past. "I have not dwelt in any house since the time that I brought up the children of Israel from Egypt, even unto this day, but have walked in a tent and in a tabernacle" (v.6). He had never commanded His people to build Him "an house of cedar" (v.7), so the former leaders of God's people had not been negligent in failing to build a house for God, and David had not been negligent either. The time for carrying out this work had not yet come. Do notice that whilst God did **not** hold His people responsible for what He had **not** told them, He **did** hold them responsible for what He **had** told them. Remember what happened to Uzzah.

The presence of God amongst his people is beautifully expressed in the words, "I...have walked in a tent *(ohel)* and in a tabernacle (*mishkan*: a dwelling)...in all the places wherein I have walked with all the children of Israel" (vv.6-7). This reminds us that centuries later "the Word was made flesh and dwelt among us" (Jn 1.14). The word "dwelt" *(skenoo)* means "to tabernacle" or "to pitch a tent." He is still with His people: "Lo, I am with you always, even unto the end of the world" (Mt 28.20). The words, "In all the places wherein I have walked...spake I a word with any of the **tribes** of Israel, whom I commanded to feed my people Israel..." (v.7), seem a little difficult to understand. The parallel passage (1 Chron 17.6) has, "Wheresoever I have walked with all Israel, spake I a word to any of the **judges** of Israel, whom I commanded to feed my people..." Keil & Delitzsch suggest that "the government of Israel, which was in the hands of the judges, was transferred to the tribes to which the judges belonged", and cite Psalm 78.67-68 in support.

B) God would build a house for David (vv.8-17)
While David was not given permission to build the temple, "the Lord valued his concern for the ark, and amply repaid him for what he did in thought, though not by hand" (A. McShane). Remember, too, that when God says "No" to our plans, it is because he has something far better in mind! The promises made to David are permeated with divine certainty. Notice the occurrences of "I will" (vv.10,12,13,14), and the assurance with which the promises end: "And thine house and thy kingdom shall be established for ever before thee: thy throne shall be established for ever" (v.16). But the "I will" also emphasises that the Lord will fulfil the promises Himself. If their fulfilment was left to David's successors, there would have been no future for the house of David. But what made God's promises reliable?

i) The assurance of the past (vv.8.-9)
"*I took thee* from the sheepcote, from following the sheep, to be ruler over my people, over Israel: and *I was with thee* whithersoever thou wentest, and have cut off all thine enemies out thy sight, and **have made thee** a great name, like unto the name of the great men that are in the earth."

God's faithfulness, ability and power could not be doubted. They were proven facts. David's greatness and success were wholly due to "the one who had accompanied him unseen through all his life" (J. Baldwin). It is certainly worth noticing that Nathan was instructed to say, "Now therefore so shalt thou say unto my servant David..." (v.10). J. Baldwin puts it like this: "My servant David" is an honoured title, but at the same time a reminder to David that, though he is king, and surrounded by those who serve him, he too has his servant role in relation to his God...If David had his eyes on greatness, it would begin with submission and service to the Lord God."

ii) The certainty of the future (vv.10-16)
God had been faithful to David in the past, and he could therefore be absolutely certain that He would be faithful in the future. Do remember that if there is no certainty that God will fulfil His promises to David, then there is no certainty that He will fulfil His promises to **us.**

a) The certainty of David's kingdom (vv.10-11a). "I will appoint a place for my people Israel, and I will plant them, that they may dwell in a place of their own, and move no more; neither shall the children of wickedness afflict them any more, as beforetime, and as since the time that I commanded judges to be over my people Israel, and have caused thee to rest from thine enemies." (Compare Amos 9.14-15). This promise is beautifully confirmed in Isaiah 66.22, "For as the new heavens and the new earth, which I will make, shall remain before me, saith the Lord, so shall your seed and your name remain." See also Jeremiah 31.35-37.

b) The certainty of David's house (vv.11b-17). It begins with, "Also the Lord telleth thee that he will make thee an house." The play on the word "house" is clear. It is now used in the sense of "dynasty." This covers the near future (vv.12-14) and the distant future (vv.15-16).

The **near future** is occupied with David's successor. "And when thy days shall be fulfilled, and thou shalt sleep with thy fathers (do notice the word "sleep" here), I will set up thy seed after thee, which shall proceed out of thy bowels, and I will establish his kingdom. He shall build an house for my name, and I will establish the throne of his kingdom for ever" (v.11b-13). It was, of course, Solomon, David's son, who built the temple. We must notice what follows. "I will be his father, and he shall be my son", and this implies discipline: "If he commit iniquity, I will chasten him with the rod of men, and with the stripes of the children of men" (v.14). But it also implies "lovingkindness" or "steadfast love", which is the meaning of the word "mercy" *(chesed)* here: "But my mercy shall not depart from him, as I took it away from Saul, whom I put away before thee" (v.15). It is most important to notice that disobedience in David's family would bring chastening, but **not** the termination of the covenant. See Amos 8.8-11. Sadly, Solomon "committed iniquity" (see 2 Kings 11) and was chastened. Many of his successors, kings of "the house and lineage of David", followed suit, and were severely chastened by God until, ultimately, the kingdom was lost, and it was said of the last king, Zedekiah, "Remove the diadem, and take off the crown...I will overturn, overturn, overturn: and it shall be no more, until he come whose right it is: and I will give it to him" (Ezek 21.25-27). The King "whose right it is", is the Lord Jesus Christ. He will sit "upon the throne of David, and upon his kingdom, to order it, and to establish it with judgment and with justice from henceforth even for ever. The zeal of the Lord of hosts will perform this" (Is 9.7).

The words, "I will be his father, and he shall be my son", are cited in Hebrews 1.5 where they are applied to the Lord Jesus. He will be the ideal King. There is no question of Him committing iniquity, and therefore the balance of 2 Samuel 7.14 is omitted. Of course!

This brings us to the **distant future**. It was the "distant future" at the time, but it must be the "imminent future" now! "And thine house and thy kingdom shall be established for ever before thee: thy throne shall be established for ever" (v.16). God's steadfast love for His people will ensure that the promises made to David are fulfilled. He has not, and will not, withdraw his "mercy." He says of Israel, "Yea, I have loved thee with an everlasting love: therefore with lovingkindness have I drawn thee. Again I will build thee, O virgin of Israel: thou shalt again be adorned with thy tabrets, and shalt go forth in the dances of them that make merry" (Jer 31.3-4).

In view of the revelation of his part in God's purposes, David can only worship. He prays that all that the Lord has spoken will be fulfilled.

3) The Prayer of David (vv.18-29)
"Then went king David in, and sat before the Lord..." This is quite an astounding verse, even though the word translated "sat" *(yashab)* is more likely to mean "abode": it is used in this way in Gen 24.55; 29.19 etc. David entered the Lord's presence, something normally reserved for the high priest. It must have been an awe-inspiring experience. Now read Heb

2 Samuel

10.19-22. Shouldn't it be an awe-inspiring experience for **us** as well? David's prayer can be divided into four parts.

A) He recognises his own unworthiness (vv.18-19)
"Who am I, O Lord God? And what is my house, that thou hast brought me hitherto? And this was yet a small thing in thy sight, O Lord God; but thou hast spoken also of thy servant's house for a great while to come. And is this the manner of man, O Lord God?" God had already done so much for David, but as if that wasn't enough, God had something even bigger in view! Don't **we** feel the same when we think of God's grace to us? "Behold, what manner of love the Father hath bestowed upon us, that we should be called the sons God" (1 Jn 3.1). We are certainly blessed for "a great while to come!" We are "heirs of God, and joint heirs with Christ" (Rom 8.17).

B) He recognises the greatness of God (vv.20-22)
"And what can David say any more unto thee? For thou, Lord God, knowest thy servant. For thy word's sake, and according to thine own heart, hast thou done all these great things, to make thy servant know them. Wherefore thou art great, O Lord God: for there is none like thee, neither is there any God beside thee, according to all that we have heard with our ears." God is sovereign: He acts according to His "own heart"; God communicates: He reveals His purposes to His servants; God is incomparable: "there is none like thee, neither is there any God beside thee."

C) He recognises the uniqueness of Israel (vv.23-24)
"And what one nation in the earth is like thy people, even like Israel, whom God went to redeem for a people to himself, and to make him a name, and to do for you great things and terrible, for thy land, before thy people, which thou redeemedst to thee from Egypt, from the nations and their gods? For thou hast confirmed to thyself thy people Israel to be a people unto thee for ever: and thou, Lord, art become their God." David looks back in v.23, and forward in v.24. Israel's national life began in Egypt, and it will continue "for ever." God's people were wonderfully privileged in other ways: see, for example, Deuteronomy 4.32-38; Psalm 147.19-20; 148.14, Romans 3.1-2; 9.4-5. We are wonderfully privileged too: see, for example, 1 Peter 2.9-10.

D) He asks God to implement His promises (vv.25-29)
"And now, O Lord God, the word that thou hast spoken concerning thy servant, and concerning his house, establish it for ever, and do as thou

hast said...let the house of David be established before thee...let it please thee to bless the house of thy servant, that it may continue for ever before thee...and with thy blessing let the house of thy servant be blessed for ever." David makes it clear that he would not have prayed like this had God not made these promises to him. "Thou hast revealed to thy servant, saying, I will build thee an house: **therefore** hath thy servant found in his heart to pray this prayer unto thee...Therefore now let it please thee to bless the house of thy servant, that it may continue for ever before thee: **for** thou, O Lord God, hast spoken it." We should always pray in accordance with the word of God, shouldn't we? "And this is the confidence that we have in him, that, if we ask anything according to his will, he heareth us" (1 Jn 5.14).

CHAPTER 8.1-22

"David gat him a name"

In this chapter, we reach the highest point in David's achievements. "And David reigned over all Israel" (v.15). Chapter 7 closes with David worshipping and praying in the Lord's presence (vv.18-29). Chapter 8 opens with David on the battlefield. The opposition was no match for him, not because of his native military genius but because "the Lord preserved David whithersoever he went" (vv.6,14). David attacked his pagan neighbours with the assurance that God had never failed him in the past (ch.7.9), and had promised that his house and his throne would "be established for ever" (ch.7.16). When David mounted his military campaigns he was armed with the promises of God as well as the usual weaponry! No wonder he was so successful! The sequence in the two chapters is therefore most significant, and the connection between them is clearly spelt out: "And after this it came to pass..." (ch.8.1). David opened his campaigns in the spirit of worship and praise. There could be no better way in which to engage the enemy.

This chapter falls into two sections. **(1) David's foreign affairs: he attacks his enemies (vv.1-14)**; he "smote the Philistines (v.1)...Moab (v.2)...Hadadezer (v.3)...slew of the Syrians two and twenty thousand men (v.5)...put garrisons in Edom" (v.14). David secured the borders of his kingdom. **(2) David's home affairs: he administers his kingdom (vv.15-18)**; "David executed judgment and justice unto all his people" (v.15). There is a parallel passage in 1 Chronicles 18.1-17.

1) David Attacks His Enemies (vv.1-14)
His enemies were located to the **west** the Philistines (v.1), to the **east** the Moabites (v.2), to the **north** Hadadezer and the Syrians (vv.3-8): but there was also a friend in Toi King of Hamath (vv.9-10), and to the **south** the Edomites (vv.13-14). It reminds us of the hymn:

Chapter 8

> Oh, let me feel Thee near me, the world is ever near;
> I see the sights that dazzle, the tempting sounds I hear:
> My foes are ever near me, around me and within;
> But, Jesus, draw Thou nearer, and shield my soul from sin.
>
> John E Bode

A) The western campaign (v.1)

"And after this it came to pass, that David smote the Philistines, and subdued them: and David took Metheg-ammah out of the hand of the Philistines." According to Keil & Delitzsch, "Metheg-ammah" means "the bridle of the mother." It was evidently a figurative name for Gath. See 1 Chronicles 18.1: "David...took Gath and her towns (literally, "daughters") out of the hand of the Philistines." Keil & Delitzsch argue that Gath had become the capital of Philistia (they quote 1 Samuel 29.2 in support) and that the city "held the bridle (or reins) of Philistia in its own hand." It is important to remember how the Philistines had attacked and harassed God's people in the past. We dealt with this in our studies in 1 Samuel, so this is revision! *(a)* **They filled wells:** "For all the wells which his (Isaac's) father's servants had digged...the Philistines had stopped them, and filled them with earth" (Gen 26.15); *(b)* **They prevented ascent:** "After that thou shalt come to the hill of God, where is a garrison of the Philistines" (1 Sam 10.5); *(c)* **They monopolised weapons:** "Now there was no smith found throughout all the land of Israel: for the Philistines said, Lest the Hebrews make them swords or spears" (1 Sam 13.19); *(d)* **They despatched spoilers:** "And the spoilers came out of the camp of the Philistines in three companies" (1 Sam 13.17); *(e)* **They exercised lordship.**: "Knowest thou not that the Philistines are rulers over us?" (Jud 15.11). These tactics are still used by *our* spiritual opponents. The Philistines have their counterpart in the satanically led "principalities and powers" (Eph 6.12).

B) The eastern campaign (v.2)

"And he smote Moab, and measured them with a line, casting them down to the ground; even with two lines measured he to put to death, and with one full line to keep alive. And so the Moabites became David's servants, and brought gifts." This partly fulfilled Balaam's prophecy: "there shall come a Star out of Jacob, and a sceptre shall arise out of Israel, and shall smite all the corners of Moab..." (Num 24.17). This prophecy will be finally fulfilled by Christ. Keil & Delitzsch suggest that the death of the Moabites here is restricted to soldiers taken as prisoners of war. This is how they describe it: "they were ordered to lie down in a row upon the earth; and then the row was measured for the purpose of putting two thirds to death, and leaving one third alive." We do not

2 Samuel

know what prompted David to act in this way, and can only conclude that he was avenging some ghastly crime against Israel. In the past, the king of Moab had provided a safe haven for David's parents (1 Sam 22.3-4), and David's great-grandmother (Ruth) was a Moabitess.

However, Moab and Ammon do remind us of Abraham's mistake about a thousand years previously. God had told him to leave his "kindred" and his "father's house" (Gen 12.1), but Lot accompanied him to Caanan (Gen 12.4) and became the father of Moab and Ammon in the most appalling circumstances (Gen 19.30-38). Incomplete obedience to God's will yields a bitter harvest.

The death of the Moabites here reminds us that we must act without mercy when dealing with the results of sin in our lives. "Mortify (put to death) therefore your members which are upon the earth: fornication, uncleanness, inordinate affection ("passion" RV), evil concupiscence ("evil desire"), and covetousness..." (Col 5). Bearing in mind that "Moab hath been at ease from his youth, and he hath settled on his lees" (Jer 48.11), it also reminds us that we must deal ruthlessly with our complacency!

C) The northern campaign (vv.3-10)
David encountered foes and friends in the north, and we must therefore subdivide this section as follows: *(i)* enemies in the north (vv.3-8,13); *(ii)* friends in the north (vv.9-10).

i) Enemies in the north (vv.3-8)
"David also smote Hadadezer, the son of Rehob, king of Zobah, as he went to recover his border at the river Euphrates...And when the Syrians of Damascus came to succour Hadadezer king of Zobah, David slew of the Syrians two and twenty thousand men" (vv.3,5). Keil & Delitzsch tell us that it is not possible to identify Zobah, but it was evidently closely allied to Syria. See 2 Samuel 10.6,8. As J. Baldwin observes, David "chose a moment when the king, Hadadezer, was campaigning to recapture territory that had belonged to him in the north, including part of the Euphrates river." This was some distance from David's territory, but Joshua was told that "from the wilderness and this Lebanon even unto the great river, the river Euphrates...shall be your coast" (Josh 1.2). It does seem that Hadadezer was endeavouring to recover territory taken from him by Saul (1 Sam 14.47), and David took steps to ensure that he didn't succeed. He "took from him a thousand chariots, and seven hundred horsemen (1 Chron 18.4) has

"seven thousand horsemen": the difference being only in two dots over the letter marking the numeral in Hebrew), and twenty thousand footmen: and David houghed all the chariot horses (made them lame by cutting the tendons in their legs), but reserved of them for an hundred chariots."

Now there's an important lesson for us! Our spiritual enemies are always ready to make a comeback. Let's look back to those early days in our Christian lives, when we kicked out things that rivalled the Lord Jesus, and gave Him first place. Are we ***still*** keeping them out, or do we have to sing

> Where is the blessedness I knew
> When first I saw the Lord?
> Where is the soul-refreshing view
> Of Jesus and His word?
> William Cowper

Don't let the things you abandoned for Christ gain a toehold in your life again. If they can regain an inch, it won't be long before they take a mile! David saw Hadadezer coming, and stopped him in his tracks. Do the same! Nip things in the bud, or you'll find yourself with very big problems.

Sometimes old enemies come back with added power, and in this case, Hadadezer was supported by the Syrians of Damascus. Since David "smote Hadadezer (a slightly different spelling here) king of Zobah unto Hamath" (1 Chron 18.3), it seems possible that the Syrians planned to attack him from behind. (Consult a map of the area, and look for Hamath). We do need to be alert. The enemy can strike from any direction. We must not be "ignorant of his devices" (2 Cor 2.11).

ii) *Friends in the north (vv.9-10)*
At this point in the narrative a grateful friend appears. "When Toi king of Hamath heard that David had smitten all the host of Hadadezer, then Toi sent Joram his son unto king David, to salute him, and to bless him, because he had fought against Hadadezer, and smitten him: for Hadadezer had wars with Toi. And Joram brought with him vessels of silver, and vessels of gold, and vessels of brass." David had defeated Hadadezer on Toi's doorstep, and the grateful king of Hamath acknowledged his debt to David in the customary manner. There may have been a little more to this: "As a result of his victory over Zobah, David's prestige rose to such an extent that the king of Hamath on the Orontes river, over a hundred miles north of

Damascus, took the precaution of forestalling any attack on his territory by sending his son as an ambassador to David...King Toi...by volunteering tribute, was pledging his support for the newly victorious Israelite king" (J. Baldwin). One thing is clear, David did not attack all and sundry. He did not wage war purely for the sake of gaining territorial advantage. These verses therefore remind us that, like Toi, we should always display our gratitude to those who help us (Paul did this in Philippians 4.14-19).

David did not take tribute for personal or national advantage. The brass taken from Hadadezer was used by Solomon in building the temple. See 1 Chronicles 18.8. He did not use the gifts sent by Toi (v.10), and the silver and gold paid as tribute by the conquered nations (vv.11-12), to build opulent palaces in the same way as Saddam Hussein, but dedicated them "unto the Lord" (v.11). Paul could say, "we are not as many which corrupt the word of God (make a trade of the word of God): but as of sincerity, but as of God, in the sight of God speak we in Christ" (2 Cor 2.17). Paul was not like some American television evangelists!

David devoted his massive income of precious and valuable metals to the Lord, and we must not forget the Lord's teaching on the subject: "Lay not up for yourselves treasures upon earth, where moth and rust doth corrupt, and where thieves break through and steal: but lay up for yourselves treasures in heaven..." (Mt 19-20). Remember too, His teaching in connection with the rich farmer in Luke 12, with its conclusion, "so is he that layeth up treasure for himself, and is not rich toward God" (v.21). David did not "lay up treasure for himself." Read 1 Chronicles 28.11-19. David's policy in this respect will be repeated at the end-time, when God will say, "Arise and thresh, O daughter of Zion: for I will make thine horn iron, and I will make thy hoofs brass: and thou shalt beat in pieces many people: and I will consecrate their gain unto the Lord, and their substance unto the Lord of the whole earth" (Mic 4.13).

D) The southern campaign (vv.13-14)
"And David gat him a name when he returned from smiting of the Syrians (JND margin has "some read Edomites") in the valley of salt, being eighteen thousand men. And he put garrisons in Edom; throughout all Edom put he garrisons, and all they of Edom became David's servants." Bearing in mind the parallel passage in 1 Chronicles 18.12, "Moreover Abishai the son of Zeruiah slew of the Edomites in the valley of salt eighteen thousand" and that Amaziah later smote the Edomites in the same place (2 Kings 14.7,

the reading "Edomites" rather than "Syrians" is evidently correct. Do notice that according to 1 Chronicles 18.12-23, it was actually Abishai who fought against the Edomites, but David received the glory. It reminds us that we should live and act in a way which brings glory to the Lord Jesus. According to Keil & Delitzsch, "valley of salt" "cannot have been any other than the Ghor adjoining the Salt Mountain on the south of the Dead Sea, which really separates the ancient territories of Judah and Edom." J. Baldwin suggests that "the large number of Edomites put to death implies an attempt to invade Israel from the south, and so preserve their monopoly on trade routes through the desert to the Red Sea port of Ezion Geber." If this was the case, it paved the way for the development of trade during the reign of Solomon. See 1 Kings 9.26-28. Like Moab, Balaam's prophecy against Edom was partly fulfilled by David; "and Edom shall be a possession, Seir also shall be a possession for his enemies: and Israel shall do valiantly" (Num 24.18).

The Edomites were the inveterate enemies of God's people. They were known for their pride. "The pride of thine heart hath deceived thee, thou that dwellest in the clefts of the rock, whose habitation is high; that saith in his heart, Who shall bring me down to the ground?" (Ob v.3). It was the mountainous terrain of their country that gave the Edomites the security in which they boasted.

David was successful in all directions because "the Lord preserved David whithersoever he went" (vv.6,14). Let's look back over the various enemies in the passage, and check our own success rate. The same Lord will help and preserve us in our battles too if we seek His face and submit to His will.

2) David Administers His Kingdom (vv.15-18)
In this section of the chapter we should notice the extent and character of his administration (v.15), and the officers in his administration (vv.16-18).

A) The extent of his administration (v.15)
"And David reigned over all Israel." This began with his anointing at Hebron by "all the elders of Israel" (2 Sam 5.1-5), and is restated here to emphasise the unity of the kingdom at the height of his reign. Does the Lord Jesus reign supreme in **all** our hearts? We talk about the need for assembly unity. It can only exist when every member recognises Him as "Lord of all." Unity is quite different to uniformity!

B) The character of his administration (v.15)

"David executed judgment and justice unto all his people." Prior to David's reign, this had been exercised by the Judges up to and including the time of Samuel. See Judges 3.10; 4.4; 15.20; 1 Samuel 7.15. Since the judiciary had been in the hands of the national leaders, it is not surprising that David became supreme judge. He ensured that "judgment" (meaning "justice") and "justice" (meaning "equity") were available to all his people without prejudice or discrimination. The men who judged Israel were to be examples to the nation: "He that ruleth over men must be just, ruling in the fear of God" (2 Sam 23.3). This has not changed. Do notice that the words "judgment" and "justice" will characterise the reign of "great David's greater Son" (Is 9.7).

C) The officers in his administration (vv.16-18)

We could call them "David's fellow-labourers" (Phil 2.25, 4.3). David didn't attempt to do everything himself, and A. McShane has some wise things to say on the subject: "It is obvious from this paragraph that while David was a just and wise ruler, he in no way was independent of the help of others. He knew how to share responsibility, and how to discern those fitted to carry it. In assembly life this is a vital feature of its wellbeing." It is said that in business "delegation is the art of good management."

i) Joab (v.16)

"Joab the son of Zeruiah was over the host." He was David's commander-in-chief. He was not chosen because he was a relative but because he was the first man to enter Zion via the water shaft. See 1 Chronicles 11.6, "And David said, Whosover smiteth the Jebusites first shall be chief and captain. So Joab the son of Zeruiah went first up, and was chief." There was no doubt about his military expertise, but he was not a very nice character. He had a nasty habit of killing people in cold blood, particularly when they looked like possible rivals. See 2 Samuel 4.23-27; 20.4-12. He supported Adonijah instead of Solomon, and was executed by Benaiah (1 Kings 2.28-35). Joab does remind us, however, that **in the assembly** we need people who will take the lead in carrying the battle to the enemy: who will "earnestly contend for the faith" (Jude v.3).

ii) Jehoshaphat (v.16)

"Jehoshaphat the son of Ahilud was recorder." We know nothing further about him. The word "recorder" comes from the Hebrew "to remember." It is worth remembering that copies of God's word were not freely available as they are today, and that men who could recall the scriptures were invaluable. According to J. Baldwin, he had "a most important role at court, with responsibility for keeping the king informed, advising him, and communicating the king's commands." See 2 Kings 18.18-37, and 2 Chronicles 34.8. Jehoshaphat reminds us that *in the assembly*, we need people who will call us to remembrance: see 2 Peter 1.12-13.

iii) Zadok and Ahimelech (v.17)
"Zadok the son of Ahitub, and Ahimelech the son of Abiathar, were the priests." It has been suggested that David's unusual choice of two priests (they are not called "high priests") was based on diplomatic grounds, because he chose a man from each of the two priestly families. It has also been suggested that one functioned at Jerusalem (where the ark was located), and the other (definitely Zadok) at Gibeon (where the tabernacle was located: 1 Chron 16.39, 21.29). Zadok and Ahimelech remind us that *in the assembly*, we need effective priesthood. See 1 Peter 1.5,9.

iv) Seriah (v.17)
"Seriah was the scribe." He acted as David's "Secretary of State." Solomon had two scribes (1 Kings 4.3). According to Gesenius, the scribes at this time were "the friends of the king whose office it was to write his letters". (They didn't have shorthand skills and lap-tops in those days!) Later, the word "scribe" describes "a person skilled in sacred writings", of which Ezra is a good example (Ezra 7.6, Neh 8.1). Seraiah reminds us that *in the assembly*, everything should be done "decently and in order" (1 Cor 14.40), including secretarial work and public relations!

v) Benaiah (v.18)
"Benaiah the son of Jehoiada was over the Cherethites and the Pelethites." Benaiah was one of David's "mighty men", and David "set him over his guard" (2 Sam 23.23). Some commentators suggest that the Cherethites (possibly meaning "executioners") and the Pelethites (possibly meaning "runners") were foreign mercenaries from Crete or Philistia. This seems highly unlikely! They evidently formed David's body-guard (2 Sam 20.7) and later, Solomon's body-guard (1 Kings 1.38,44). This reminds us that in *the assembly,* we need people who will "guard the deposit" (1 Tim 6.20 RV margin: AV "keep that which is committed to thy trust").

vi) David's sons (v.18)
"David's sons were chief rulers." The phrase "chief rulers" is usually

translated "priests" and the same word *(cohen)* is translated "friend" in 1 Kings 4.5, "Zabud…was principal officer, and the king's friend." It could therefore be translated, "David's sons were confidential advisers" (Keil & Delitzsch). (1 Chron 18.17 has "chief about the king"). This reminds us that **in the assembly**, there should be a plurality of elders. "In the multitude of counsellors there is safety" (Prov 11.14).

CHAPTER 9.1-13

"Jonathan hath yet a son"

David's kindness to Mephibosheth is one of the better-known events in his life. It is certainly a "happy hunting ground" for gospel preachers, and beautifully illustrates the message of God's love and mercy.

We must start by noticing its position in the book. Chapters 8 & 10 record David's conquests. Chapter 8 describes his foreign policy, with campaigns to the west, east, north and south of his territory (vv.1-14), and his domestic policy (vv.15-18). Military conquest was accompanied by administrative efficiency. Chapter 10 describes what C. I. Scofield calls "the Ammonite-Syrian war." Between these two passages lies the story of David's kindness to the crippled grandson of a man who once hunted him "from pillar to post."

David's kindness to Mephibosheth fulfilled his promise to Jonathan: "And thou shalt not only while I yet live shew me the kindness of the Lord, that I die not: but also thou shalt not cut off thy kindness to my house for ever: no, not when the Lord hath cut off the enemies of David every one from the face of the earth. So Jonathan made a covenant with the house of David...and Jonathan caused David to swear again, because he loved him: for he loved him as he loved his own soul" (1 Sam 20.14-17). The word "kindness" *(chesed)* means "loving-kindness" and is sometimes translated "steadfast love." David now uses the same word: "Is there yet any that is left of the house of Saul, that I may shew him kindness *(chesed)* for Jonathan's sake?" As A. McShane observes, "Quite often people make solemn promises when in times of difficulty, but once the storm passes they conveniently forget all about them. Not so with David...who...did not forget the promises he had made to Jonathan."

The king of Israel was not a blood-thirsty despot whose sole object was to "feather his own nest" without the slightest regard for other people. The great conqueror had a compassionate heart, and this reminds us that although the Lord Jesus is "The mighty God", He is also "The everlasting Father" (Is 9.6).

This delightful chapter can be divided as follows: **(1)** the initiative of David (v.1); **(2)** the information of Ziba (vv.2-4); **(3)** the intervention of David (vv.5-6); **(4)** the inheritance of Mephibosheth (vv.7-13). There is a sequel to the story in 2 Samuel 16.1-4; 19.24-30; 21.7.

1) The Initiative of David (v.1)
"And David said, Is there yet any that is left of the house of Saul, that I may shew him kindness for Jonathan's sake?" The "house of Saul" had faded away into oblivion. It was no longer noteworthy, and any survivors were complete nonentities, reminding us of our own unimportance. There was nothing outstanding about us, and we sing:

> I wonder what He saw in me,
> To suffer such deep agony?

Mephibosheth owed his place at the king's table to David's "loving-kindness" alone. He made the first move, and God has taken the initiative in our blessing. "Herein is love, not that we loved God, but that he loved us, and sent his Son to be the propitiation for our sins" (1 Jn 4.10). Compare Titus 3.3-5. The Bible is not the record of human initiative in seeking God, but His initiative in seeking us. It all began in the garden of Eden, when God said to Adam, "Where art thou?" (Gen 3.9). Adam and Eve "hid themselves from the presence of the Lord God amongst the trees of the garden", but God actively sought them. Centuries later, the Lord Jesus came "to seek and to save that which was lost" (Lk 19.10).

The basis of David's interest and provision for Mephibosheth was the love of Jonathan, of which David said "I am distressed for thee, my brother Jonathan: very pleasant hast thou been unto me: thy love to me was wonderful, passing the love of women" (2 Sam 1.26). We could say that Mephibosheth was accepted in Jonathan, in the same way that we are "accepted in the beloved" (Eph 1.6). This is how Paul puts it: "And be ye kind one to another, tenderhearted, forgiving one another, even as **God for Christ's sake hath forgiven you**" (Eph 4.32).

Whilst we have emphasised the picture here of God's love for us in Christ, we must not overlook the practical lessons. David was not a hard, unforgiving man. It has been said that

> He little knows of God and heaven,
> Who never breathes the word "Forgiven."

It is therefore not surprising to hear David say, "Is there not yet any of the house of Saul, that I may shew **the kindness of God** unto him?" (v.3). Compare Luke 6.36, "Be ye therefore merciful, as your Father also is merciful." A. McShane points out that "had David not known God he would not have acted as he did" and continues "Vital it is that every leader should drink deeply from the well of love in the heart of God. In all dealings with the saints righteousness is essential, but it must be accompanied with love, otherwise it becomes cold and harsh."

2) The Information of Ziba (vv.2-4)

"And Ziba said unto the king, Jonathan hath yet a son, which is lame on his feet. And the king said, Where is he? And Ziba said unto the king, Behold, he is in the house of Machir, the son of Ammiel, in Lo-debar" (vv.3-4). Ziba mention's Mephibosheth's lameness and location, but we'll complete the picture by adding two further pieces of information. The result looks like this:

A) His lineage
He belonged to an enemy family. "Is there yet any that is left of the house of **Saul**...?" (v.1). Mephibosheth's family background did not bode well for him, and he must have wondered what was in store for him when he was summoned by David (v.5). We must remember that sin does not only alienate us from God. It makes us enemies of God. This is clearly stated in the New Testament: "For if, when we were **enemies**, we were reconciled to God by the death of his Son, much more, being reconciled, we shall be saved by his life" (Rom 5.10). We are told that "the carnal mind is **enmity** against God: for it is not subject to the law of God, neither indeed can be" (Rom 8.7).

B) His lameness
"Jonathan hath yet a son, which is lame on his feet" (v.3). We have the details in 2 Samuel 4.4: "And Jonathan, Saul's son, had a son that was lame of his feet, He was five years old when the tidings came of Saul and Jonathan out of Jezreel, and his nurse took him up, and fled: and it came to

pass, as she made haste to flee, that he fell, and became lame. And his name was Mephibosheth." (We discussed this with reference to 1 Thess 2.7-8). His lameness illustrates another aspect of our sad spiritual ruin. Mephibosheth could not help himself, and Paul reminds us that "when we were yet **without strength**, in due time Christ died for the ungodly" (Rom 5.6). Like the impotent by the pool of Bethesda, we had "no man" (Jn 5.7).

C) His location
"Behold, he is in the house of Machir, the son of Ammiel, in Lo-debar" (v.4). It seems that Machir was a wealthy man for, with others, he supplied "beds, and basons, and earthen vessels" and various foodstuffs to David in exile. See 2 Sam 17.27. Lo-debar was evidently near Mahanaim, and was probably the same place as Lidbir (Josh 13.26). It seems therefore that Mephibosheth lodged in the same area as his assassinated uncle Ish-bosheth (2 Sam 2.8), to the east of Jordan.

According to Gesenius, Lo-debar means "without pasture", and this is a further reminder of our poor spiritual condition. The world is like a wilderness: it cannot provide and sustain spiritual life. It is full of "broken cisterns, that can hold no water" (Jer 2.13). The Lord Jesus likened the crowds to "sheep not having a shepherd", and fed them in "a desert place" (Mk 6.34-35). He said, "I am the door: by me if any man enter in, he shall be saved, and shall go in and out, and find **pasture**" (Jn 10.9). David said, "He maketh me to lie down in **green pastures**: he leadeth me beside the still waters" (Ps 23.2). God does not want us in barren land! He wants to "satiate" our souls "with fatness" (Jer 31.14).

D) His lament
Mephibosheth describes himself as a "dead dog" here (v.8), and refers to his "father's house" as "dead men before my lord the king" in 2 Samuel 19.28. This accurately describes our spiritual position apart from the grace of God. Men and women without Christ are "dead in trespasses and sins" (Eph 2.1). They are "alienated from the life of God through the ignorance that is in them, because of the blindness of their heart" (Eph 4.18). It is possible to be dead and alive at the same time: "she that liveth in pleasure is dead while she liveth" (1Tim 5.6).

3) The Intervention of David (vv.5-6)
David did not merely have an academic interest in Mephibosheth, reminding us that God has an active love for us: "Hereby perceive we the love of God,

because he laid down his life for us" (1 Jn 3.16). These verses illustrate the twin truths of divine sovereignty and human responsibility. David "sent, and fetched", and Mephibosheth "fell on his face, and did reverence."

A) David's sovereignty (v.5)
"Then king David sent, and fetched him out of the house of Machir, the son of Ammiel, from Lo-debar." It is phrased rather beautifully. Not, "then David sent", but "then **king** David sent." The emphasis on David's royal status here stresses his grace to Mephibosheth. This was in Paul's mind when he wrote, "The Son of God, who loved me, and gave himself for me" (Gal 2.20); he emphasises the greatness of his Saviour; He is none other than "the Son of God!" The fact that "king David **sent, and fetched**" Mephibosheth, reminds us of God's compelling grace. The Lord Jesus said, "No man can come to me, except the Father which hath sent me draw him" (Jn 6.44). Left to ourselves, we would be like the invited supper guests who "with one consent began to make excuse." But the servant was commanded to "bring in hither the poor, and the maimed, and the halt, and the blind", and when that wasn't enough, "to compel them to come in" (Lk 14.16-24). In the words of Isaac Watts:

> How sweet and sacred is the place,
> With Christ within the doors,
> While everlasting love displays
> The choicest of her stores!
>
> While all our hearts and all our songs
> Praise Him who makes the feast,
> We can but cry, with thankful tongues,
> "Lord, why am I a guest?"
>
> "Twas that same love that spread the feast
> That sweetly forced us in;
> Else we had still refused to taste,
> And perished in our sin.
>
> Isaac Watts

B) Mephibosheth's response (v.6)
"Now when Mephibosheth, the son of Jonathan, the son of Saul, was come unto David, he fell on his face and did reverence. And David said, Mephibosheth. And he answered, Behold thy servant!" Mephibosheth certainly didn't enter David's presence with poise and assurance. He

probably feared the worst, but his fears were allayed by David's opening words, "Fear not: for I will surely shew thee kindness for Jonathan thy father's sake" (v.7). However, Mephibosheth's response reminds us that "the sacrifices of God are a broken spirit: a broken and a contrite heart, O God, thou wilt not despise" (Ps 51.17). He was astonished at what followed.

4) The Inheritance of Mephibosheth (vv.7-13)

We must notice **(A)** The promise to him (v.7); **(B)** The provision for him (vv.9-10); **(C)** The place for him (vv.10-13). No wonder Mephibosheth cried, "What is thy servant, that thou shouldest look upon such a dead dog as I am?" Away in Lo-debar, he had no idea what David planned for him, and we had no idea of God's plans for us!

A) The promise to Mephibosheth (v.7)

"Fear not: for I will surely shew thee kindness for Jonathan thy father's sake, and will restore thee all the land of Saul thy father; and thou shalt eat bread at my table continually." It reminds us of Gerhard Tersteegen's hymn:

> Trembling, I had hoped for mercy -
> Some low place within His door,
> But the crown, the throne, the mansion,
> All were ready long before.

David could have said, "I restored that which I took not away" (Psalm 69.4), but these are the words of "great David's greater Son." Saul had forfeited everything, and his family shared his loss, in the same way that we shared all that Adam lost in the garden of Eden. But "where sin abounded, grace did much more abound" (Rom 5.20). Mephibosheth had been "far off": but now he had been "made nigh" (Eph 2.13), and "given exceeding great and precious promises" (2 Pet 1.4). We too have become "landed gentry." Listen to this: "Blessed be the God and Father of our Lord Jesus Christ, which according to his abundant mercy hath begotten us again unto a lively hope by the resurrection of Jesus Christ from the dead, to an inheritance incorruptible and undefiled, and that fadeth not away, reserved in heaven for you..." (1 Pet 1.3-4). That's even better than Mephibosheth's inheritance! We too are going to feast at the king's table. Listen to this: God "hath raised us up together, and made us sit together in heavenly places in Christ Jesus: that in the ages to come he might shew the exceeding riches of his grace toward us through Christ Jesus" (Eph 2.6-7). That's even better than the place given to Mephibosheth!

B) The provision for Mephibosheth (vv.9-10)

As J. Baldwin observes, "Mephibosheth, who had apparently been dependent up to this point on the hospitality of a generous individual, suddenly became a rich man, the owner of wealth-producing property." Whilst he himself ate daily as a guest at the king's table, "he had to make provision as a royal prince for the maintenance of his own family and servants" (Keil & Delitzsch). He had at least one son (v.12) and was given a retinue of servants (v.10). David made arrangements for the upkeep of the property, reminding us that God has made arrangements for our spiritual progress and prosperity. His "divine power hath given unto us all things that pertain unto life and godliness" (2 Pet 1.3). Mephibosheth benefited from the labours of others, and we benefit from the service of our fellow-believers. We are told that "the manifestation of the Spirit (in the various gifts bestowed on believers) is given to every man to profit withal (for mutual profit)" (1 Cor 12.7). Ziba and his servants had to work hard to support Mephibosheth, reminding us that we too need to "till the land" and "bring in the fruits" so that there can be spiritual food and nourishment for God's people.

C) The place of Mephibosheth (vv.11-13)

These verses describe not only the place given to him, but the position that he enjoyed. His place was at "the king's table" (v.13), and he was there as "one of the king's sons" (v.11). J. Baldwin puts it nicely: "Jonathan had given gracious help to David when he was driven from the king's table, and now David has been able to show kindness in return by giving to Jonathan's son security and honour."

i) "At the king's table"

This is mentioned four times in the chapter: "thou shalt eat bread at **my table** continually (v.7)...thy master's son shall eat bread alway at **my table** (v.10)...he shall eat at **my table** (v.11)...he did eat continually at the **king's table** (v.13)."

The fact that Mephibosheth was to "eat continually at the king's table" reminds us that we are always at "the Lord's table" (1 Cor 10.21). In the Old Testament, the Lord's table was the altar (Mal 1.7) and the sacrifices were called "the bread of God" (Mal 1.7, Lev 21.21-22). When Paul describes believers as "partakers of the Lord's table", he refers to the blessings which belong to us as a result of the death of the Lord Jesus Christ. This is why, in 1 Corinthians 10.16, the cup, reminding us of the blood of Christ, is mentioned first. His precious blood is the basis of every blessing that we enjoy. We took our place at the Lord's table at the moment of our conversion, we have never ceased to be there since that event, and we will be there for ever. We are continually enjoying the blessings of the Lord's table, not just at meetings, but all the time! In the language of this chapter, we "**eat continually** at the king's table!"

The Lord's supper (1 Cor 11.20) refers to our weekly remembrance of the Lord Jesus. The historical order is emphasised here: "My body...my blood" (vv.24-25). Paul uses the same symbols in connection with the Lord's table (1 Cor 10.21) but there they are reversed. In 1 Corinthians 10 he is writing about fellowship, and in 1 Corinthians 11 about remembrance.

ii) "One of the king's sons"
Hannah said, "He raiseth the poor out of the dust, and lifteth up the beggar from the dunghill, to set them among princes, and to make them inherit the throne of glory" (1 Sam 2.8). Perhaps Mephibosheth remembered this as he found himself amongst "the king's sons." He confessed himself to be a servant (vv.6,8) and was given the place of a son. The New Testament has something even more staggering to say: "But when the fulness of the time was come, God sent forth his Son, made of a woman, made under the law, to redeem them that were under the law, that we might receive the adoption of sons. And because ye are sons, God hath sent forth the Spirit of his Son into your hearts, crying, Abba, Father. Wherefore thou art no more a servant, but a son; and if a son, then an heir of God through Christ" (Gal 4.4-7). Paul says something similar in Romans 8.16-17, but there he describes believers as "children of God." We are "children of God" by birth, and "sons of God" by adoption. But "adoption" does not mean something less than birth: it refers to our position and dignity in God's family.

The chapter ends with the words, "So Mephibosheth dwelt in Jerusalem: for he did eat continually at the king's table; and was **lame on both his feet**." This emphasises the grace and kindness of David. A. McShane reminds us that "There should be room for the feeble and helpless...as well as for the strong and sturdy. Some brethren have no time for those who are not going to be useful and active, but here David shows us how to make happy one who is unable to do anything but sit and eat. Mephibosheth was viewed by David as one related to Jonathan, so we must learn to value saints because they belong to Christ."

CHAPTER 10.1-19

"The children of Ammon...stank before David"

In our studies in 2 Samuel, we have reached the stage in David's life which he describes in Psalm 18. "Thou hast delivered me from the strivings of the people; and thou hast made me head of the heathen: a people whom I have not known shall serve me. As soon as they hear of me, they shall obey me" (vv.43-45). This is a faint picture of the coming reign of the "Son of David" (Mt 20.30-31). He will be "head of the heathen" as well as "King of Israel" (Jn 1.49).

Each part of 2 Samuel contains valuable lessons for us, and as we shall see, this chapter is certainly no exception. It has the added merit of explaining why David did not campaign against Ammon in Chapter 8, although they were certainly subject to him (v.12), and explaining the background to the sad events described in Chapter 11. In the first case, David was appreciative of kindness shown to him by Nahash, the "king of the children of Ammon" (v.2), and in the second case, he responded to the antagonism of Ammon by sending his army across the Jordan for the second time to besiege Rabbah, whilst he "tarried still at Jerusalem" (11.1).

The chapter can be analysed in the following way: **(1)** The insult to David (vv.1-5); **(2)** The assault on Ammon (vv.6-8); **(3)** The encouragement for the battle (vv.9-12); **(4)** The effect of defeat (vv.13-14); **(5)** The resilience of the enemy (vv.15-19).

1) The Insult to David (vv.1-5)
This paragraph describes *(A)* David's kindly intentions (vv.1-2) and *(B)* Hanun's rude insult (vv.3-5).

A) David's intentions (vv.1-2)
David never forgot people who showed him kindness. In chapter 9 he

remembered the kindness of Jonathan (v.1) and in chapter 10 he remembered the kindness of Nahash (v.2). In both cases he responded with kindness. "Is there yet any that is left of the house of Saul, that I may shew him kindness *(chesed)* for Jonathan's sake" (9.1); "I will shew kindness *(chesed)* unto Hanun the son of Nahash, as his father shewed kindness *(chesed)* unto me" (10.2). It has been suggested (J. Baldwin, *Tyndale Old Testament Commentaries: 1 and 2 Samuel*) that *"chesed"* carries the idea of faithfulness to a covenant. As we have already noted, the word means "loving-kindness" and is sometimes translated "steadfast love." We do not know what particular kindness David had in mind here (v.2). Presumably, it was something that happened during his years as a fugitive. Keil & Delitzsch are quite certain that Nahash was the same Ammonite king who threatened Jabesh-gilead (1 Sam 11), but not everybody agrees! F. Gardiner *(Ellicott's Commentary)* is of the opinion that "he was probably a son or a grandson of the Nahash whom Saul conquered, as more than fifty years must have passed away since that event." However this isn't important and we must concentrate on the practical lessons here.

i) God's people should always be appreciative of kindness shown to them. They should not cry "Give, give", like the two daughters of the horseleach" (Prov 30.15). According to Henry M. Morris *(The Remarkable Wisdom of Solomon)* the words, "two daughters", refer to the "two-forked tongue" of the "never-satisfied leech." Some people are like that: they take all, and give nothing!

It's worth pointing out that David was consistent. Jonathan was one of his own people, and Nahash was an Ammonite. The Lord Jesus made it clear that His disciples should not have double-standards in their relationships with other people. See Matthew 5.43-48.

ii) God's people should always be sympathetic. David "sent to comfort him (Hanun)...for his father." God is appreciative of kindness (see Jer 2.2) and the Lord Jesus is "touched *(sumpatheo)* with the feeling of our infirmities" (Heb 4.15).

B) Hanun's insult (vv.3-5)
"Rabbah of the children of Ammon...the royal city" (2 Sam 12.26) was about fifty miles from Jerusalem. It is the present-day Amman, capital of Jordan. David's servants were not welcome. We do not know how Hanun initially responded to David's courtesy, but he certainly seems to have

succumbed to pressure from his princes. David's courtesy was completely misrepresented by the "princes of the children of Ammon", and Hanun returned his servants minus half their beards and half their clothing. As H. Mowvley observes, David "could have sent them new tunics, but there was nothing he could do about their beards!" Keil & Delitzsch emphasise the gravity of the insult as follows: "With the value universally set upon the beard by the Hebrews and other oriental nations, as being man's greatest ornament, the cutting off of one-half of it was the greatest insult that could have been offered to the ambassadors, and through them to David their king." Hanun and his princes showed true Ammonite character. Compare 1 Samuel 11. The enmity between Israel and Ammon went back a long way. See Judges 11. Notice Deuteronomy 23.3-6.

We should notice David's care and concern for his representatives. "He sent to meet them" and made arrangements for them to remain at Jericho to save them further embarrassment. We are to "consider one another to provoke unto love and to good works" (Heb 10.24).

The Lord Jesus was treated even more despicably. "I gave my back to the smiters, and my cheeks to them that plucked off the hair" (Is 50.6). They did not shave off our Lord's beard, they tore it off, with such physical damage that we read "his visage was so marred more than any man, and his form more than the sons of men" (Is 52.14).

The response of Hanun and the "princes of Ammon" to David's kindness is very much akin to the response of men and women to the "kindness and love of God our Saviour...toward man" (Tit 3.4). As A. McShane observes, "not only do they refuse the message, but shame and abuse the messengers. Paul, the great ambassador to the Gentiles, knew what it was to be shamefully treated." In his January-March 2004 prayer requests, E. Jaminson refers to "a Palestinian convert to Christianity. In July he set off with Bibles, Christian cassettes and videos, but disappeared. Some ten days later his body was returned, cut into four pieces. Pray for his widow and two young children." We too must expect refusal and rejection, albeit to a much lesser degree.

2) The Assault on Ammon (vv.6-8)
F. Gardiner *(Ellicott's Commentary)* rightly observes that "it is remarkable that in none of David's wars does he appear as the aggressor." But he certainly responded to people who attacked or threatened Israel, and the

treatment of his representatives certainly looks like a deliberate act of provocation. The Ammonites clearly expected reprisals, and prepared for battle by hiring mercenaries from the Syrians. It cost them "a thousand talents of silver" (1 Chron 19.6). In response, David "sent Joab, and all the host of the mighty men" across the Jordan. They faced formidable odds. There were the Ammonites themselves plus "the Syrians of Beth-rehob, and the Syrians of Zoba, twenty thousand footmen, and of king Maachah a thousand men, and of Ish-tob twelve thousand men" (v.6). "Ish-tob" may not be a proper name: it means "the men of Tob." 1 Chronicles 19 mentions "chariots and horsemen", but not men: 2 Samuel 8 only mentions the foot-soldiers.

Joab faced a "pincer movement." The Ammonites made a sortie out of the city and took up positions in front of the gate, whereas the Syrian mercenaries were encamped in the open country (v.8). The "front of the battle was against him before and behind" (v.9). Once again, there are simple but important lessons here.

i) People who do wrong often become militant. The Ammonites rejected David's kindness, and assembled an army against him. When it came to actual warfare, they made the first move (v.6). This still happens. The message and messengers of God's love are not only rejected, but attacked, especially by the religious world that regards the Gospel of God's grace as "fundamentalism", and its adherents as "cultist." Anyone who dares to condemn the vile sin of sodomy (that's the Bible word) attracts vilification and abuse. "Political correctness" and the word of God are mutually exclusive.

ii) People from different backgrounds often combine against the truth. Nehemiah was opposed by an alliance between "Sanballat the Horonite, and Tobiah the servant, the Ammonite" (Neh 2.10) plus "Geshem the Arabian" (Neh 6.1). The Pharisees and Herodians were united against the Lord Jesus (Mk 12.13). Pilate and Herod became friends in rejecting Him (Lk 23.12). The Ecumenical Movement comprises a wide variety of different religious bodies. The literature advertising Christmas services in Broxbourne covers all shades of religious opinion, including midnight mass at the Roman Catholic church. Just imagine the reaction if the gospel was preached at the annual Borough of Broxbourne Civic Service, to which invitations are issued by the mayor!

iii) People who unite against the Gospel sometimes seem to have the upper hand. The Ammonites and Syrians endeavoured to "squeeze" Joab and "the mighty men" of Israel. Those who love the word of God and all that it contains sometimes seem bound for oblivion. Erroneous teaching seems to be running like the flood tide. So let's take encouragement from what happened next.

3) The Encouragement for the Battle (vv.9-12)
Joab was well aware of the enemy's strategy. He noted their positions, and knew that he was "caught between two fires." But this did not deter him. He did not panic in the face of extreme danger, but "strategically deployed his forces so as to allow for flexibility as the battle progressed" (J. Baldwin). We must notice how he tackled the danger. **(A)** The deployment of the army (vv.9-10); **(B)** The mutual support (v.11); **(C)** The encouragement to fight (v.12). Each of these has significant lessons for us.

A) The deployment of the army (vv.9-10)
"He chose of all the choice men of Israel, and put them in array against the Syrians; and the rest of the people he delivered into the hand of Abishai his brother, that he might put them in array against the children of Ammon." Quite obviously, Joab faced the Syrians with a picked body of men because they were the stronger of the two opposing forces. This was good leadership. Joab knew how to use his men to the very best advantage. This reminds us that whilst God has given ability to every believer, not everybody can do everything! Paul sets out the position in Romans 12.4-8 as follows: "For as we all have many members in one body, and all members have not the same office: so we, being many, are one body in Christ, and every one members one of another, Having then gifts differing according to the grace that is given unto us, whether prophecy, let us prophesy according to the proportion of faith; or ministry, let us wait on our ministering: or he that teacheth on teaching; or he that exhorteth on exhortation: he that giveth, let him do it with simplicity; he that ruleth with diligence; he that sheweth mercy, with cheerfulness."

Elders cannot *impart* gifts to assembly members, but they can *identify* them, and take steps to ensure that assembly resources are used to the best advantage. It is important to remember that preaching is not the only work available. Harold St.John once observed that whilst he saw lots of young men queuing up for the platform, he didn't see many queuing up to push old ladies in their wheel-chairs to the meetings!

B) The mutual support (v.11)
"If the Syrians be too strong for me, then thou shalt help me: but if the

children of Ammon be too strong for thee, then I will come and help thee." Nehemiah adopted the same strategy: "And I said unto the nobles, and to the rulers, and to the rest of the people, The work is great and large, and we are separated upon the wall, one far from another. In what place therefore ye hear the voice of the trumpet, resort ye hither to us: our God shall fight for us" (Neh 4.19-20). Whatever we may think about Joab's conduct on other occasions, he was certainly thinking about other people here rather than his own personal interests.

In the New Testament, Paul discusses the importance of mutual sympathy and support. "God hath tempered the body together…that there should be no schism in the body; but that the members should have the same care one for another. And whether one member suffer, all the members suffer with it; or one member be honoured, all the members rejoice with it" (1 Cor 12.25-26). Onesiphorus was a great help to Paul when he was in prison at Rome: "he oft refreshed me, and was not ashamed of my chain; but, when he was in Rome, he sought me out very diligently, and found me" (2 Tim 1.16-17). Phebe is described as "a succourer (meaning 'protectress" or 'patroness') of many, and of myself also" (Rom 16.1-20). We should always be willing to give help and support in areas of assembly life and gospel work where "the labourers are few" and under pressure. It's nice, like Peter, to have a "strengthening" ministry. See Luke 22.31-32.

C) The encouragement to fight (v.12)
"Be of good courage, and let us play the men for our people, and for the cities of our God: and the Lord do that which seemeth him good." Paul puts it like this: "Be ye stedfast, unmoveable, always abounding in the work of the Lord, forasmuch as ye know that your labour is not in vain in the Lord" (1 Cor 15.58). Joshua was told, "Be strong and of a good courage; be not afraid, neither be thou dismayed: for the Lord thy God is with thee whithersoever thou goest" (Josh 1.9). There are at least three things to notice here:

i) The courage. "Be of good courage, and let us play the men…" or "Be strong, and let us show ourselves valiant…" (JND). The parallel passage (1 Chron 10.13) has "Be of good courage, and let us behave ourselves valiantly." Paul says something similar in 1 Cor 16.13, "Watch ye, stand fast in the faith, quit you like men, be strong." Our work and warfare requires spiritual strength and determination, particularly when difficulty and discouragement stare us in the face. David knew what that was like at

Ziklag, and "encouraged himself in the Lord his God" (1 Sam 30.6). Paul didn't say "be strong", but "be strong in **the Lord**, and in the power of **his might"** (Eph 6.10).

ii) The cause. "Let us play the men for our people, and for the cities of our God." Joab was very conscious that there was a great deal at stake. Defeat at the hands of the Ammonites and Syrians could have dire consequences for Israel at large. Nehemiah knew that as well: "Be not ye afraid of them: remember the Lord, which is great and terrible, and fight for your brethren, your sons, and your daughters, your wives, and your houses" (Neh 4.14). Joab was concerned, not only for the interests of the people, but for the honour of God. "Let us play the men…for the cities of **our God**." Any insult levelled at God's people is an insult against God Himself.

iii) The confidence. "And the Lord do that which seemeth him good." Compare Eli's response to Samuel: "It is the Lord: let him do what seemeth him good" (1 Sam 3.18). As J. Baldwin observes, Joab prayed "not expressly for victory, but for the Lord's outworking of his will." J. P. Fokkelman puts it like this: "Joab will apply his forces and strategic genius to the full but, as a believer, he remains aware at the same time that the decision rests in God's hand, and he resolves himself to this". J. Baldwin continues by saying, "It comes as something of a surprise to find the tough Joab exhibiting faith in this way; now we know him a little better, and see him as a worthy general of David's army." We must certainly give credit where credit is due.

4) The Effect of Defeat (vv.13-14)
No, not on Israel! The effect of the Syrians defeat on the Ammonites! "And Joab drew nigh, and the people that were with him, unto the battle against the Syrians: and they fled before him. And when the children of Ammon saw that the **Syrians were fled**, then **fled they also** before Abishai, and entered into the city." For the time being, fighting against the "children of Ammon" then stopped. Joab and his army came home, and went back again in the next chapter or, to put it more accurately, "after the year was expired, at the time when kings go forth to battle" (2 Sam 11.1).

There's an important lesson in all this for us. We can have the same sort of affect on each other as the Syrians did on the Ammonites. Our own discouragement and defeat can effect other people. See Deuteronomy 20.8. Whether we are conscious of it or not, we do have an influence on each other. When the spies returned from reconnoitring Canaan (Numbers 13-

14), the people of Israel were influenced by the dismal report of the ten spies, rather than the encouragement of Caleb and Joshua. Just listen to them: "Whither shall we go up? Our brethren have discouraged our heart" (Deut 1.28). It's all too easy to be "wet blankets!" It is so important for us to be in tip-top spiritual health, not only for our own sake, but for the sake of other believers as well. We need people like Barnabas who "exhorted them all, that with purpose of heart they would cleave unto the Lord" (Acts 11.23).

5) The Resilience of the Enemy (vv.15-19)
Whilst the Ammonites stayed within their city walls (v.14), and remained there until Joab and David took the city (12.26-31), the Syrians immediately regrouped. "And when the Syrians saw that they were smitten before Israel, they gathered themselves together. And Hadarezer sent, and brought out the Syrians that were beyond the river: and they came to Helam; and Shobach the captain of the host of Hadarezer went before them" (vv.15-16). Hadadezer (8.3) and Hadarezer are evidently one and the same person. This time, David himself took command (v.17), and the Syrians were routed (v.18). This brought an end to Syrian opposition, and deprived the Ammonites of any further help (v.19).

But it isn't quite like that in our case. We face a very resilient enemy. His power has already been annulled (Heb 2.14), but he is still very active. Like the Syrians, he is adept at regrouping, and unlike the Syrians, even a second defeat doesn't put him out of action. Sometimes he acts like "a roaring lion...seeking whom he may devour" (1 Pet 5.8), and sometimes he is "transformed into an angel of light" (2 Cor 11.14). But one way or another, he is always there. No wonder Paul says, "Put on the whole armour of God, that ye may be able to stand against the wiles of the devil" (Eph 6.11). He is called, "the god of this world" (2 Cor 4.4), but not "the god of the world to come!" One day, like the Syrians, he will be utterly and finally defeated, and never rear his head again-read Revelation 20.10. The enemy was not "too strong" (v.11) and the chapter ends with David's supremacy.

CHAPTER 11.1-27

"The thing that David had done displeased the Lord"

We now come to the heart of the book, only to discover that it describes the heart of man, "deceitful above all things, and desperately wicked" (Jer 17.9). This is a good time to take another look at the structure of 2 Samuel, from which it is clear that David's sin changed the whole course of his life. This is how we divided the book in our introduction: **(1)** David's triumphs (chs.1-10); **(2)** David's tragedy (chs.11-12); **(3)** David's troubles (chs.13-24). The teaching in chapters 11 & 12 can be summed up by Proverbs 28.13: "He that covereth his sins shall not prosper" (1 Sam 11): "but whoso confesseth and forsaketh them shall have mercy" (1 Sam 12).

David's tragedy is summed up in one verse: "David did that which was right in the eyes of the Lord, and turned not aside from anything that he commanded him all the days of his life, **save only** in the matter of Uriah the Hittite" (1 Kings 15.5). Whilst there have been some sad events in chapters 1-10, the Holy Spirit charts the steady progress of David from his fugitive days to his complete supremacy in the Middle East. "The Lord preserved David whithersoever he went" (2 Sam 8.6,14).

The remaining chapters, in the main, make most unpleasant reading, but do remember that "whatsoever things were written aforetime were written for our learning" (Rom 15.4), and we must therefore read them carefully and thoughtfully. They clearly teach us, amongst other things, that "whatsoever a man soweth that shall he also reap" (Gal 6.7), or to put it in Old Testament language, "they have sown the wind, and they shall reap the whirlwind" (Hos 8.7). The word of God faithfully records the failures of great Bible characters to prevent us from failing in the same way. Let's remember too that "the fall of such a devoted and God-fearing man tells us to beware lest we conclude that our past spiritual development is proof against present failure" (A. McShane). The warning is still needed, "let him that thinketh he standeth take heed lest he fall" (1 Cor 10.12).

2 Samuel 11 can be divided in the following way: **(1)** David's sinful desire (vv.1-5); **(2)** David's attempted deceit (vv.6-13); **(3)** Uriah's arranged death (vv.14-27a); **(4)** God's grave displeasure (v.27b). David does not mention the Lord's name once in the chapter. In fact, the only reference to His name at all is in the final verse, emphasising the fact that David was completely out of touch with Him.

1) David's Sinful Desire (vv.1-5)

The chapter begins with the resumption of the war against the Ammonites. Strange as it may seem to us in our modern world, hostilities normally ceased during the inclement weather of the winter months, and were resumed in the spring when travelling became bearable. It is more important to notice, however, that whilst the time had come for "kings to go forth to battle", David stayed at home. "And it came to pass, after the year was expired, at the times when kings go forth to battle, David sent Joab, and his servants with him, and all Israel; and they destroyed the children of Ammon, and besieged Rabbah. **But David tarried still at Jerusalem**." He appears to have abdicated his responsibility in favour of Joab, and he was very forcibly reminded of this later: see v.11. It has often been pointed out that the temptation to which David succumbed would not have occurred had he been campaigning with his army instead of relaxing in Jerusalem. It's a bad policy to be idle, and there is some mileage in the old proverb that "the devil finds work for idle hands to do." See 1 Timothy 5.13. David took a holiday from the war, but Satan certainly didn't take a holiday in his war against David – and he doesn't take a holiday in his war against us either! David certainly appears to have preferred his bed (v.2) to the battle. The Bible has a great deal to say about sleep. See, for example, Proverbs 24.30-34; Jonah 1.6; Matthew 13.24; Matthew 26.40.

We certainly do need to remember that we are all on active service, and there is no prospect of leave until we meet the Lord! We can't afford to relax when it comes to the spiritual battle.

David's downfall began when he didn't avert his eyes during a stroll on the roof of his house after an afternoon siesta. Solomon gave his son some very sound advice when he said, "Let thine eyes look straight on, and let thine eyelids look straight before thee. Ponder the path of thy feet, and let all thy ways be established. Turn not to the right hand nor to the left: remove thy foot from evil" (Prov 4.25-27). We must carefully notice the three stages that led to the disaster in David's life: he **"saw"** (v.2); he **"enquired"** (v.3); he **"took her"** (v.4).

i) He "saw" (v.2). "From the roof he saw a woman washing herself; and the woman was very beautiful to look upon." David's glance became a gaze. Solomon said, "Lust not after her beauty in thine heart" (Prov 6.25). We must "beware of the second look", and in this context, of the second thought as well. The New Testament calls it "the lust of the eyes" (1 Jn 2.16). It was a pity that David didn't follow his own teaching: "I will walk within my house with a perfect heart. I will set no wicked thing before mine eyes..." (Ps 101.2-3). Job said, "I made a covenant with mine eyes; why then should I think upon a maid" (Job 31.1). When the question is asked, "Who among us shall dwell with the devouring fire? who among us shall dwell with everlasting burnings?" the answer is, amongst other things, "He that...shutteth his eyes from seeing evil" (Is 33.14-16). Sadly, the Lord's teaching in Matthew 5.27-28 applied to David. We must make sure that our glances don't turn into anything more when we call at our local newsagents, or when a questionable book comes to hand, or something sensual appears on the screen, or... There's no need to say any more, is there? Except to quote the Chinese (so we are told) proverb:

> You can't stop a bird flying over your head,
> But you can stop it making a nest in your hair!

ii) He "enquired" (v.3). "And David sent and enquired after the woman. And one said, Is not this Bath-sheba, the daughter of Eliam, the wife of Uriah the Hittite?" Having seen the woman, David wants to find out all about her. This is perfectly acceptable when "boy meets girl" and courtship begins, but David's interest in Bath-sheba was unwholesome. Sin has a curiosity value. If something looks questionable, it is a terrible mistake to try and find out as much about it as you can. It will only absorb your attention, and then dominate you. See Proverbs 5.22. When Joseph was deliberately tempted by Potiphar's wife, he took steps to ensure that he was out of the sphere of temptation as much as possible. See Genesis 39.10, "he hearkened not unto her...or to be with her."

The picture darkens when we learn that Bath-sheba was not only a married woman, but the wife of one of David's serving troops. This information should have stopped David immediately. In any case, he had plenty of wives already. See 1 Samuel 3.2-6. Uriah was away from home. So was Potiphar. So was the husband of the woman in Proverbs 7: "Come, let us take our fill of love until the morning...for the goodman is not at home, he is gone on a long journey: he hath taken a bag of money with him, and will come home at the day appointed" (vv.18-20). There is no need to elaborate.

iii) He "took her" (v.4). "And David sent messengers and took her; and she came in unto him, and he lay with her." (Compare 9.5, "Then king David sent, and fetched him..." Mephibosheth was sent for out of love: Bath-sheba was sent for out of lust). James gives us the best commentary here: "Every man is tempted, when he is drawn away of his own lust and enticed. Then when lust hath conceived, it bringeth forth sin...." (Jas 1.15). Let's listen again to Solomon: "Can a man take fire in his bosom, and his clothes not be burned? Can one go upon hot coals, and his feet not be burned? So he that goeth in to his neighbour's wife; whosoever toucheth her shall not be innocent" (Prov 6.27-29).

The whole emphasis is upon David's sin. We can only assume that he overrode Bath-sheba's personal feelings in the matter, although the words, "and she came in unto him" imply her willingness. The words, "for she was purified from her uncleanness: and she returned unto her house", could be a delicate way of saying that she was not already pregnant at the time. Alternatively, on the basis of JND's margin reading ("and she purified herself from her uncleanness; and she returned to her house"), this could refer to Leviticus 15.18. As J. Baldwin observes, "no mention is made of the agony of uncertainty" suffered by Bath-sheba, "all the more so because the child of a king was involved." But "now it was David's turn to be dismayed." "And the woman conceived, and sent and told David, and said, I am with child" (v.5). The Bible says, "Be sure your sin will find you out" (Num 32.23). He immediately attempted to "cover his tracks."

2) David's Attempted Deceit (vv.6-13)
As we said in introduction, the words, "he that covereth his sins shall not prosper" (Prov 28.13), could be written over this chapter. His first attempts at "cover-up" didn't work at all.

"And David sent to Joab, saying, Send me Uriah the Hittite. And Joab sent Uriah to David." You can almost see question marks sprouting over the heads of Joab and Uriah. Uriah was one of David's "mighty men" (2

Sam 23.39), and in this case he proved to be mightier than even David himself. This is even more remarkable when we remember that Uriah was a Hittite! His name means "light of Jehovah" (Scofield) or "flame of Jehovah" (Gesenius). He was like "a light that shineth in a dark place" (2 Pet 1.19). We met a Hittite earlier (Ahimelech) who had presumably joined David's men in the cave of Adullam (1 Sam 26.6), and quite possibly Uriah joined David at the same time. David's questions were quite superficial: how was Joab?; how were the men?; what about the war? (v.7). But he was really grappling with the problem of an illegitimate child, and as J. P. Fokkelman notes, "The answer Uriah gives is not included in the narrative - a significant gap which symbolises that David just lets him talk, not paying any particular attention to his account." (Incidentally, someone has said that there is no such thing as an illegitimate child – but there are certainly many illegitimate parents). David addressed his problem in two ways:

A) He encouraged him to go home sober (vv.8-12)
"And David said to Uriah, Go down to thy house, and wash thy feet. And Uriah departed out of the king's house, and there followed him a mess of meat from the king." The royal gift was intended to impress upon Uriah that he was specially favoured, and therefore able to relax and enjoy the opportunity to go home and be with his wife." But we are told three times that he "went not down to his house" (vv.9-10). This does not tell us that Uriah had fallen out of love with his wife, and didn't want to see her. It tells us that at that moment, he was totally committed to his duty as a soldier. Notice what he said:

i) "The ark, and Israel, and Judah, abide in tents; and my lord Joab, and the servants of my lord, are encamped in the open fields..." (v.11), reminding us of Philippians 2.25 and Colossians 2.1. He was not on leave! He expressed solidarity with the men at the front. He was loyal to his commander. In fact, he was loyal to David as well for "he slept at the door of the king's house with all the servants of **his lord**" (v.9). There's commitment for you! Paul puts it like this: "No man that warreth entangleth himself with the affairs of this life; that he may please him who hath chosen him to be a soldier" (2 Tim 2.4). It would be quite wrong to suppose that Uriah was implying that David should have been at the front as well, but it's worth remembering that elders are to be "ensamples to the flock" (1 Pet 5.3). It is rather remarkable that a Hittite should mention the ark before everything else that influenced his behaviour!

ii) "Shall I then go into mine house, to eat and to drink, and to lie with my wife?" (v.11). He showed remarkable self-restraint, whereas David had completely lost self-control.

We have to say that in a sordid situation, though unknown to him, Uriah's conduct is exemplary. He was quite determined: "as thou livest, and as thy soul liveth, I will not do this thing" (v.11). He didn't go home during the day, or at night (v.12). He was "stedfast, unmoveable..." (1 Cor 15.58).

B) He encouraged him to go home drunk (v.13)
David now resorts to desperate measures. "And when David had called him, he did eat and drink before him; and he made him drunk: and at even he went out to lie on his bed with the servants of **his lord**, but went not down to his house." Yes, he was loyal to David, even when he was under the influence of alcohol. There were sad results when Noah became drunk (Gen 9.20-27) and even worse in the case of Lot (Gen 19.30-38). But Uriah's resolution was not impaired by David's lavish (and despicable) hospitality. Now, a "word to the wise." Please don't think that a little drink will leave you unscathed. Uriah was a remarkable man, but a glass (or tankard) in **your** hand might prove disastrous for you. You are **not** under an obligation to conform when it comes to social drinking amongst family or friends, or entertaining business contacts. Leave it alone.

David's strategy failed. The coming baby could not be attributed to Uriah. There was only one answer: Uriah must die.

3) Uriah's Arranged Death (vv.14-27a)
As A. McShane observes, "seldom does sin end without further sin being committed in an attempt to cover it over." Deceit is "a slippery slope." The narrative speaks for itself, and all we need to do is to note the sad sequence of events:

A) The return of Uriah (vv.14-15)
Uriah returned to the battle at Rabbah carrying his own death-warrant. The letter to Joab was written in his blood. "And it came to pass in the morning, that David wrote a letter to Joab, and sent it by the hand of Uriah. And he wrote in the letter, saying, Set ye Uriah in the forefront of the hottest battle, and retire ye from him, that he may be smitten, and die." It was a case of "murder by proxy." Nathan made this clear: "**thou** hast killed Uriah the Hittite with the sword"

(12.9). In order to 'legalise' his relationship with Bath-sheba, David deliberately exposed Uriah to danger.

B) The removal of Uriah (vv.16-17)
"And it came to pass, when Joab observed the city, that he assigned Uriah unto a place where he knew the valiant men (referring to the Ammonites) were. And the men of the city went out, and fought with Joab: and there fell some of the people of the servants of David; and Uriah the Hittite died also." Let's look at it like this:

i) Uriah died. So David's plan succeeded. Or did it? David went to great lengths to screen himself from exposure, but ironically the incident has become one of the best known in scripture.

ii) Other people died as well. This was not intended. David said, "retire from him, that he may be smitten and die." But other soldiers died too. This reminds us that our wrong-doing will almost inevitably affect unconnected and innocent people.

iii) Joab himself was put at risk. Joab was in the most unenviable position of trying to balance loyalty to David and his own conscience. Joab must have wondered why David wanted Uriah killed in battle. He certainly found out later, and we can only imagine what this did to his confidence in David. But David also put Joab's professional competence at risk by asking him to do something which wasn't in the "training manual." As Joab knew (v.20), it was bad practice to get too close to the city wall when you were conducting a siege. He had been asked to act against his better judgment. That's not uncommon! How do we act when it is a question of loyalty to a close friend (perhaps a close Christian friend, or even someone in leadership) versus loyalty to God's word? It isn't always easy, is it?

C) The report to David (vv.18-24)
"Then Joab sent and told David all things concerning the war." Joab is clearly very unhappy about the whole incident, and makes it very clear that David himself was responsible for the avoidable bloodshed and heavy death toll. If the king was angry with Joab for getting too near the wall, forgetting the lesson at Thebez (see Judges 9.50-53), the messenger was to say, "thy servant Uriah the Hittite is dead also" (vv.19-21). Having described the course of the battle, during which the army got into serious difficulties ("the men prevailed against us"), the messenger added, "and thy servant

Uriah the Hittite is dead also" (vv.22-24). Joab wanted David to know that in order to carry out his instructions, unnecessary risks had been taken and unnecessary blood had been shed.

D) The response of David (vv.25-27a)
"Thus shalt thou say unto Joab, Let not this thing displease thee, for the sword devoureth one as well as another: make the battle more strong against the city, and overthrow it: and encourage thou him" (v.25). There's not the slightest hint of sorrow or remorse in David's voice. He ignores Joab's implied rebuke, passes off the whole incident as part of "the fortunes of war", and urges Joab not to worry too much about it: "let not this thing displease thee" (don't get upset, old chap). "David is at the same time speaking to himself and placating his own conscience" (J. Baldwin). The contrast with his attitude in the previous chapter could not be greater. In chapter 10, he showed care and kindness to his men (v.5): in chapter 11, he showed callous disregard for Uriah. A man out of touch with God will lose his love for God's people. David had cause to regret his words, "the sword devoureth one as well as another." The sword returned to his own house: "thou hast killed Uriah the Hittite with the sword...now therefore the sword shall never depart from thine house..." (2 Sam 12.9-10). David certainly reaped "the whirlwind."

This meant that the "coast was clear." Bath-sheba was now a war widow, and therefore free to marry David. "And when the wife of Uriah heard that Uriah was dead, she mourned for her husband. And when the mourning was past, David sent and fetched her to his house, and she became his wife, and bare him a son." This is the second time that David "sent" for Bath-sheba. (Compare v.4). J. Baldwin points out that she is called "the wife of Uriah", referring to her status rather than her name. "In this way, the writer detaches himself from the new liaison and pays his respect to *Uriah her husband*, who *was dead*. At no point is the reader permitted to gather that Uriah's death was regarded as a matter of indifference."

4) God's Grave Displeasure (v.27b)
Everything had gone according to David's plan. Uriah was dead, Bath-sheba was now his wife, the child was born (conceived by adultery, but born within marriage), time had passed, and the king could heave a big sigh of relief. Everything now continued as it had before. The future was assured. But was it? David had failed to look up, and we read, "But the thing that David had done **displeased the Lord.**" David had blithely said to Joab, "let not

this thing displease **thee**": the fact that it had **"displeased the Lord"** wasn't so important. What is most important to us? Paul said, "Wherefore also we make it our aim (margin, "are ambitious")...to be well-pleasing unto him" (2 Cor 5.9 RV).

This is a salutary reminder to us all that "neither is there any creature that is not manifest in his sight: but all things are naked and opened unto him with whom we have to do" (Heb 4.13), and that "the ways of man are before the eyes of the Lord, and he pondereth all his goings" (Prov 5.21). David did not know it, but God was about to intervene. "The Lord in his infinite grace (note this) had allowed David's attempt at cover-up to fail, and was about to confront him" (J. Baldwin). Nathan was on his way. Even the king was not above the law, and A. McShane makes the important point that "whatever power the overseers in an assembly have, this gives them no licence to do wrong. They are as much under the Lord's authority as the weakest saint in the company".

CHAPTER 12.1-31

"Thou art the man"

As we saw in our last study, the lessons in chapters 11 and 12 can be summed up by Proverbs 28.13: "He that covereth his sins shall not prosper" (1 Sam 11): "but whoso confesseth and forsaketh them shall have mercy" (2 Sam 12). In chapter 11, apart from the final verse, the Lord's name is conspicuously absent. David does not mention Him once in the chapter. He does not speak to the Lord, and the Lord does not speak to him. When Abraham "went down into Egypt" (Gen 12.10), there was no communication with God or from God. Sin robs us of fellowship with Him. But the silence of God does not mean that He is indifferent: "The ways of men are before the eyes of the Lord, and he pondereth all his goings" (Prov 5.21). Chapter 11 concludes with the words, "But the thing that David had done displeased the Lord." (v.27). The Lord now intervenes. David had "sown the wind": now he "reaps the whirlwind" (Hos 8.7).

The chapter can be divided in the following way: **(1)** The message of Nathan (vv.1-12); **(2)** The repentance of David (vv.13-14); **(3)** The death of the child (vv.15-23); **(4)** The birth of Solomon (vv.24-25); **(5)** The fall of Rabbah (vv.26-31).

1) The Message of Nathan (vv.1-12)
"And the **Lord** sent Nathan unto David" (v.1), although Nathan does not reveal this until verse 7. His work is described in Galatians 6.1. We met Nathan in chapter 7. He was obviously in close contact with David (vv.2-3), and close contact with the Lord (vv.4-5). He conveyed a very pleasant message in chapter 7, but now he has something very unpleasant to say. The Bible says, "Faithful are the wounds of a friend" (Prov 27.6). We don't help each other by avoiding serious issues. Nathan did not spare David, but he acted in his best interests. It isn't always easy to confront people with their sins and failures, but properly handled, the object should always

be their repentance and forgiveness. Saul had stubbornly refused to accept the rebukes of Samuel (1 Sam 13.11-12; 15.14-15; 19-21), and we await David's response to Nathan. We should notice **(A)** The parable (vv.1-4); **(B)** The response (vv.5-6); **(C)** The application (vv.7-12).

A) The parable (vv.1-4)
Perhaps we should call it "case study." Nathan presented the case skilfully. After all, David was an excellent judge. He "executed judgment and justice unto all his people" (1 Sam 8.15). There is no need to recount the details of the "case study" here, except to say that it accurately reflected the situation. The "rich man had exceeding many flocks and herds" (David had plenty of wives) and the "poor man had nothing save one little ewe lamb" (Uriah had one wife). You can take it from there.

B) The response (vv.5-6)
David reacted with righteous anger. He is quite vehement: "As the Lord liveth, the man that hath done this thing shall surely die ("is worthy of death" JND). And he shall restore the lamb fourfold, because he did this thing, and because he had no pity." As J. Baldwin observes, "David passes the death sentence on the rich man. But why? He had not committed murder." The strength of David's reaction strongly suggests that he was attempting to rid himself of his guilty conscience by passing judgment on someone else. It also proves that "humanity is endowed with a keen sense of justice which operates effectively, providing that the individual passing judgment is not personally part of the case" (J. Baldwin). David had unconsciously passed judgment on himself. He **was** "worthy of death" and he certainly paid "fourfold" for his sin. It is often pointed out that he lost the baby son (12.17), Amnon (13.28-29), Absalom (18.14), and Adonijah (1 Kings 2.24-25). It's also worth pointing out that David was familiar with God's word. When he said, "he shall restore the lamb fourfold", he was referring to Exodus 22.1, "If a man shall steal an ox, or a sheep, and kill it; he shall **restore** five oxen for an ox, and **four sheep for a sheep."**

C) The application (vv.7-12)
David now has to face the consequences of his own verdict. In this section we must solemnly consider the following:

i) God's favour towards David (vv.7-8). "I anointed thee...I delivered thee...I gave thee...and if that had been too little, I would moreover have given unto thee such and such things." David owed everything to God. We too have been wonderfully blessed by God. He has anointed us: "Now he which stablisheth us with you in Christ, and hath **anointed us**, is God; who hath also sealed us, and given the earnest of the Spirit in our hearts" (2 Cor 1.21-22). He has delivered us: "Who hath **delivered us** from the power of darkness, and hath translated us into the kingdom of his dear Son" (Col 1.13). He has given so much to us: "He that spared not his own Son, but delivered him up for us all, how shall he not with him also freely **give us** all things?" (Rom 8.32). His "divine power hath **given unto us** all things that pertain to life and godliness." He has also "**given unto us** exceeding great and precious promises" (2 Pet 1.3-4).

The reference to "thy master's wives" is strange language to us! "Evidently the custom was that the harem of the dead monarch was inherited by his successor, and by this rule David had already added to his household" (J. Baldwin).

David had every reason to **obey** God's word. His sin was an affront to the goodness of God. What a way to repay God for all His kindness! David had despised "the riches of his (God's) goodness" (Rom 2.4).

ii) God's condemnation of David (v.9). "Wherefore hast thou despised the commandment of the Lord, to do evil in his sight? Thou hast killed Uriah the Hittite with the sword, and hast taken his wife to be thy wife, and hast slain him with the sword of the children of Ammon." David had despised the law of God. He had broken at least three commandments: "Thou shalt not kill…Thou shat not commit adultery…Thou shalt not covet thy neighbour's wife…" (Ex 20.13,14,17). We must also notice that if we despise the word of God (v.9), we despise God Himself (v.10). Paul made this clear in Galatians 1: "I marvel that ye are so soon removed from him that called you into the grace of Christ unto another gospel." Paul does not say, "I marvel that ye are soon removed from the gospel", but "from **him that called you** into ("in" JND) the grace of Christ unto another gospel."

iii) God's punishment of David (vv.10-12). This clearly illustrates the law of sowing and reaping: "Be not deceived; God is not mocked: for whatsoever a man soweth, that shall he also reap" (Gal 6.7).

David had "killed Uriah the Hittite with the **sword**…and hast slain him with the **sword** of the children of Ammon" (v.9). God's judgment would fit the crime: "Now therefore the **sword** shall never depart from thine own house…" (v.10).

David had destroyed the family life of Uriah. God's judgment would fit the crime. His own family life would be destroyed. "Now therefore the sword shall never depart from **thine own house** (v.10)...I will raise up evil against thee out of **thine own house**" (v.11).

David had taken "the wife of Uriah the Hittite" **secretly** (v.12). Uriah knew nothing about it. God's judgment would fit the crime. "I will take thy wives before **thine eyes**, and give them unto thy neighbour, and he shall lie with thy wives in the sight of **this sun**. For thou didst it secretly: but I will do this thing before all Israel, and before **the sun**" (v.11).

Subsequent chapters will prove that God meant exactly what he said. Amnon, Absalom, and Adonjah all died violently, and "they spread Absalom a tent upon the top of the house; and Absalom went in unto his father's concubines in the sight of all Israel" (2 Sam 16.22). We must not forget that God "abideth faithful: he cannot deny himself" (2 Tim 2.13). The Lord Jesus taught that "there is nothing covered that shall not be revealed; neither hid that shall not be made known. Therefore whatsoever ye have spoken in darkness shall be heard in the light; and that which ye have spoken in the ear in closets shall be proclaimed upon the housetops" (Lk 12.2-3). It is important to notice that Nathan did not mention Bath-sheba by name. He deliberately calls her "the wife of Uriah the Hittite", stressing her status, to emphasise the gravity of David's sin. (See also 11.26).

2) The Repentance of David (vv.13-14).
These important verses stress two aspects of God's character. They emphasise **(A)** The grace of God (v.13) and **(B)** The government of God (v.14).

A) The grace of God (v.13)
"And David said unto Nathan, I have sinned against the Lord. And Nathan said unto David, The Lord also hath put away thy sin; thou shalt not die." There was no provision in the law for either the adulterer or the murderer to escape the death penalty (see Ex 21.12; Lev 20.10), and we can only attribute David's forgiveness to the grace of God. The fact that he was allowed to continue his reign must also be attributed to God's grace. As J. Baldwin observes, "the worrying feature is that David apparently benefits from his wrongdoing...the woman he desired, but should not have had, became his wife...Did not the fact that the Lord granted to David restoration of fellowship encourage wrongdoing?"

2 Samuel

The answer to this problem must lie in David's thorough repentance, and we should now read Psalm 51 in its entirety. It is headed, "To the chief musician, A Psalm of David, when Nathan the prophet came unto him, after he had gone in to Bath-sheba." Here are some extracts:

"Have mercy upon me, O God, according to thy lovingkindness: according to the multitude of thy tender mercies blot out my transgressions. Wash me throughly from mine iniquity, and cleanse me from my sin. For I acknowledge my transgressions: and my sin is ever before me. Against thee, thee only, have I sinned, and done this evil in thy sight...For thou desirest not sacrifice; else would I give it: thou delightest not in burnt-offering. The sacrifices of God are a broken spirit: a broken and a contrite heart, O God, thou wilt not despise" (vv.1-4,16-17).

It is traditional to connect Psalm 32 with this sad occasion in David's life. As J. Flanigan observes *(What the Bible Teaches - Psalms)* in connection with this Psalm, "there seems to be little reason to doubt that it was, like Psalm 51, occasioned by the sin of David's adultery with Bath-sheba, and the untimely death of Uriah as recorded in 2 Samuel chapter 11." Here are some extracts.

"Blessed is he whose transgression is forgiven, whose sin is covered. Blessed is the man unto whom the Lord imputeth not iniquity, and in whose spirit there is no guile. When I kept silence, my bones waxed old through my roaring all the day long. For day and night thy hand was heavy upon me: my moisture is turned into the drought of summer. Selah. I acknowledged my sin unto thee, and mine iniquity have I not hid. I said, I will confess my transgressions unto the Lord; and thou forgavest the iniquity of my sin. Selah" (vv.1-5).

The **ground** of David's forgiveness was the all-sufficient death of the Lord Jesus. Sins have only and ever been forgiven on this basis. See Romans 3.24-26: "Being justified freely by his grace through the redemption that is in Christ Jesus: Whom God hath set forth to be a propitiation through faith in his blood, to declare his righteousness for the remission of sins **that are past**, through the forbearance of God; To declare, I say, at **this time** his righteousness: that he might be just, and the justifier of him that believeth in Jesus." The **means** by which David obtained forgiveness was repentance.

B) *The government of God (v.14)*

"Howbeit, because by this deed thou hast given great occasion to the enemies of the Lord to blaspheme, the child also that is born unto thee shall surely die." Confession and forgiveness do not necessarily remove the consequences of sin. An additional result of David's sin was the dishonour he brought on the Lord's name. The "enemies of the Lord" must refer to the surrounding nations, amongst whom the news must have spread like wildfire. Centuries later, Paul was obliged to say of the Jewish nation, "For the name of God is blasphemed among the Gentiles through you..." (Rom 2.24). But what was the nature of their blasphemy here? We almost hear them saying, "The God of Israel allows His own people to flout His laws, and get away with it. What sort of a God is that?" David had brought the Lord's name into disrepute, and now the time had come for God to display His righteousness. David is told that the child, born within marriage but conceived in adultery, would die. God would not tolerate the slur on his name. David must reap the consequences of dishonouring God. This is a solemn warning to us all. In this connection, it is interesting to notice that the surrounding nations **did** recognise that God would not tolerate sin in His people. See for example Jeremiah 22.8-9, "And many nations shall pass by this city, and they shall say every man to his neighbour, Wherefore hath the Lord done thus unto this great city? Then they shall answer, Because they have forsaken the covenant of the Lord their God, and worshipped other gods, and served them."

3) The Death of the Child (vv.15-23)

We must notice first of all that "the Lord struck the child that **Uriah's wife** (there it is again) bare unto David, and it was very sick." This is the one occasion in Scripture where illness is associated with the sin of a parent. The welfare of the innocent child is not in question. It would be "well with the child" (2 Kings 4.26). There are at least three important lessons for us from the way in which David reacted to the child's illness and death.

A) *His prayer (vv.16-17)*

"David therefore besought God for the child; and David fasted, and **went in**, and lay all night upon the earth." Compare this with 2 Samuel 7.18, "Then **went** king David **in**, and sat before the Lord..." We are not told exactly **where** he went (either to the "tent", 2 Sam 6.17, or his own house) but we do know to **whom** he went and what he did. He prayed and fasted for a week. Yes, he had been told that the child would die (v.14), but he saw the possibility that God would alter His decision (see v.22). Compare Zephaniah 2.1-3: "Gather yourselves together, yea, gather together, O nation not desired; before the day pass as the chaff, before the fierce anger of the Lord come upon you...it **may be** ye shall be hid in the day of the Lord's anger." Whilst the child was alive there was hope. We know that "he that believeth not is condemned already", but that does not mean that we should not pray for their salvation.

B) His worship (vv.18-20)

The deep concern of David's servants was unfounded. Having heard that his baby son was dead, he "arose from the earth, and washed, and anointed himself, and changed his apparel, and came into the house of the Lord, and **worshipped:** then he came to his own house..." (v.20). After his catastrophic losses, Job "rent his mantle, and shaved his head, and fell down upon the ground, and **worshipped:** And said...the Lord gave, and the Lord hath taken away; blessed be the name of the Lord" (Job 1.20-21). There was no bitter complaint or recrimination on the part of either David or Job. David accepted the Lord's judgment, and Job accepted the Lord's will. Both said in effect, "As for God, his way is perfect" (Ps 18.30). But this doesn't mean that the sorrows and disappointments of life are easily dismissed. The Lord Jesus prayed, "Abba, Father, all things are possible unto thee; take away this cup from me: nevertheless not what I will, but what thou wilt" (Mk 14.36).

C) His explanation (vv.21-23)

David explained his reversal of convention as follows: "While the child was yet alive, I fasted and wept: for I said, Who can tell whether God will be gracious unto me, and that the child may live? But now he is dead, wherefore should I fast? Can I bring him back again? I shall go to him, but he shall not return to me." We mustn't think that all David's concern disappeared when he realised that there was nothing more he could do. As H.Mowvley observes, "The writer does not put this negative 'spin' on it. Instead he shows David's realism, his readiness to accept what God had decreed, and then to get on with his life". Whilst H. Mowvley suggests that David's final remark (v.23) is "simply an acknowledgement that there was no way back from the dead and that all, at death, went to Sheol", it seems preferable to see David's hope for the future. "David comes to terms with his own mortality, and even in that finds hope, because he looks forward to being reunited with his child" (J. Baldwin).

4) The Birth of Solomon (vv.24-25)

"Bathsheba...bare a son, and he called his name Solomon: and the Lord loved him. And he sent by the hand of Nathan the prophet; and he called his name Jedidiah, because of the Lord." The two names are significant:

A) Solomon

His name is explained in 1 Chronicles 22.9; "Behold, a son shall be born unto thee, who shall be a man of rest." Solomon means "peaceable." The name comes from the same Hebrew root as *"shalom"*, meaning "peace" or "well-being." David certainly reminds us of the Lord Jesus as the Warrior-King (Rev 19.11-16), and Solomon reminds us of the Lord Jesus as the coming "Prince of Peace" (Is 9.6) in whose reign "nation shall not lift up sword against nation, neither shall they earn war any more" (Is 2.4). If David called his new son "Solomon", reflecting his hope for the future as opposed to past distress, then he received confirmation from God through Nathan.

B) Jedidiah

"And the Lord loved him. And he sent by the hand of Nathan the prophet; and he called him Jedidiah, because of the Lord." Jedidiah means "beloved of the Lord." Perhaps the fact that Jedidiah was never actually adopted as Solomon's name means that it was given to him as a symbol of the Lord's love for him. The Lord Jesus, "greater than Solomon", is the true Jedidiah. Read John 15.9-10. Do notice that another of David's sons by Bath-sheba was called **Nathan** (1 Chron 3.5). It seems that David commemorated the faithfulness of "Nathan the prophet" in this way!

5) The Fall of Rabbah (vv.26-31)

During all this time, Joab was busy besieging Rabbah, but as J. Baldwin observes, the settlement of David's sin takes priority over the settling of accounts with the Ammonites. The lesson is clear. However, Joab was on the point of total victory. "I have fought against Rabbah, and have taken the city of waters (Rabbah was situated near the source of the river Jabbok). Now therefore gather the rest of the people together, and encamp against the city (the citadel area which, as excavations have proved, was heavily fortified), and take it: lest I take the city, and it be called after my name." Joab wanted David to have the honour of capturing the city and its king, and in the same way it should be our desire that "in all things he (the Lord Jesus) might have the pre-eminence (Col 1.18). The transfer of the crown from the head of the Ammonite king (Hebrew *"malkam"*, leading some to suggest that it was the crown worn by the idol Milcom) symbolised the transfer of power to David. The final verse makes horrifying reading, and attempts have been made to make it refer to forced labour. See RV margin. But this does require a small alteration to the text. The Ammonites were a cruel people (see 1 Sam 11.2 and Amos 1.3), and it does seem that David treated them in the same way as they treated their enemies.

CHAPTER 13.1-39

"Such thing ought to be done in Israel"

Having considered David's triumphs (chs.1-10) and David's tragedy (chs.11-12), we now come to David's troubles (chs.13-24). As we shall see, he encounters troubles in his family (chs.13-19) and troubles in the nation (chs.20-24). Nathan had warned David that his adultery with Bath-sheba and the murder of her husband would bring dire consequences: "Now therefore the sword shall never depart from thine house; because thou hast despised me, and hast taken the wife of Uriah the Hittite to be thy wife" (12.10). We must never forget that "whatsoever a man soweth, that shall he also reap." The reaping begins in this chapter, and we discover "the sombre lesson that children are more likely to copy our vices than our virtues" (A. McShane).

In one sense, chapter 13 is a rerun of chapter 11. See the addendum. The Lord is not mentioned in chapter 11 until the last verse: "But the thing that David had done displeased the Lord" (v.27). In this chapter He is not mentioned at all, and the two chapters therefore prove that disaster is inevitable when people live without reference to Him. 2 Samuel 13 makes very unpleasant reading, and must be handled with care and sensitivity. We should carefully note that the passage provides only sufficient information to emphasise the gravity of Amnon's sin, and that is all. The unwholesome incident is intended to appal us, not to interest the public and sell more newspapers.

We can divide the chapter in the following way: **(1)** The sin of Amnon (vv.1-14); **(2)** The distress of Tamar (vv.15-20); **(3)** The vengeance of Absalom (vv.21-29); **(4)** The sorrow of David (vv.30-39).

1) The Sin of Amnon (vv.1-14)
These verses tell us at least three unpalatable things about Amnon: *(a)* he

harboured an evil desire (vv.1-2); **(b)** he received some evil advice (vv.3-10); **(c)** he committed an evil act (vv.11-14).

a) He harboured an evil desire (vv.1-2)
Events in this chapter demonstrate yet again the sad consequences of polygamy. "Absalom...had a fair sister, whose name was Tamar; and Amnon the son of David loved her. And Amnon was so vexed (distressed, *yatsar*), that he fell sick for his sister Tamar; for she was a virgin; and Amnon thought it hard for him to do anything to her." Amnon was David's son by Ahinoam, and Absalom and Tamar were David's son and daughter by Maacah (2 Sam 3.2-3). The purity of Tamar ("she was a virgin") is contrasted with the illicit love of Amnon, if love is the right word. Subsequent events proved that it was lust rather than love. Incest was prohibited by the law. See Leviticus 20.17, "if a man shall take his sister, his father's daughter, or his mother's daughter...they shall be cut off in the sight of their people." See also Leviticus 18.6-9. Amnon was therefore in an impossible situation. There was nothing he could do about it, and it made him ill in the sense that he was beside himself with lust (v.2).

The Lord Jesus taught that "from within, out of the heart of men, proceed evil thoughts, adulteries, fornications...lasciviousness..." (Mk 7.21-22). As a man "thinketh in his heart, so is he" (Prov 23.7). No wonder Solomon said, "Keep thy heart with all diligence; for out of it are the issues of life" (Prov 4.23). If sinful thoughts are allowed to persist in our minds, there is every possibility that they will become actions. Amnon followed in his fathers footsteps. David "saw a woman" and then he "sent and enquired" about her, and then "he sent messengers, and took her" (11.2-4). We all do well to follow the example of Job: "I made a covenant with mine eyes; why should I then think upon a maid? (Job 31.1).

b) He received some evil advice (vv.3-10)
"But Amnon had a friend, whose name was Jonadab, the son of Shimeah (Shammah, 1 Sam 16.9) David's brother: and Jonadab was a very subtil man" (v.3). Cousin Jonadab was worldly-wise. The word "subtil" *(chakam)* means "wise", and is usually translated in that way. But there was nothing commendable about Jonadab's wisdom, and this may be the reason for the way in which it has been translated here. The context suggests that he was wise in the sense of "artful."

Jonadab was observant: "Why art thou, being the king's son, lean from day to day" (v.4). The only thing we can say in his favour is that he noticed that

Amnon was losing weight, and was concerned about it. The son of a king was expected to look well, and whilst the sons of the King of kings have their due share of physical problems, they ought to be in good spiritual health like Gaius (3 Jn 2). Notice that even David didn't seem to have spotted that something was amiss. Sadly, it has to be said that Christians sometimes appear to be so disinterested in each other, that they don't notice when things seem to be going wrong. We should "consider one another" (Heb 10.24) and remember that "the members should have the same care one for another" so that "whether one member suffer, all the members suffer with it" (1 Cor 12.25-26).

But that's about the only favourable thing we can say about Jonadab. He certainly wasn't much of a friend. The Bible says "faithful are the wounds of a friend (Prov 27.6), but instead of correcting Amnon, Jonadab helped him in the wrong direction. Being a very subtle man (yes, a play on words here!), he put only half an idea into Amnon's head, knowing that the rest would take care of itself. Whilst Jonadab's advice was wrong, it seems improbable that he foresaw its terrible outcome. "His proposed deception, "admittedly not very morally elevated", was meant to secure a private meeting between Amnon and Tamar" (J. P. Fokkelman quoted by J. Baldwin).

Against this dark background, unsuspecting Tamar acted in a most commendable way. She responded to her father's request, "Go now to thy brother Amnon's house, and dress him meat" (v.7), and showed her care for Amnon by taking time to make him a meal (v.8). She was totally oblivious of his evil intentions.

c) He committed an evil act (vv.11-14)
We now reach the second stage of the sequence described by James: "when lust hath conceived, **it bringeth forth sin**: and sin, when it is finished, bringeth forth death" (Jas 1.15). Whilst Amnon was completely blinded by his lust, Tamar fully understood the fearful consequences of his intentions: "Nay, my brother, do not force me; for no such thing ought to be done in Israel: do not thou this folly. And I, whither shall I cause my shame to go? And as for thee, thou shalt be as one of the fools in Israel" (vv.12-13). She made a threefold plea to Amnon:

i) She asked him to consider the word of God. "No such thing ought to be done in Israel: do not thou this folly." Compare Genesis 34.7, "the men (Jacob's sons) were grieved...because he (Shechem) had wrought folly in

Israel in lying with Jacob's daughter; which thing ought not to be done." To ignore or disobey God's word is always "folly." As we have noticed, the word of God prohibited incest.

It is noteworthy that Tamar places the word of God first. This is the proper basis of moral conduct. When Joseph was tempted by Potiphar's wife, he said "how then can I do this great wickedness, and **sin against God?**" (Gen 39.9).

ii) She asked him to consider her. "And I, whither shall I cause my shame to go?" Shame and contempt would meet her everywhere. Her entire future would be jeopardised.

iii) She asked him to consider his own future. "And as for thee, thou shalt be as one of the fools in Israel." It has been pointed out that as his first-born son (2 Sam 3.2). Amnon was the heir-apparent. "Was this the sort of person Israel would want for a king, a man without principles, who took the law into his own hands and offended the ordinary standards of morality in the land?" (J. Baldwin). His entire future would be jeopardised as well. Tamar's desperate suggestion, "Now therefore, I pray thee, speak unto the king; for he will not withhold me from thee", does not infer that David would have broken the law in the circumstances. It was an attempt to "escape from his hands by any means in her power, and to avoid inflaming him still more by precluding all hope of marriage and driving him to sin" (quoted by Keil & Delitzsch).

But it was to no avail. In this case a "threefold cord" (Eccl 4.12) **was** "quickly broken" by Amnon.

2) The Distress of Tamar (vv.15-20)
Amnon's alleged love for Tamar (v4) suddenly turns into burning hatred. "Then Amnon hated her exceedingly; so that the hatred wherewith he hated her was greater than the love wherewith he loved her" (v.15). In these verses we must notice *(a)* Amnon's animosity (vv.15-18), and *(b)* Tamar's anguish (vv.19-20).

a) Amnon's animosity (vv.15-18)
J. Baldwin suggests that "the sudden reversal from love to hate, and the dismissal, "Arise, be gone", are cruel, most of all to Tamar, but also in their revelation of Amnon's inadequacy as a person." However, this does seem

an understatement, and it is more appropriate to say that Amnon was perverse. Tamar's second plea (see also v.14) was ignored (v.16), and she was bundled through the door. "My sister" (v.11) now becomes "this woman" (v.17): the literal rendering is "put this...out from me." The contemptuous way he spoke about her and the command to the servant, "bolt the door after her", imply that she was the guilty party. It implies that she was put out, and in no way was she coming back. No wonder Tamar said, "this evil in sending me away is greater than the other that thou didst unto me" (v.16).

b) Tamar's anguish (vv.19-20)
"And Tamar put ashes on her head, and rent her garment of divers colours that was on her, and laid her hand on her head, and went on crying." These were the customary signs of mourning over the loss of a loved one, but here it was the loss of her virginity. Her "garment of divers colours" was distinctive, "for with such robes were the king's daughters that were virgins apparelled" (v.18). The "garment of divers colours" recalls "the coat of many colours" worn by Joseph (Gen 37.3). We are told that in both cases it was "a coat with sleeves" (Gen 37.3 JND margin) or "a long dress with sleeves" (2 Sam 13.18-19, Keil & Delitzsch). As J. Baldwin observes, "though the details are obscure, the dress was no doubt splendid, but all that it stood for was gone for ever."

Absalom quickly realised what had happened (v.20), and the way in which he apparently made light of her experience concealed hatred for Amnon. It would be two years before he had the opportunity to avenge his sister's dishonour. (He showed his affection for Tamar by naming his own daughter after her: see 14.27). The words, "So Tamar remained desolate in her brother Absalom's house", imply that she was 'a desolate woman (Heb. *somema*), isolated from society, disqualified through no fault of her own from marriage" (J. Baldwin). This brings us to:

3) The Vengeance of Absalom (vv.21-29)
David was "very wroth", but "Absalom spake unto his brother neither good nor bad: for Absalom hated Amnon because he had forced his sister Tamar" (vv.21-22). David appears to have had little control over his sons. He was "very wroth" over Amnon's crime, but that was all. David's own conduct had robbed him of the moral right to deal with the situation, and his family knew it. He failed to impose the required penalty on Absalom for murdering Amnon, and according to 1 Kings 1.6 he made

no attempt to discipline or correct Adonijah: "his father had not displeased him at any time in saying, Why hast thou done so?" Although in his "last words", David said, "he that ruleth over men must be just, ruling in the fear of God" (2 Sam 23.3), he didn't always practice what he preached. In the New Testament, an overseer (AV "bishop") must be "one that ruleth well his own house, having his children in subjection with all gravity; (for if a man know not how to rule his own house, how shall he take care of the church of God?)..." (1 Tim 3.4-5).

But Absalom was not content to let the matter rest. His hatred for Amnon is suppressed in v.22, but it is expressed in vv.23-29, and we must notice *(a)* his invitation (vv.23-25); *(b)* his intention (vv.26-27); *(c)* his instructions (vv.28-29).

a) His invitation (vv.23-25)
Sheep-shearing had long been regarded as a time for festivities. See Genesis 38 12-13 and 1 Samuel 25.2 etc. The precise location of "Baal-hazor, which is beside Ephraim" is not known, and we have every right to be suspicious when we read, "the text says it was near "Ephraim" but almost certainly this is a miscopying, the familiar word "Ephraim" being copied for the less common "Ephron." Ephron was a hill just a few miles north-west of the capital" (H. Mowvley). It is all too common for commentators to alter the text when they can't explain it! Whether Absalom really wanted David to attend the festivities is doubtful, but there is no doubt about his desire for Amnon to be there. The general invitation to the whole family was a smokescreen.

b) His intention (vv.26-27)
Absalom's real motive becomes clear when David declined the invitation. "Then said Absalom, If not, I pray thee, let my brother Amnon go with us. And the king said unto him, Why should he go with thee?" No satisfactory answer was forthcoming, but "Absalom pressed him, that he let Amnon and all the king's sons go with him." Jonadab **may** have been aware of Absalom's intentions (v.32), but although David was puzzled at first, he evidently had no idea that there was a "hidden agenda." Although Absalom had suppressed his ill-will (v.22) it seems unlikely that David did not know that strained relationships existed between his two sons. Perhaps he concluded that after two years, Absalom had decided that "enough was enough" and wanted to "let bygones be bygones." We certainly get the impression that Absalom was David's favourite son (see 18.33).

Let's just say that as believers, we should be "straight up and down" in our relationships with each other. Paul put it like this: "For our rejoicing is this, the testimony of our conscience, that in simplicity and godly sincerity, not with fleshly wisdom, but by the grace of God, we have had our conversation in the world, and more abundantly to you-ward. For we write none other things unto you, than what ye read or acknowledge" (2 Cor 1.12-13).

c) His instructions (vv.28-29)

People are very vulnerable when they are "merry with wine." It does mean rather more than being full of "le joie de vivre". Nabal's "heart was merry within him, for he was very drunken" (1 Sam 25.36). We mustn't forget king Ahasuerus either (Est 1.10). The first mention of wine in the Bible involved drunkenness. See Gen 9.20-21. Don't ignore the clear lesson here. The London Transport tube trains (Piccadilly Line) used to carry the following advertisement: "Total abstinence from intoxicating liquor promotes accuracy in skilled movements."

The words, "have not I commanded you? be courageous, and be valiant", imply that Absalom would take full responsibility for his brother's murder. But they also recall similar words in a different context. "Have not I commanded thee? Be strong and of a good courage" (Josh 1.9). The servants of Absalom were to be "courageous" in disobeying God's word: Joshua was to be "courageous" in obeying God's word. See also 1 Chronicles 28.20, where David uses the same exhortation.

"And the servants of Absalom did unto Amnon as Absalom had commanded." He had avenged his sister's dishonour, and "all the king's sons, and every man gat him up upon his mule, and fled." As Nathan had predicted, "the sword" had been wielded in David's house, and more was to follow.

4) The Sorrow of David (vv.30-39)

David's sorrow in these verses was caused by *(a)* incorrect information (vv.30-35); *(b)* Amnon's death (vv.36-37); *(c)* Absalom's exile (vv.38-39).

a) Sorrow over incorrect information (vv.30-35)

"And it came to pass, while they were in the way, that tidings came to David, saying, Absalom hath slain all the king's sons, and there is not one of them left. Then the king arose, and tare his garments, and lay on the earth; and all his servants stood by with their clothes rent." David took the *communiqué* at face value, and his sorrow must have been heightened by the fact that he had permitted his sons to leave Jerusalem, and Amnon in particular. Amongst other things, this reminds us that exaggeration can be highly dangerous. Unlike ourselves, David had no immediate means of verifying this terrible news. Modern communications (even such old-fashioned things as telephones) enable **us** to check information, but in spite of this we do tend to repeat things without making sure of our facts, and this can sometimes cause unnecessary distress. We should be particularly careful when relating something critical or discreditable about somebody else. Whilst Deuteronomy 13 deals with procedure when idolatry was reported in Israel, the following instructions make very good advice whenever rumours start to fly: "Then shalt thou enquire, and make search, and ask diligently; and, behold, if it be truth, and the thing certain…" (v.14). Some rumours are started deliberately, and the apostle Paul knew what it was like to be on the receiving end. Read Romans 3.8.

Jonadab, the "subtil" friend of Amnon (v.3) reached the right conclusion, not because he knew in advance that Amnon would be murdered at Baal-hazor, but because he knew that Absalom was intent on reprisals. "Let not my lord suppose that they have slain all the young men the king's sons; for Amnon only is dead: for by the appointment of Absalom this hath been determined from the day that he (Amnon) forced his sister Tamar." In spite of this, it seems clear that Jonadab, who continued to be "artful", made no attempt to warn David at any time that trouble was brewing. There is all the difference in the world between telling stories, and seriously drawing someone's attention to a possible disaster. Paul had been informed by "them which are of the house of Chloe" that there were "contentions" (strife or rivalry) at Corinth (1 Cor 1.11), but this wasn't mere tittle-tattle. "The house of Chloe" knew that Paul was a competent man who could deal with the situation. Jonadab was soon proved right, and seemed very pleased to say, "I told you so!" (v.35).

b) Sorrow over Amnon's death (vv.36-37)
"And it came to pass, as soon as he had made an end of speaking, that, behold, the king's sons came, and lifted up their voice and wept: and the king also and all his servants wept very sore…And David wept for his son every day." Christians are not exempted from grief and sorrow. "Devout men carried Stephen to his burial, and made great lamentation over him" (Acts 8.2). But where fellow-Christians are concerned, we "sorrow not, even as others which have no hope" (1 Thess 4.13).

c) Sorrow over Absalom's exile (vv.38-39)
"But Absalom fled (v.34)…But Absalom fled (v.37)…So Absalom fled" (v.38). As each occurrence gives us extra information, this isn't quite the repetition it seems. The last reference implies his eventual return, and whets our appetite for the next instalment in the story! Talmai was his grandfather on his mother's side (2 Sam 3.3). According to J. Baldwin, Geshur was "a buffer state between Israel and Syria, to the north of Gilead." We say that "time is a great healer" and it certainly seems that way here: "And the soul of king David longed to go forth unto Absalom: for he was comforted concerning Amnon, seeing he was dead" (v.39). However, in his love for Absalom David evidently overlooked the interests of justice, and this reminds us that family interests should not take precedence over the word of God. It is not unknown for preachers to take a very firm stand on the teaching of God's word, that is, until their families start to transgress. If you take time to delve into commentaries, you will discover that the final verse is sometimes translated quite differently, but the AV rendering makes perfectly good sense, and this is confirmed by the opening words of ch 14: "Now Joab…perceived that the king's heart was towards Absalom" (v.1).

The chapter ends with disaster for the house of David. The heir-apparent is dead; the next in line would have been Chileab, but we know nothing about him; and Absalom, the third son, is in exile. As A. McShane observes, "David paid dearly for his sin, but in spite of it he retained the throne and finished his life in honour." "The gifts and calling of God are without repentance" (Rom 11.29).

Addendum
The parallels between the murder of Uriah and the murder of Amnon are most significant:

i) David made Uriah drunk at a feast: "And when David had called him, he did eat and drink before him; and he made him drunk" (11.13). Absalom did the same to Amnon. His heart was "merry with wine" at a feast (13.28).

ii) David gave instructions for Uriah's death (11.15). Absalom gave instructions for Amnon's death (13.28).

iii) David showed no remorse over Uriah's death: "Let not this thing displease thee, for the sword devoureth one as well as another" (11.25). Jonadab showed no sorrow over the death of Amnon: "Let not my lord suppose that they have slain all the young men the king's sons; for Amnon only is dead" (13.32).

iv) David "mourned" for his son" (13.37), just as Bath-sheba "mourned for her husband" (11.26).

In the world this would be called "poetic justice." In the Bible it is called "reaping the whirlwind" (Hos 8.7).

CHAPTER 14.1-33

"Yet doth he devise means,
that his banished be not expelled from him"

Many gospel messages have been based on the words of the "wise woman" of Tekoah in this chapter: "for we must needs die, and are as water spilt on the ground, which cannot be gathered up again; neither doth God respect any person: yet doth he devise means, that his banished be not expelled from him" (v.14). We will highlight the major points here in due course. But it could be said of this chapter that "Joab devised means whereby David's banished be not expelled from him." Whilst David's rather reluctant forgiveness of Absalom seemed a step forward, his return from exile brought a fresh crop of troubles for David. As we have noted more than once, David's successes in chs.1-10 were followed by David's sins in chs.11-12 and David's sufferings in chs.13-24. Absalom's return from exile resulted in David's exile (15.14), and still further sorrow for David when Absalom was killed (18.33).

This chapter can be divided in the following way: **(1)** The woman's request (vv.1-20); **(2)** Absalom's repatriation (vv.21-27); **(3)** Absalom's reconciliation (vv.28-33).

1) The Woman's Request (vv.1-20)
David was certainly impressed by a good story. Nathan was so successful that David unconsciously passed judgment on himself (12.1-7), and the woman from Tekoah succeeded in pointing out to David that he was willing to do something for her that he was not willing to do for himself: "the king doth speak this thing as one which is faulty, in that the king doth not fetch home again his banished" (v.13). We should notice **(A)** the role of Joab (vv.1-3) and **(B)** the role of the woman (vv.4-20).

A) The role of Joab (vv.1-3)
"Now Joab the son of Zeruiah perceived that the king's heart was towards

Absalom." Some commentators suggest that the words "towards Absalom" should read "against Absalom", but the AV translation (supported by JND, RV and RSV) seems perfectly reasonable. David evidently wanted his son back, but was reluctant to make the first move in view of his crime in murdering Amnon. Joab does not appear to have a "hidden agenda." As far as we can see, he acted purely in the interests of David, but in actual fact it was the complete reverse. It ultimately caused David untold grief. Whilst A. McShane describes the woman as "only a puppet in the crafty hand of Joab", she is rightly described as a "wise woman", although it was "the wisdom of this world" (1 Cor 1.20). "Though Joab prescribed her dress and her words, she needed all her wit and tact to parry the response of the king which could not be foreseen" (J. Baldwin).

C. I. Scofield calls this paragraph "Joab's craft" and his heading is certainly justified. He said to the woman, "I pray thee, feign thyself to be a mourner", and "put the words in her mouth." It was a very clever plan. In pretending to be "a woman that had a long time mourned for the dead", she would have the sympathy of David who mourned the loss of a son. However, we should notice that Joab embarked on this without any reference to the Lord. The whole procedure reeks of worldly wisdom. While the woman uses the Lord's name frequently, David only mentions it once, and that was in connection with his oath (v.11). No doubt the "wise woman" willingly complied with Joab's request, but we should be careful about "firing other people's bullets!" As we shall see, "the penny dropped" eventually with David (v.19), but some people do like to hide behind others in achieving their objectives.

B) The role of the woman (vv.4-20)
The "wise woman" evidently followed Joab's instructions in approaching David and in making him look at the problem objectively, but she was certainly skilful in her own right. This is clear from the way in which she directed the conversation, which she moved on from stage to stage in the following way:

i) Her problem (vv.4-8)
Although this was what we would call today a "put up job", we do learn that David was evidently accessible to ordinary people, and continued to execute judgment and justice unto all his people" (8.15). Absalom was quite wrong in saying "there is no man deputed of the king to hear thee" (15.3). David listened to people personally. The king of Israel was approachable, and we must remember that the "King of kings" is also accessible to His people. We can come "boldly unto the throne of grace that we may obtain mercy,

and find grace to help in time of need" (Heb 4.16). The woman "fell on her face to the ground, and did obeisance, and said, Help, O king" (v.4), and this reminds us that we should approach the Lord with reverence. We are not talking to our neighbour over the garden fence.

There is no need to repeat the details of her story, but we should notice the skill of the story-teller: "thy handmaid had two sons…but one smote the other, and slew him" (v.6). David could certainly empathise with that! On one hand stood the family crying for justice, for the law said that if a man "in enmity smite him with his hand, that he die: he that smote him shall surely be put to death; for he is a murderer" (Num 35.21). On the other hand stood the mother who loved the remaining son in whom lay the family future (v.7). "He was her one remaining *coal* in a dying fire" (J. Baldwin). David could certainly empathise with that as well! It was his own dilemma. As we have seen, with the death of Amnon, and the absence of reference to Chileab, Abslalom was now the heir-apparent. See 2 Samuel 2.2-3. We have to admire the story-line! (In actual fact Absalom was not David's heir at all: if David had prayed about it, he might have discovered that his successor was to be Solomon).

David responds by promising consideration of the case. "Go to thine house, and I will give charge concerning thee" (v.8). But the "wise woman" was not easily dismissed!

2) Her perseverance (vv.9-11)
She continues to press her case. It needed to be settled urgently, and she was not prepared to wait for the promised decision. Her words, "My lord, O king, the iniquity be on me, and on my father's house: and the king and his throne be guiltless" (v.9) evidently mean that if it was wrong **not** to punish this bloodshed, she and her family would bear the guilt. This wrung from David the promise that "whosoever saith ought to thee, bring him to me, and he shall not touch thee any more" (v.10), but that wasn't sufficient for the woman. She wanted his assurance on oath! "Let the king remember the Lord thy God, that thou wouldest not suffer the avengers of blood to destroy any more, lest they destroy my son", and she got what she wanted: "And he said, As the Lord liveth, there shall not one hair of thy son fall to the earth" (v.11). David swore to her on solemn oath.

Let's remember that while the woman certainly "twisted David's arm", we do not have to put pressure on God to answer our prayers and meet our needs. The Lord Jesus said, "your heavenly Father knoweth that ye have need of all these things" (Mt 6.32). But we are to "continue (persevere) in prayer" (Col 4.2). We are not heard for empty and repetitious "much speaking" (Mt 6.7), but for continuing and believing prayer.

3) Her purpose (vv.12-14)

Although David did not yet know it, he was now committed to protect the life of Absalom against the death penalty for murdering his brother. This is now made very clear to him by the woman. She now reaches the purpose of her visit. "Wherefore then hast thou thought such a thing against the people of God? For the king doth speak this thing as one that is faulty, in that the king doth not fetch home again his banished" (v.13). This must have come as something of a bombshell to David. The woman is very blunt! David was inconsistent. He was prepared to protect her son, but he wasn't prepared to protect his own son.

Doesn't this remind us of the need for consistency between what we say and what we do? What we **say** may be right, but are **we** right? The Lord Jesus charged the religious leaders with inconsistency: "they say, and do not" (Mt 23.3). He was the perfect exemplar of His own teaching: "The former treatise have I made, O Theophilus, of all that Jesus began both to do and teach" (Acts 1.1). Timothy was told: "Take heed unto **thyself**, and unto the **doctrine**" (2 Tim 4.16). There was to be no discrepancy between his personal life and his teaching.

We should notice her words, "Wherefore then hast thou thought such a thing **against the people of God?** Whilst this could be regarded as an indefinite statement which paves the way for something specific, it seems more likely that the woman is stressing that Absalom's exile was a loss to the nation. This reminds us that each child of God is not only precious to Him, but of immense value to the assembly. The absence of any member, particularly because of wrongdoing or disinterest, means that the assembly suffers

This brings us to the well-known verse: "for we must needs die, and are as water spilt on the ground, which cannot be gathered up again; neither doth God respect any person: yet doth he devise means, that his banished be not expelled from him" (v.14). As Keil & Deltizsch rightly point out, "in order to persuade the king to forgive, she reminded him of the brevity of human life, and of the mercy of God." Her point is clear: if David does not act, he might never see his son again. At death, life is irrevocably gone. But God does not stand by, and let sinful men perish without making provision for their recovery and blessing. The "wise woman" is telling David to act in the same way as God Himself. We must not forget that the woman was pressurising David to do something contrary to God's will, but taken in isolation, her words can be applied in the following way:

a) As an illustration of the gospel message: the **inevitability of death** ("we must needs die"); the **impossibility of further opportunity** ("and are as water spilt on the ground, which cannot be gathered up again"); the **impartiality of God** ("neither doth God respect any person"); the **initiative of God** ("yet doth he devise means, that his banished be not expelled from him"). This will do for a start! Plenty of scope for expansion here, especially the words "yet doth he devise means, that his banished be not expelled from him." The "means" by which God has so wonderfully blessed us is the death of His own Son. See, for example, Romans 3.21-26. (It should be pointed out that the RV has "neither doth God take away life" in the place of "neither doth God respect any person").

b) As an illustration of the way in which "the love of Christ" should "constrain" us (hold us fast) in our service for Him. See 2 Corinthians 5.14. If God has acted in such love and mercy towards us, we should act in love and mercy towards others.

iv) Her plea (vv.15-17)

Having made the intended point, although David has not yet realised that this was the purpose of her visit, the "wise woman" returns to her story. Once again she displays her wisdom. She pleads her vulnerability (v.15) which led to her decision to bring her case to the king, who was sure to listen and act on her behalf (vv.15-16). "For the king will hear, to deliver his handmaid out of the hand of the man that would destroy me and my son altogether out of the inheritance of God." In deciding to ask for David's help, she was confident that such a great and wise king would not fail to help her. "Then thine handmaid said, The word of my lord the king shall now be comfortable: for as an angel of god, so is my lord the king to discern good and bad: therefore the Lord thy God will be with thee" (v.17). As we would say, this was certainly "laying it on a bit!" But it was all intended to give David a feeling of deep satisfaction. However, at this stage David "smelt a rat" (perhaps we should say, "became suspicious!").

v) Her praise (vv.18-20)

At last "the penny dropped!" "Then the king answered and said unto the woman, Hide not from me, I pray thee, the thing that I shall ask thee. And the woman said, Let my lord the king now speak. And the king said, Is not the hand of Joab with thee in all this?" It was a tense moment, but once again the "wise woman" is equal to the situation. Before and after admitting that Joab had been "the author of her role play" (J. Baldwin), she acknowledged the king's astuteness in suspecting that Joab had been lurking behind the scenes. Just listen to her! "As thy soul liveth, my lord the king, none can turn to the right hand or to the left from ought that my lord the king hath spoken: for thy servant Joab, he bade me, and he put all these words in the mouth of thine handmaid: to fetch about this form of speech (or, "in order to turn the appearance of the thing, JND) hath thy servant Joab done this thing: and my lord is wise, according to the wisdom of an angel of God, to know all things that are in the earth" (vv.19-20). She emphasised David's wisdom rather than Joab's craftiness! But even Joab's role is cast in the best possible light: it was "in order to turn the appearance of the thing", that is, to enable David to resolve the problem of Absalom's exile. As J. Baldwin says, "with a flattering reference to the wisdom of the king, the woman brings her audience to an end. Her fictional story has done its work and she has achieved her purpose." We now see the result:

2) Absalom's Repatriation (vv.21-27)

Exit the "wise woman", and enter Joab. "And the king said unto Joab, Behold now, I have done this thing: go therefore, bring the young man Absalom again" (v.21). We must notice two things in this section of the chapter: **(A)** Absalom's arrival in Jerusalem (vv.21-24) and **(B)** Absalom's attractiveness to Israel (vv.25-27).

A) His arrival in Jerusalem (vv.21-24)

Having expressed his gratitude to David for agreeing to Absalom's return (v.22), Joab "arose and went to Geshur, and brought Absalom to Jerusalem" (v.23). A. McShane refers to this, and to a string of events commencing with David's adultery with Bath-sheba, with the comment that "if success proves matters to be right, then all these happenings were correct, but we know that they were evil crimes in the sight of the Lord." The fact that evil men appear to "get away with it" doesn't mean that sin has triumphed over righteousness. Success is not a safe standard by which to judge. David, Amnon and Absalom all appeared to escape the consequences of their sin at first, but not for long. We have only one criterion: "What saith the scripture?"

Quite clearly, David could not bring himself to receive Absalom, and continued to show his disfavour by banishing him to his own house. F. Gardiner summarises the situation as follows: the recall of Absalom was "done in weakness", and he was excluded from the palace "through a sense of justice." David's half-hearted forgiveness worked against his best interests. As we shall see, Absalom "resented his father's limited and reserved acceptance of him, and reacted with hostility" (J. Baldwin). Leaving aside the immediate circumstances, how genuine and whole-hearted are **we** in forgiving people? If we are the guilty party, remember that forgiveness can only follow repentance. Our repentance led to God's forgiveness of our sins. There is no evidence that Absalom repented of his crime in slaying Amnon.

B) His attractiveness to Israel (vv.25-27)
Absalom was "so handsome that he put everyone else in the shade" (J. Baldwin). "But in all Israel there was none to be so much praised as Absalom for his beauty: from the sole of his foot even unto the crown of his head there was no blemish in him" (v.25). Events were to prove that this was deceptive, and that "favour is deceitful, and beauty is vain" (Prov 31.30). Inwardly he was more like Isaiah's description of Israel: "From the sole of the foot even unto the head there is no soundness in it; but wounds, and bruises, and putrifying sores" (Is 1.6).

It does seem that Absalom was occupied with his appearance: "And when he polled his head, (for it was at every year's end that he polled it: because the hair was heavy upon him, therefore he polled it) **he** weighed the hair of his head at two hundred shekels after the king's weight" (v.26). This was about 5 lb. or 2.5 kg. (We are usually told that his hair caused his death, but this is not actually stated. Read 18.9-14 carefully). He evidently thought very highly of himself, and like Satan (acting as the unseen "king of Tyre"), he was "lifted up" because of his beauty. See Ezekiel 28.17. Further evidence of his self-importance occurs in 2 Sam 18.18. "Now Absalom in his lifetime had taken and reared up for himself a pillar...for he said I have no son to keep my name in remembrance." This does not conflict with the statement, "And unto Absalom there were born three sons and one daughter" (v.27). As C. I. Scofield explains, "the pillar...must have been reared before the birth of his sons" or "his sons died in youth." Tamar inherited her father's good looks (v.27). Her name enshrined Absalom's regard for his desolate sister.

We ought to be deeply concerned about **our** beauty. "Let thy work appear unto thy servants, and thy glory unto their children. And let the beauty of the Lord our God be upon us" (Ps 90.17): "O worship the Lord in the beauty of holiness" (Ps 90.7). We ought to be deeply concerned about *our* name: "A good name is better than precious ointment" (Eccl 7.1). This means that we must be occupied with "the beauty of the Lord" (Ps 27.4), and acknowledge the "name which is above every name" (Phil 2.9).

3) Absalom's Reconciliation (vv.28-33)
Absalom's patience was worn out after two years, and he took matters into his own hands yet again. He was evidently under some kind of "house arrest" (v.24), and his secret ambitions could never be achieved whilst his movements were restricted. We must therefore notice *(A)* His anger with Joab (vv.28-32) and *(B)* His acceptance with David (v.33).

A) His anger with Joab (vv.28-32)
The only way to reach David was through Joab, who obviously thought that he had gone far enough. There was a touch of arrogance in the way he sent messengers to tell Joab to come and see him. Joab was probably old enough to be his father. Absalom's blazing anger at Joab's refusal to negotiate on his behalf resulted in a blaze amongst Joab's barley. His bitter condemnation of Joab for refusing to help him is most significant: "now therefore let me see the king's face; and if there be any iniquity in me, let him kill me." Absalom certainly seems to be arguing that he is free from guilt. There is no sign whatever of regret or repentance. He may have persuaded himself that in avenging the wrong done to Tamar he was only doing what David should have done.

B) His audience with David (v.33)
"So Joab came to the king, and told him: and when he had called for Absalom, he came to the king, and bowed himself on his face to the ground before the king: and the king kissed Absalom." David and Absalom were formally reconciled, but that was all. Absalom showed no remorse for slaying his brother. David showed little evidence of true forgiveness. Unlike the reconciliation between Joseph and his brothers, there is no record of tears and joy. Outwardly, five cold years of alienation had ended, but in reality nothing had changed. We cannot emphasise too strongly that when sin has destroyed harmony and fellowship, restoration and reconciliation can only take place after repentance. "Godly sorrow worketh repentance to salvation not to be repented of" (2 Cor 7.10). But there was no "godly sorrow" with Absalom. Disaster loomed.

CHAPTER 15.1-37

"The conspiracy was strong"

David had been told: "the sword shall never depart from thine house" (2 Sam 12.10), and already Amnon had been murdered at Baal-hazor on the instructions of Absalom. He had also been told: "thus saith the Lord, Behold, I will raise up evil against thee out of thine **own house**" (2 Sam 12.11), and this chapter relates the sad story of Absalom's rebellion against David, and his flight into exile.

Joab could never have foreseen the results of his carefully laid plan to repatriate Absalom, and David never foresaw the consequences of his mistake in reinstating Absalom without his repentance. But these things have been "written for *our* learning." (Rom 15.4). Unlike Joab and the "wise woman" of Tekoah, we should not be people with a "hidden agenda." Paul was able to say "we write none other things unto you, than what ye read or acknowledge" (2 Cor 1.13). We would say that he was "up front." Let's remember too that fellowship is based on righteousness and holiness. "If we walk in the light, as he is in the light, we have fellowship one with another" (1 Jn 1.7). David ultimately kissed Absalom (2 Sam 14.33), but there is not the slightest hint of any remorse or repentance on Absalom's part. Alas, David had lost the moral right to discipline his sons, but that does not alter the principle that only true repentance can lead to true forgiveness and renewed fellowship. Because this never happened, David stored up trouble for himself, and Absalom, freed from house arrest, was able to plot his father's overthrow.

2 Samuel 15 can be easily divided into two major sections: **(1)** Absalom's subversive activities (vv.1-12) and **(2)** David's flight into exile (vv.13-37). "Subversion" emphasises the underhand way in which Absalom achieved his goal.

1) Absalom's Subversive Activities (vv.1-12)

"And it came to pass after this, that Absalom prepared him chariots and horses, and fifty men to run before him." You could call it "pomp and circumstance!" He certainly knew how to get people's attention. It is difficult to understand why David allowed him to do this. He evidently saw no wrong now in his favourite son, which reminds us that our judgment can be impaired by our personal likes and dislikes. Notice that Adonijah, Absalom's younger brother eventually copied him: "Then Adonijah the son of Haggith exalted himself, saying, I will be king: and he prepared him chariots and horsemen, and fifty men to run before him…and he was also a very goodly man; and his mother bare him after Absalom" (1 Kings 1.5-6). Absalom's bad behaviour influenced his brother. Need we say more?

It is interesting to compare David and Absalom. Although David had been anointed king, he was not averse to performing the somewhat menial task of carrying bread and cheese to his brothers! (1 Sam 17.17). David exhibited the lesson that "before honour is humility" (Prov 15.33; 18.12), but not Absalom! He was out to make a name for himself. But that was only the beginning of his strategy, and we must now notice how he proceeded: **(A)** He sowed discord (vv.1-4); **(B)** He stole hearts (vv.5-6); **(C)** He spoke piously (vv.7-9); **(D)** He sent spies (v.10); **(E)** He selected servants (vv.11-12).

A) He sowed discord (vv.1-4)

Absalom would have made a first class "Leader of the Opposition" in Parliament! First of all attack the shortcomings of the Government, and then say you can do so much better! "See, thy matters are good and right; but there is no man deputed of the king to hear thee…Oh that I were made judge in the land, that every man which hath any suit or cause might come unto me, and I would do him justice!" (vv.3-4). A little flattery goes a long way ("thy matters are good and right"), especially from the lips of such a handsome and appealing candidate like Absalom! He made sure that the electorate got the impression that he really did want to help them, by getting up early to catch them *en route* to David. This was his equivalent of a "walkabout." Like a great many political activists (perhaps all of them, but let's be generous), Absalom completely misrepresented the truth. It was true that David did not depute other people to deal with controversies (v.2) for the simple reason that he dealt with them ***himself!*** See 2 Samuel 8.15. After all, the "wise woman" of Tekoah had no trouble in getting an audience with him. But this seems to have conveniently escaped Absalom's memory! A half truth is as bad as a downright lie.

2 Samuel

But we mustn't throw all the mud at the politicians. Listen to this: "These six things doth the Lord hate: yea, seven are an abomination unto him: a proud look...a false witness that speaketh lies, and he **that soweth discord among brethren**" (Prov 6.19). Absalom certainly created discord between David and Israel. People who do that reveal their true character: "He that is of a proud heart stirreth up strife" (Prov 28.25).

B) He stole hearts (vv. 5-6)

Absalom had plenty of charisma about him. "And it was so, that when any man came nigh to him to do him obeisance, he put forth his hand, and took him, and kissed him...so Absalom stole the hearts of the men of Israel." His arrogance (vv.1-4) and his extravagance (vv.5-6) certainly achieved the desired result. He used every trick in the book: he sowed the seeds of discontent and dissatisfaction, and threw in a charm offensive with plenty of personality and appeal. Modern politicians kiss babies: Absalom kissed everybody who came his way! Paul probably had Absalom in mind when he wrote: "Now I beseech you, brethren, mark them which cause divisions and offences contrary to the doctrine which ye have learned; and avoid them. For they that are such serve not our Lord Jesus Christ, but their own belly; and by good words and fair speeches deceive the hearts of the simple" (Rom 16.17-18). We must remember that the most important thing about a person is what they believe and practice. Don't be swept off your feet by someone's charm and personality. Absalom's strategy reminds us of the "wiles (craft or deceit) of the devil" (Eph 6.11). We must not be "ignorant of his devices" (2 Cor 2.11).

We know that Satan still steals the hearts of men and women generally in this way: sometimes he steals the hearts of **believers** by the same means. Whilst we have been highlighting Absalom's infamous conduct, we mustn't forget that the people he influenced were gullible. They should have known better than to allow themselves to be influenced by Absalom, and therefore they contributed to the looming disaster. This reminds us that "the time will come when they will not endure sound doctrine; but after their own lusts shall they heap to themselves teachers, having itching ears; and they shall turn away their ears from the truth, and shall be turned unto fables" (2 Tim 4. 3-4). The "itching ears" belong to the hearers, not the teachers. We do like to hear what we like to hear, don't we? People evidently "hung on every word" that Absalom said.

C) He spoke piously (vv. 7-9)

Absalom mentions the Lord's name three times in these verses: "let me go and pay my vow, which I have vowed unto the **Lord**, in Hebron (where he was born 3.2-3). For thy servant vowed a vow while I abode at Geshur in Syria, saying, If the **Lord** shall bring me again indeed to Jerusalem, then I will serve the **Lord**." It looks good! But it was sheer pretence, and Absalom intended to launch his *coup d'etat* under the pretext of paying his vow at Hebron. Absalom "knew the form": he could use the right language, and apparently offered the required sacrifices (v.12). But it concealed a wicked heart. "Go in peace" are the very last words of David to Absalom, who then ironically goes off to prepare for war against his father. He could be placed amongst those described in 2 Timothy 3.4-5, "Traitors, heady, highminded…having a form of godliness, but denying the power thereof." Absalom's religious veneer reminds us that "Satan himself is transformed into an angel of light. Therefore it is no great thing if his ministers also be transformed as the ministers of righteousness" (2 Cor 11.14-15). (Translators and commentators seem unanimous in substituting "four years" for "forty years" in v.7).

D) He sent spies (v.10)
He was well organised: "But Absalom sent spies throughout all the tribes of Israel, saying, As soon as ye hear the sound of the trumpet, then ye shall say, Absalom reigneth in Hebron." Satan too is well-organised: "we wrestle not against flesh and blood, but against principalities, against powers, against the rulers of the darkness of this world, against spiritual wickedness in high places" (Eph 6.12).

E) He selected servants (vv.11-12)
Very clearly, Absalom was supported by two very different categories of people. The first category could be called "the deceived" (v.11) and the second category could be called "the defector" (v.12).

i) The deceived. "And with Absalom went two hundred men from Jerusalem, they were called; and they went in their simplicity, and they knew not any thing" (v.11). J. Baldwin describes them as invited guests who "suspected nothing, and therefore gave the proceedings a genuine air of normality. By the time they realised what was happening…they were powerless to intervene." We do need to be "nourished up in the words of faith and of good doctrine" (1 Tim 4.6). The false cults feed on people's ignorance of God's word. We have noticed that Paul evidently refers to these events in Romans 16.17-18, and it does seem likely that he continues to do so in the same passage: "I would have you wise unto that which is good, and simple concerning evil" (Rom 16.19). We must never think that our love for God's people means that we accept everything that they do and say. Paul prayed that the love of the Philippians would "abound yet more and more in knowledge and in all judgment" (Phil 1.9).

ii) The defector. "And Absalom sent for Ahithophel the Gilonite, David's counsellor, from his city, even from Giloh, while he offered sacrifices" (v.12). If you put 2 Samuel 11.3 and 2 Samuel 23.34 together, you will come to the conclusion that Ahithophel was Bath-sheba's grandfather. According to J. Baldwin, Giloh was a village in the hills to the north of Hebron. (Hebron was about twenty miles south-west of Jerusalem). Ahithophel's defection was a great blow to David (see v.31). We can only speculate about the reason for his defection. Perhaps he thought that he was "on a hiding to nothing" if he continued to support David, and that his future now lay with the new king. Let's remember that loyalty to the Lord Jesus can be costly. He is "despised and rejected of men", and those who follow Him share His rejection. This may become much more obvious in the future for us westerners. Ahithophel "swapped horses in mid-stream." The Saviour said, "Remember the word that I said unto you, The servant is not above his lord. If they have persecuted me, they will persecute you" (Jn 15.20).

Absalom looks unstoppable. "And the conspiracy was strong; for the people increased continually with Absalom." We now turn to David.

2. David's Flight into Exile (vv.13-37)
"And there came a messenger to David, saying, The hearts of the men of Israel are after Absalom." David has no misconceptions about Absalom's intentions: "And David said unto all his servants that were with him at Jerusalem, Arise, and let us flee; for we shall not else escape from Absalom: make speed to depart, lest he overtake us suddenly, and bring evil upon us, and smite the city with the edge of the sword" (vv.13-14). The king prepares to leave for exile. He is assured of the loyalty of all his servants. It is worth noticing that David is "repeatedly and deliberately referred to as **the king**" (J. Baldwin). It is also worth noticing that David was not only thinking of himself, but of the safety of his people in Jerusalem.

We must now follow David out of the city (v.17), "over the brook Kidron" (v.23) and "up by the ascent of mount Olivet" (v.30). Our attention is drawn particularly to David's servants (vv.15-18) and to David's friends (vv.19-37).

A) David's servants (vv.15-18)

"And the king's servants said unto the king, Behold, thy servants are ready to do whatsoever my lord the king shall appoint" (v.15). We could say that they were "sanctified, and meet for the master's use, and prepared unto every good work" (2 Tim 2. 21). They were ready, not only to serve the king in his glory, but also in his rejection. Are **we** prepared to do the Lord's will in adverse circumstances? David's servants knew that he was the anointed king, and that God's promise could not be thwarted by a rival.

Notice the expressions, "after him" (vv.16-17), "beside him" (v.18) and "before the king" (v.18). J. Baldwin describes it as a review: "Once out of the city, the king halts to take stock, and to make sure who is accompanying him. It is a true march-past, a review of long-valued servants and troops, whose years of allegiance made them doubly precious in such an emergency." The Cherethites and Pelethites formed David's bodyguard (see our comments on 2 Samuel 8.18), and the "six hundred men which came after him from Gath" were his "well-tried veterans" (Keil & Delitzsch). See 1 Samuel 27.2-3,8; 29.2; 30.1,9. They were not "fair weather friends." The Lord Jesus described His disciples as "ye are they which have continued with me in my temptations" (Lk 22. 28). Can it be said of us, "thou hast a little strength, and hast kept my word, and hast not denied my name?" (Rev 3. 9).

On a technical note, the "place that was far off" can be rendered "the house of the distance" and "is probably a proper name given to a house in the neighbourhood of the city and on the road to Jericho, which was called "the farthest house", viz, from the city" (Keil & Delitzsch).

B) David's friends (vv.19-37)

No doubt "all his servants" were equally his friends, but now we have individuals named: **(i)** Ittai (vv.19-22), **(ii)** Zadok and Abiathar (vv.24-29), and **(iii)** Hushai (vv.31-37). Hushai is called "David's friend" (v.37).

i) Ittai (vv.19-22)

As Keil & Delitzsch point out, "It is evident from 2 Samuel 18.2, where Ittai is said to have commanded a third part of the army against Absalom, and to have been placed on an equality with Joab and Abishai the most experienced generals, that Ittai was a Philistine general who had entered David's service." David describes him as "a stranger, and also an exile." He had recently joined David's ranks, and for that reason David endeavoured to dissuade Ittai from joining him in his own exile. Now listen to his reply: "As the Lord liveth, and as my lord the king liveth, surely in what place my lord the king shall be, whether in death or life, even there also will thy servant be" (v.21). Do remember that these were the words of "a new convert!" Ittai was not brought up amongst God's people. He was a Philistine! But he confessed that he now belonged to Jehovah. He was "under new management!" Ittai was well-aware that his loyalty to David could prove costly: "surely in what place my lord the king shall be, whether in **death** or life, even there also will thy servant be." His allegiance to the rejected king involved entire families: "And Ittai the Gittite passed over, and all his men, and all the little ones that were with him." Many servants of God have taken their families out of the comparative security of the homeland into the uncertainty and insecurity of overseas mission fields.

It was another "stranger" who said, "Intreat me not to leave thee, or to return from following after thee: for whither thou goest, I will go; and where thou lodgest, I will lodge: thy people shall be my people, and thy God my God: where thou diest I will die, and there will I be buried: the Lord do so to me, and more also, if ought but death part thee and me" (Ruth 1.16-17). No wonder that when Naomi saw Ruth "was steadfastly minded to go with her, then she left speaking unto her." No wonder either that David said to Ittai, "Go and pass over!" Both Ittai (v.20) and Ruth (1.15) had the opportunity to "return", but their minds were made up. Can we *really* sing

> O Jesus, I have promised
> To serve Thee to the end?

The Lord Jesus said, "If any man serve me, let him follow me; and where I am, there shall also my servant be if any man serve me, him will my Father honour" (Jn 12. 26).

It has been frequently pointed out that both David and the Lord Jesus "passed over the brook Kidron" (v.23), and the parallel is well worth noticing. "The two were rejected kings; they both passed over Kidron; they both wept, Christ in the Garden and David as he walked along (v.30); they both went to the Mount of Olives; and they were both followed by men with heavy hearts. The defection of Ahithophel reminds us of the treachery of Judas. David was never more like his Lord (Ps 110.1) than he was on this occasion. There was, however, this great difference: David was suffering for his former sins, but the Lord was rejected in spite of His sinlessness" (A. McShane,

Lessons for Leaders). We could add that David crossed the Kidron as the result of his sin, but the Lord Jesus crossed the brook to give His life for sinners.

ii) Zadok and Abiathar (vv.24-29)
"And lo Zadok also, and all the Levites were with him, bearing the ark of the covenant of God. and they set down the ark of God; and Abiathar went up, until all the people had done passing out of the city" (v.24). Although Zadok is placed first and was evidently in charge of the ark, Abiathar had proved trustworthy over many years. See 1 Samuel 22.20-23. Notice that the ark was carried. They did not repeat the earlier mistake and put it on "a new cart" (2 Sam 6.3), even though the urgency of the situation called for quick transportation. God's word was obeyed, even in dire circumstances!

No doubt the two priests brought the ark "because they knew that David valued it, and felt that it would give him the assurance of the Lord's presence" (A. McShane). Quite clearly, David did not believe that the presence of the ark guaranteed his preservation and success. He placed his future firmly in the hands of God Himself: "If I shall find favour in the eyes of the Lord, he will bring me again, and shew me both it, and his habitation: but if he thus say, I have no delight in thee; behold, here am I, let him do to me as seemeth good unto him" (vv.25-26). David is evidently referring here to the judgment for his sin pronounced on him by Nathan (12.10-11). He was willing to bow to God's will, whatever it may hold for him. Although circumstances were totally different, the presence of the ark did nothing to avert defeat by the Philistines years before. See 1 Samuel ch.4. It's worth remembering that we can only enjoy God's blessing and help if we honour Him in our lives. We can "go through the motions" as much as we like, but are our hearts right with God? David knew that it was so important to "find favour in the eyes of the Lord."

On a practical note, Zadok and Abiathar could be far more use to David in Jerusalem than they would be to him in the wilderness. "The king said also unto Zadok the priest, Art thou not a seer? Return into the city in peace, and your two sons with you, Ahimaaz thy son, and Jonathan the son of Abiathar. See, I will tarry in the plain (or "passage", referring to the fords of Jordan) of the wilderness, until there come word from you to certify me." The words, "Art thou not a seer" have been rendered "can you make good use of your eyes?" (NEB) but this is a paraphrase rather than a translation. The words, "Thou art the seer" (JND) may be deliberately ambiguous. After all, as J. Baldwin observes, "this was no private conversation...David needed informers, and he sent the priestly group "in peace" to act as his spies in the city (v.27).

Zadok and Abiahar "carried the ark of God again to Jerusalem...and David went up by the ascent of mount Olivet, and wept as he went up, and had his head covered, and he went barefoot: and all the people that was with him covered every man his head, and they went up, weeping as they went up" (vv.29-30). David's grief was shared by his companions. See Rom 12.15. The covering of the head and the bare feet were signs of deep mourning. See Esther 6.12 and Ezekiel 24.17. "All the country wept with a loud voice when David crossed the Kidron" (v.23), and it was a sorrowful party that ascended Olivet. David's sorrow was heightened by the news that Ahithophel had defected. There can be little doubt that David is referring to Ahithophel in Psalm 55.12-14. We must also read Psalm 41.9, "Yea, mine own familiar friend, in whom I trusted, which did eat of my bread, hath lifted up his heel against me." This is cited in John 13.18-19. Ahithophel betrayed David and eventually hanged himself; Judas betrayed the Lord Jesus, and also hanged himself (Mt 27.3-5). David's prayer, "O Lord...turn the counsel of Ahithophel into foolishness", was answered in full. See 2 Samuel 17.14, 23. It is noteworthy that in both Psalm 55 & Psalm 41, David anticipates the fall of his enemies, and the vindication of his faith in God. See Psalm 55.22-23; 41.10-13.

iii) Hushai (vv.32-37)

Almost immediately, God gave David the assurance that his prayer had been heard. Enter Hushai the Archite, whom David sent to Jerusalem to "defeat the counsel of Ahithophel" (v.34). In his adversity, David both prayed (v.31) and worshipped: "and it came to pass, that when David was come to the top of the mount, where he worshipped God, behold, Hushai the Archite came to meet him with his coat rent, and earth upon his head" (v.32). Do notice this: David "worshipped God." Yes, in those circumstances! Job worshipped the Lord in even worse circumstances: "the Lord gave, and the Lord hath taken away; blessed be the name of the Lord (Job 1.20-21). Prayer and worship were followed by help and fellowship. We are not told how Hushai, from Archi (Josh 16.2), would have been a burden to David in exile (possibly because he was a very old man), but he certainly proved to be "an invaluable ambassador to counter the suggestions of Ahithophel at Jerusalem" (J. Baldwin). "So Hushai David's friend came into the city", possibly at the same time as Absalom was entering from the south. See chapter 16.15-16. The right man was there at the right time! There can be no doubt that Hushai exposed himself to considerable risk by returning to Jerusalem. Absalom was obviously suspicious. See 16.17. Paul described Priscilla and Aquila as people "who have for my life laid down their own necks ("staked their own neck" JND)" (Rom 16.4). However, we cannot escape the impression that David was guided in all this by worldly wisdom. Absalom employed "spies" (v.10), and David did the same. He now has Zadok, Abiathar, Ahimaaz, Jonathan and Hushai working for him in Jerusalem. There is no record that he asked God for guidance in the circumstances.

However, we must end on a positive note. This sad chapter does conclude with "David's friend", and David went into exile with the assurance that he was accompanied by loyal and devoted men like Ittai, and that his interests were represented at Jerusalem by loyal men like Zadok and Abiathar, with their sons, and Hushai. Many of God's children are under pressure from different sources, and the fellowship and loyalty of fellow-believers is of immense encouragement to them. But let's take this further. Remember that our devotion and loyalty to the Lord Jesus will bring **Him** joy and delight in His rejection, and it is our business to represent **His interests** in a hostile world.

CHAPTER 16.1-23

"It may be that the Lord will look on mine affliction"

Although David's exile was short-lived, it was extremely painful. According to the dates given in the Scofield Bible, he was about sixty-two when Absalom usurped the throne. (David died at seventy in B.C.1015, and his exile took place in B.C.1023). The treachery of Absalom and the defection of Ahithophel (15.31) were terrible blows, and it is not surprising that "David went up by the ascent of mount Olivet, and wept as he went up, and had his head covered, and he went barefoot" (15.30). But as we have seen, David was not friendless. He was accompanied into exile by his faithful servants who said, "Behold, thy servants are ready to do whatsoever my lord the king shall appoint" (15.5). Ittai was there: "As the Lord liveth, and as my lord the king liveth, surely in what place my lord the king shall be, whether in death or life, even there also will thy servant be" (15.21). At the same time he was represented in Jerusalem by men who deliberately concealed their loyalty to him. Amongst them was "Hushai David's friend" (15.37; 16.16), and we must not forget Zadok and Abiathar with their sons, Ahimaaz and Jonathan. Hushai is called "the king's companion" in 1 Chron 27.33.

Chapter 16 describes the role of four men in the sad story of David's rejection in favour of Absalom. Only one of them, Shimei, is a complete newcomer. We have already met Ziba (9.2 etc), heard about Ahithophel (15.12), and briefly made the acquaintance of Hushai (15.32 etc). The chapter centres on **(1)** David in exile (vv.1-14) and **(2)** Absalom in Jerusalem (vv.15-23). David is met by a friend (Ziba v.1) and an enemy (Shimei v.5). Absalom is accompanied by a friend (Ahithophel v.15) and met by an enemy (Hushai v.16). As we shall see, Ziba was not all that David imagined, and Hushai certainly was not all that Absalom imagined. David accepted Ziba's explanation of Mephibosheth's absence, and Absalom accepted Hushai's explanation of his presence in Jerusalem.

Chapter 16

1) David in Exile (vv.1-14)
We now renew our acquaintance with Ziba, and meet Shimei for the first time. This section of the chapter can be divided as follows: **(A)** The assistance of Ziba (vv.1-4); **(B)** The antagonism of Shimei (vv.5-14). Ziba brought stores, and Shimei threw stones. Both men met David again on his return journey. See 19.16 and 19.24.

A) The assistance of Ziba (vv.1-4)
"And when David was a little past the top of the hill, behold, Ziba the servant of Mephibosheth met him, with a couple of asses saddled, and upon them two hundred loaves of bread, and an hundred bunches of raisins (or 'a hundred raisin-cakes'), and an hundred of summer fruits (or 'hundred date or fig-cakes'), and a bottle of wine" (v.1). (If you feel that one "bottle of wine" wouldn't go very far, remember that it means "a skin of wine!"). David asked Ziba two questions:

i) "What meanest thou by these?"(v.2)
The answer seems perfectly reasonable. "The asses be for the king's household to ride on; and the bread and summer fruit for the young men to eat; and the wine, that such as be faint in the wilderness may drink." The second question was far more searching:

ii) "And where is thy master's son?" (vv.3-4)
The answer seems to fit the facts. Mephibosheth wasn't there. So, "Behold, he abideth at Jerusalem: for he said, Today shall the house of Israel restore me the kingdom of my father." David accepted his explanation without query, "Behold, thine are all that pertained unto Mephibosheth", and Ziba was duly grateful: "I humbly beseech thee that I may find grace in thy sight, my lord, O king." There the matter remained until David returned, and listened to an entirely different story from Mephibosheth, who "had neither dressed his feet, nor trimmed his beard, nor washed his clothes, from the day that the king departed until the day he came again in peace" (19.24). The record of his interview with David (19.25-30) leaves no doubt about his integrity. Mephibosheth had been deceived and slandered by Ziba (19.26-27).

Ziba's liberality towards David masked his desire for personal gain. He was an opportunist, and made the most of the circumstances to "feather his own nest." Since Ziba had been appointed by David to farm Mephibosheth's land, the produce was probably part of the owner's harvest, and hardly

2 Samuel

Ziba's to give (9.10). However, as J. Baldwin observes, "if Ziba was trying to curry favour with the king, he certainly succeeded." Let's notice three lessons:

a) We must have pure motives in our service for God. Paul wrote about this as follows: "we are not as many, which corrupt the word of God (make a trade of the word of God): but as of sincerity, but as of God, in the sight of God speak we in Christ" (2 Cor 2.17). The word translated "corrupt" (*kapeleuo*) was especially applied to retailers of wine, "with whom adulteration and short measures were matters of course" (Vincent's Word Studies). Paul and his colleagues did not preach the gospel for personal gain. We may not have any desire for financial profit from our service for God, but we might want to be highly esteemed amongst our fellow-Christians, and take all the necessary steps to ensure that we are noticed. Do remember 1 Corinthians 13.3: "though I bestow all my goods to feed the poor…and have not charity (love) it profiteth **me** nothing." It might "profit" other people, but not "me."

b) We must be careful not to be influenced by people's generosity. Especially when it is accompanied by criticism of other people. "Thou shalt take no gift: for the gift blindeth the wise, and perverteth the words of the righteous" (Ex 23.8). Do note the context of this quotation. It does not mean that servants of God should not be financially supported! Remember too that we can be influenced by praise and popularity. "A flattering mouth worketh ruin" (Prov 26.28); "A man that flattereth his neighbour spreadeth a net for his feet" (Prov 29.5).

c) We must endeavour to ascertain the accuracy of reports about other people. David acted in "the heat of the moment" and whilst it was probably impossible to verify Ziba's story at the time, he could have waited before giving him Mephibosheth's inheritance. As A. McShane points out, "If David had only thought for a moment he would have seen through this fabric of lies, for there was no possibility of a crippled man becoming king." Bearing in mind Absalom's popularity, it is highly unlikely that Mephibosheth would have even thought of becoming king. All too often we act on faulty information, and incur the censure in Proverbs 8.13, "He that answereth a matter before he heareth it, it is folly and shame unto him." We really do need to ask the question, "Doth our law judge any man before it hear him, and know what he doeth?" (Jn 7.51). Read Deuteronomy 13.12-15, and 1 Timothy 5.19.

While Ziba evidently concealed his real motive in supplying David and his men, Shimei made no attempt to disguise his true feelings.

B) The antagonism of Shimei (vv.5-14)

"And when king David came to Bahurim, behold, thence came out a man of the family of the house of Saul, whose name was Shimei, the son of Gera: he came forth, and cursed still as he came." Although Absalom has usurped the throne, the Bible is careful to say "***king*** David!" The Lord Jesus is rejected, and people continue to say, "we will not have this man to reign over us" (Lk 19.14), but He is still the King! Bahurim had bitter memories for Phaltiel (2 Sam 3.14-16). Unlike Mephibosheth, who was directly descended from Saul (2 Sam 9.1-2), Shimei was evidently a distant relative. We must notice ***(i)*** the rage of Shimei (vv.5-8); ***(ii)*** the restraint of David (vv.9-14).

i) The rage of Shimei (vv.5-8)

Shimei expressed his animosity verbally ("cursed") and physically ("cast stones"). He was evidently on a parallel path to David, but separated by a ravine. This is clear from Abishai's request to "go over…and take off his head" (v.9). Shimei tracked David from a safe distance, but he could obviously be heard and could reach David with a hail of stones. "And as David and his men went by the way, Shimei went along the hill's side over against him, and cursed as he went, and threw stones at him, and cast dust" (v.13). Whilst Psalm 109 does not carry a superscript, other than "To the chief Musician, A Psalm of David", it could have been written in connection with Shimei: "As he loved cursing, so let it come unto him…As he clothed himself with cursing like as with his garment, so let it come into his bowels like water…Let them curse, but bless thou…" (vv.17,18,28). As a Benjamite "of the family of the house of Saul" he had obviously nursed a bitter spirit against David, which reminds us of the New Testament warning, "Follow peace with all men…lest any root of bitterness springing up trouble you" (Heb 12.14-15).

His words, "Come out, come out, thou bloody man, and thou man of Belial" ("Away, away, thou man of blood and man of Belial", JND), show that he regarded David as a murderer and worthless (Belial means "worthless"), and was glad to see the back of him. He held David responsible for "all the blood of the house of Saul", which may refer particularly to the deaths of Abner (2 Sam 3.27) and Ish-bosheth (2 Sam 4.5-6), of which David was completely innocent. Shimei claimed to know the Lord's will, but this was completely negated by his abusive language. He transgressed the third commandment in saying, "The **Lord** hath returned upon thee all the blood of the house of Saul, in whose stead thou hast reigned; and the **Lord** hath delivered the kingdom into the hand of Absalom thy son…" (v.8). His language and conduct proved that he had no knowledge whatsoever of the Lord's will, but this was not the case with David. As we shall now see, He **did** know the Lord!

ii) The restraint of David (vv.9-14)

David restrained Abishai when he wanted to kill Saul (1 Sam 26.8), and now he forbids him to "take off" Shimei's head. In both cases, David chose to leave retribution to the Lord. "As the Lord liveth, the Lord shall smite him…The Lord forbid that I should stretch forth mine hand against the Lord's anointed" (1 Sam 26.10-11). Once again, David refuses to take matters into his own hands: "What have I to do with you, ye sons of Zeruiah? (Joab evidently joined Abishai here: compare 3.39). So let him curse, because God hath said unto him, Curse David. Who then shall say, Wherefore hast thou done so? And David said to Abishai, and to all his servants, Behold, my son, which came forth out of my bowels, seeketh my life: how much more now may this Benjamite do it? Let him alone, and let him curse; for the Lord hath bidden him" (vv.10-11).

This is a remarkable passage. In his adversity, David bows to the will of God. He regarded the animosity of Shimei as divine judgment upon him, and there can be little doubt that he had in mind the solemn words of Nathan: "Thus saith the Lord God of Israel…the sword shall never depart from thine house; because thou hast despised me, and hast taken the wife of Uriah the Hittite to be thy wife. Thus saith the Lord, Behold, I will raise up evil against thee out of thine own house" (2 Sam 12.7-11). This emphasises David's thorough repentance. He recognised that Shimei's shameful conduct towards him was the result of his own sin against the Lord. As F. Gardiner (Ellicott's Commentary) observes, "He does not, of course, mean to justify Shimei's wrong; but only to say that, as far as his sin bears upon himself, it is of divine appointment, and he cannot resent it." David knew that the promises made to him (2 Samuel ch.7) could not be broken, but his own future was clouded with uncertainty, obliging him to say, "It may be that the Lord will look on mine affliction, and that the Lord will requite me good for his cursing this day" (v.12). Compare 15.25.

We know that David did reoccupy the throne, and that on his return journey he had to restrain Abishai yet again: "Shall not Shimei be put to death for this, because he cursed the Lord's anointed? And David said, What have I to do with you, ye sons of Zeruiah...Shall there any man be put to death this day in Israel?" (19.2-23). Shimei was eventually put to death by Solomon for disobeying the curfew placed on him See 1 Kings 2.36-46. In pronouncing sentence, Solomon said, "Thou knowest the wickedness which thine heart is privy to, that thou didst to David my father: therefore the Lord shall return thy wickedness upon thine own head." The Lord **did** "look on David's affliction", and "requited him good for his cursing this day."

The lesson for us from these verses is clearly stated in Romans 12.17-19: "Recompense to no man evil for evil...Dearly beloved, avenge not yourselves; but rather give place unto wrath: for it is written, Vengeance is mine; I will repay, saith the Lord." David clearly lived in the good of his own ministry: "Fret not thyself because of evildoers, neither be thou envious against the workers of iniquity...Trust in the Lord, and do good: so shalt thou dwell in the land, and verily thou shalt be fed" (Ps 37.1-3).

The paragraph ends with the words, "And the king, and all the people that were with him, came weary, and refreshed themselves there." The RSV reads "And the king, and all the people that were with him, arrived weary at the Jordan; and there he refreshed himself", with the footnote: "Hebrew lacks *at the Jordan.*" These words have been imported from the Greek version of the Old Testament known as the Septuagint or LXX. It is wiser to stay with the Hebrew text! But even so, the sentence does seem unusual, and it has been suggested that the words "came weary" actually refer to a place name, "Ayephim." The Hebrew word for "weary" is "*ayeph.*" As you can see, it isn't likely to be a divisive issue! We must now leave David heading into exile, and join Hushai in Jerusalem to witness the arrival of Absalom and Ahithophel.

2) Absalom in Jerusalem (vv.15-23)
This section of the chapter can be divided as follows: *(A)* The allegiance of Hushai (vv.15-19); *(B)* The advice of Athithophel (vv.20-23).

A) *The allegiance of Hushai (vv.15-19)*
"And Absalom, and all the people, the men of Israel, came to Jerusalem, and Ahithophel with him." This was a powerful combination. Absalom had endeared himself to the nation with his good looks (14.25-26) and winning ways (15.1-6), and "the counsel of Ahithophel, which he counselled in those days, was as if a man had enquired at the oracle of God" (16.23).

2 Samuel

i) The greeting of Hushai (v.16)

"And it came to pass, when Hushai, the Archite, David's friend, was come unto Absalom, that Hushai said unto Absalom, God save the king, God save the king." It is worth noticing that Hushai did not say "God save king Absalom!" Compare the following, "God save king Adonijah...Let my lord king David live for ever...God save king Solomon" (1 Kings 1.25,31,34). As J. Baldwin observes, "Hushai's double "Long live the king!", music in the ears of ambitious Absalom, raised no question in his mind, despite their ambiguity as to who was king." Some people would call this a "smart move", or perhaps "diplomatic", but it is questionable whether **we** should act in this way: certainly not to each other. Paul made his position perfectly clear when he said, "there stood by me this night the angel of God, **whose I am** and **whom I serve**" (Acts 27.23). However, we do need to be "wise as serpents and harmless as doves" (Mt 10.16), and to act in a way that will "give none offence, neither to the Jews, nor to the Gentiles, nor to the church of God" (1 Cor 10.32).

ii) The suspicion of Absalom (v.17)

"And Absalom said to Hushai, Is this thy kindness to thy friend? Why wentest thou not with thy friend?" We might have thought the same: after all the Bible does say, "thine own friend, and thy father's friend, forsake not" (Prov 27.10). We are glad to know that "there is a friend that sticketh closer than a brother" (Prov 18.24).

iii) The reassurance of Hushai (vv.18-19)

Notice again Hushai's ambiguity: "And Hushai said unto Absalom, Nay; but whom the Lord, and this people, and all the men of Israel, choose, his will I be, and with him will I abide." Hushai avoids mentioning names. He **did** remain loyal to his master, David, who had been chosen by God and by "all the men of Israel" (see 2 Sam 5.1-3). But the inference of Hushai's reply did not dawn on Absalom. Notice how Hushai continues: "And again, whom should I serve? Should I not serve in the presence of his son? As I have served in thy father's presence, so will I be in thy presence." (This is what David told him to say: see 15.34). Absalom was evidently quite satisfied with this explanation, but Hushai meant something entirely different. He would certainly serve in Absalom's presence, but he would actually be serving **David,** not Absalom! Friendly Hushai wasn't so friendly after all! He was Absalom's enemy.

B) The advice of Ahithophel (vv.20-23)

"And Ahithophel said unto Absalom, Go in unto thy father's concubines, which he hath left to keep the house; and all Israel shall hear that thou art abhorred of thy father; then shall the hands of all that are with thee be strong." Jacob censured Reuben because he "lay with Bilhah his father's concubine" (Gen 35.22; 49.4), and the purpose of Ahithophel's advice was:

i) To completely alienate David from Absalom. We must not forget that "David was reaping what he had sown. He had failed to punish the sin of Amnon, and now Absalom was taking his enmity against his father to its furthest extreme. By invading his father's most intimate and private world, and doing so blatantly and publicly, he would indeed make himself odious to his father, and to all right-minded people in Israel" (J. Baldwin).

ii) To stiffen the resolve of Absalom's supporters. "Then shall the hands of all that are with thee be strong." Once Absalom's men could see that the breach between Absalom and David was "absolute and irreconcilable" (F. Gardiner), they would realise that he was a determined leader who was worthy of their support.

Nathan's prophecy was fulfilled: he had said, "Thus saith the Lord, Behold, I will raise up evil against thee out of thine own house, and I will take thy wives before thine eyes, and give them unto thy neighbour, and he shall lie with thy wives in the sight of this sun. For thou didst it secretly: but I will do this thing before all Israel, and before the sun" (2 Sam 12.11-12). We therefore read that "they spread a tent upon the top of the house; and Absalom went in unto his father's concubines in the sight of all Israel" (v.22). It is particularly significant that this took place "on the very roof where David had first yielded to his guilty passion" (F. Gardiner).

The chapter ends with Absalom in a commanding position, not least because he had the benefit of Ahithophel's wisdom which, humanly speaking, was second to none. "And the counsel of Ahithophel, which he counselled in those days, was as if a man had enquired at the oracle of God: so was all the counsel of Ahithophel, both with David and with Absalom." Things looked black for David. How could Hushai possibly "defeat the counsel of Ahithophel?" (15.34). We shall see, however, that through Hushai, God would "destroy the wisdom of the wise" and "bring to nought the understanding of the prudent" (1 Cor 1.19).

Leaving Ahithophel aside for a moment, we should notice that servants of

God who address God's people should "speak...as the oracles of God" (1 Pet 4.11). This statement places great responsibility on the person who speaks publicly. The words "as the oracles of God" evidently refer to the "breastplate of judgment" containing "the Urim and the Thummim" (Ex 28.30). This means that the preacher or teacher has good cause to "tremble at God's word" (Is 66.2). When a man stands up to teach or preach, his ministry must come from God Himself, and this should apply to a Bible Class leader or Sunday School teacher in exactly the same way.

CHAPTER 17.1-29

"The counsel of Hushai...is better than the counsel of Ahithophel"

Having succeeded in driving an immense wedge between David and Absalom (16.21-22), Ahithophel now attempts to eliminate David completely. It seems almost unbelievable that the life of the man who had led Israel to supremacy in the Middle East should be in jeopardy from his own people. Absalom, with no proven track record whatever, had managed to swing public opinion against David and was now poised to administer the *coup de grace.* This just illustrates the fickleness of human nature. All too frequently people are swayed by strong personalities and attractive ideas, and jettison men who have laid solid foundations and achieved good results. The New Testament urges us to "remember them which have the rule over you, who have spoken unto you the word of God: whose faith follow, considering the end of their conversation" or "Remember your leaders who have spoken unto you the word of God; and considering the issue of their conversation, imitate their faith" (Heb 13.7 JND).

It never seemed to occur to Absalom or Ahithophel that they were attempting to overturn the will of God. While David was reaping the bitter harvest of his own sin, he was still God's anointed king, which reminds us that we cannot disobey God's word and God's will without opposing God Himself. As events begin to unfold it becomes evident that He was not standing on the touchline as a spectator. "And Absalom and all the men of Israel said, The counsel of Hushai the Archite is better than the counsel of Ahithophel. For the Lord had appointed to defeat the good counsel of Ahithophel, to the intent that the Lord might bring evil upon Absalom" (v.14). These are the only references to the Lord in the chapter, and they are made by the historian. He is not mentioned at the "cabinet meeting" in Jerusalem or by anyone else. In fact, He is only mentioned once in chapter 18 (but not directly: see v.33) and only once in chapter 19 (but not directly: see v.7). But this does not imply His absence.

The chapter can be divided as follows: **(1)** The counsel of Ahithophel (vv.1-4); **(2)** The counsel of Hushai (vv.5-14); **(3)** The warning to David (vv.15-22); **(4)** The death of Ahithophel (v.23); **(5)** The pursuit by Absalom (vv.24-26); **(6)** The provision for David (vv.27-29). As always, we can expect to find spiritual lessons in the narrative.

1) The Counsel of Ahithophel (vv.1-4)

"Moreover, Ahithophel said unto Absalom, Let me now choose out twelve thousand men (possibly representing the twelve tribes), and *I* will arise and pursue after David this night: and *I* will come upon him while he is weary and weak handed, and will make him afraid: and all the people that are with him shall flee; and *I* will smite the king only. And *I* will bring back all the people unto thee: the man whom thou seekest is as if all returned: so all the people shall be in peace." Ahithophel reminds us of the Pharisee: "*I* thank thee, that *I* am not as other men are…*I* fast…*I* give…" (Lk 18.11-12). It reminds us that "pride goeth before destruction, and an haughty spirit before a fall" (Prov 16.18). This was certainly true in Ahithophel's case!

Ahithophel realised that Absalom's success depended on striking an immediate blow. He felt confident, for good reason, that David was in no condition to resist a sudden attack. He was weary and disorganised ("weak handed"), and his men were likely to desert him. Perhaps he made a slip of the tongue in saying "I will smite the **king** only!" But with David's death, the nation would be reunited, and there would be peace. According to F. Gardiner, the translation "will make him afraid" is "hardly strong enough. The thought is that Ahithophel will throw David's band into a panic by a sudden night attack, and in the confusion will easily secure the person of the king. David would not even contemplate the possibility of striking "the Lord's anointed" (1 Sam 26.9), but Ahithophel had no scruples in the matter. There are two important lessons for us here:

i) The enemy will exploit our weakness. The Amalekites used this tactic against Israel: "he met thee by the way, and smote the hindmost of thee, even all that were feeble behind thee, when thou wast faint and weary; and he feared not God" (Deut 25.17-19). Satan endeavoured to do the same with the Lord Jesus: "And when he had fasted forty days and forty nights, he was afterward an hungred. And when the tempter came to him, he said, If thou be the Son of God, command that these stones be made bread" (Mt 4.1-3). The Lord Jesus defeated him with "the sword of the Spirit" in saying, three times, "It is written." Whilst we are never immune from attack, weakness in whatever form makes us particularly vulnerable. We do need to be on our guard when we feel disappointed or dispirited. We need to be on our guard when we are physically or mentally below par. The enemy knows exactly when "to put the boot in", and he can only be repulsed by recalling and applying Scriptures. This is why it is so important to stock our minds with the word of God. Let's remember that God's "divine power hath given unto us all things that pertain unto life and godliness" and amongst these are "exceeding great and precious promises" (2 Pet 1.3-4).

ii) The enemy will attack the leadership. Ahithophel was quite confident that if he could kill David, then the battle would be over. The lesson is exemplified in the words, which refer particularly to the Lord Jesus, "smite the shepherd, and the sheep shall be scattered" (Zech 13.7). This prophecy was fulfilled in Matthew 26.31, but the divine shepherd regathered His sheep after He had risen from the dead. Like Ahithophel, Satan evidently imagined that if he could get rid of the Lord Jesus, he would control "all the people." We should remember as well that Satan is well on the way to destroying the effectiveness of an assembly if he can successfully attack or undermine its elders.

The historian had no doubt about the worldly wisdom of Ahithophel's counsel. He calls it the "good counsel of Ahithophel" (v.14). But the Lord knew that David was weak and vulnerable, and used Hushai to defeat Ahithophel's plan, which beautifully illustrates 1 Corinthians 10.13, "God is faithful, who will not suffer you to be tempted above that ye are able; but will with the temptation also make a way to escape, that ye may be able to bear it."

2) The Counsel of Hushai (vv.5-14)
In view of Ahithophel's reputation as a counsellor (16.23) it is rather surprising that Absalom should bother with Hushai at all! But the Lord was putting in place a "way to escape" for David. We know that Hushai's role was to "defeat the counsel of Ahithophel" (15.34), and he clearly faced an uphill task. However, "the Lord had appointed to defeat the good counsel of Ahithophel" (v.14). It is worth noticing that Hushai carefully avoided an all-out attack on Ahithophel's wisdom. He simply said, "The counsel that Ahithophel hath given is not good **at this time**" (v.7), and did not cast aspersions on him generally. Hushai was obliged to "think on his feet", and tackled the problem by **(a)** criticising Ahithophel's plan (vv.8-10) and **(b)** advocating his own (vv.11-14).

a) The shortcomings of Ahithophel's plan (vv.8-10)
Hushai set about undermining the "good counsel of Ahithophel" by dwelling on the difficulties of apprehending David. This would not be so easy as Ahithophel suggested. David was a formidable enemy!

i) David and his men had an awesome reputation, and their present circumstances would make them absolutely lethal! "Thou knowest thy father and his men, that they be mighty men, and they be chafed in their minds ("of exasperated spirit", JND), as a bear robbed of her whelps in the field" (v.8). They were ferocious! As J. Baldwin points out, "As a son of the royal house, Absalom could not deny the prowess of his father, which had become proverbial."

ii) David was an experienced warrior and was not likely to sleep with his men. It would therefore be quite impossible to track him down easily. "Thy father is a man of war and will not lodge with the people. Behold he is hid now in some pit, or in some other place" (vv.8-9). Ahithophel had assumed that David would be with his men (v.2). Hushai probably had in mind the lessons David learnt in his fugitive years. He knew how to evade capture.

iii) David was likely to kill some of his pursuers and the news would be reported as a wholesale defeat for Absalom's army. "The report that David has made an attack will be sufficient to give rise to the belief that our men have sustained a severe defeat" (Quoted by Keil & Delitzsch). The death of "some" would be changed into a "slaughter" (v.9), and what is more, the story would be readily believed in view of David's reputation. "And he that is valiant, whose heart is as the heart of a lion, shall utterly melt: for all Israel knoweth that thy father is a valiant man, and they which be with him are valiant men" (v.10).

b) The merits of Hushai's plan (vv.11-14)
This was much more impressive. More to the point, it appealed to Absalom's pride. Hushai's plan called for:

i) Total mobilisation. Instead of sending a limited force, Absalom should send a large army drawn from all over Israel. "I counsel that all Israel be generally gathered unto thee, from Dan even to Beer-sheba, as the sand that is by the sea for multitude" (v.11). This would, of course, take time, and give David valuable "breathing space." Hushai omitted to say that huge armies had never been any problem to David!

ii) Total command. Read it again: "I counsel that all Israel be generally gathered unto **thee**, from Dan even to Beer-sheba." Once this vast army was assembled, Absalom himself would inspire them with his personal leadership: "that thou go to battle in thine own person" (v.11). Now that must have appealed to Absalom! He saw himself at the head of a huge victorious army. We must beware of any suggestion that appeals to our pride. "Yea, all of you be subject one to another, and be clothed with humility: for God resisteth the proud, and giveth grace to the humble" (1 Pet 5.5).

iii) Total saturation. "So shall we come upon him in some place where he shall be found, and we will light upon him as the dew falleth on the ground" (v.12). There could be no escape.

iv) Total victory. "And of him and of all the men that are with him there shall not be left so much as one." Not only would David be killed, but also his bodyguard with him. Should they escape and become holed up in a city, then the city could be reduced and destroyed: "then shall all Israel bring ropes to that city, and we will draw it into the river, until there be not one small stone found there" (v.13).

Hushai's arguments won the day, not because they were superior, but because "the Lord had appointed to defeat the good counsel of Ahithophel, to the intent that the Lord might bring evil upon Absalom" (v.14). Absalom accepted Hushai's inferior plan, which reminds us that "the king's heart is in the hand of the Lord, as the rivers of water: he turneth it whithersoever he will" (Prov 21.1). Absalom was impressed by a well-presented bad plan. The man who gained his position by deceit (15.1-12) was deceived by Hushai, reminding us yet again of Galatians 6.7, "Be not deceived; God is not mocked: for whatsoever a man soweth, that shall he also reap." H. Mowvley's comments here are worth repeating: "Behind all the scheming of these two men, there is another at work. They may be thought to be giving their advice on the basis of their own understanding of how things were, but, in fact, it was the Lord who was really at work...Things are not haphazard; they are not controlled by some impersonal fate. It is the Lord who is in control." We should also notice that the fact that Absalom and Ahithophel appear to "hold all the aces" did not guarantee their success against David, which reminds us that "If God be for us, who can be against us?" (Rom 8.31).

> Jehovah is our strength,
> And He shall be our song;
> We shall o'ercome at length,
> Although our foes be strong;
> In vain doth Satan now oppose,
> For God is stronger than His foes
>
> Samuel Bernard

The acceptance of Hushai's counsel "gave David the opportunity to shape his troops, recover strength, and decide on the terrain advantageous to him in the coming battle. But first he needed news of Absalom's intentions" (J. Baldwin). The "spy network" is now activated.

3) The Warning to David (vv.15-22)

There is no need to repeat the narrative. Jonathan and Ahimaaz advised David to get across the Jordan as quickly as possible (v.21). Since they only mention Ahithophel's counsel (v.21), they appear to have been uncertain whether Absalom would change his mind, and follow his adviser's counsel after all. In the interests of safety, they urged David to cross the river. "Then David arose, and all the people that were with him, and they passed over Jordan: by the morning light there lacked not one of them that was not gone over Jordan" (v.22). It would have been disastrous for David if he had not taken the advice of Hushai (vv.15-16), and it will be disastrous for us if we ignore the advice of God's word. He does "make a way to escape", but we must use it! Our spiritual safety depends on our obedience to God's word.

There is, however, a most important lesson embedded in the narrative. The success of the mission depended as much on unnamed people as it did on Hushai, Zadok, Abiathar, Jonathan and Ahimaaz. We do not know the name of "the wench" (v.17) who went from Jerusalem to En-rogel with the message for Jonathan and Ahimaaz, and we do not know the name of the woman at Bahurim (so not everybody there agreed with Shimei: 16.5) who "spread a covering over the well's mouth, and spread ground corn thereon" (v.19). But we do know that they played a vital role in ensuring David's safety.

We do not know the name of the "little maid" whose concern for Naaman prompted her to speak to his wife about Elisha (2 Kings 5.2-3), and we do not know the name of the "lad" (Jn 6.9) whose loaves and fishes were so wonderfully multiplied by the Lord Jesus. The "little maid" and the "lad" played their part, and then disappeared, but their roles are recorded in the

Bible. God does not overlook anybody! Hatach does not come readily to mind as one of the characters in the book of Esther, but he played a vital role as the intermediary between Esther and Mordecai. See Esther 4.5-9. Lack of prominence does not mean that we have no part to play in the Lord's work. In fact, He delights to use people who seem unlikely and unqualified. Just think about Gideon! Read Judges 6.15. If you think that you are too small and insignificant for God to use, then **you** are just the kind of person that He does use! However, we should also notice that there is another unnamed person in the narrative: "a lad saw them (Ahimaaz and Jonathan), and told Absalom" (v.18). Satan can use unnamed people too!

4) The Death Of Ahithophel (v.23)
"And when Ahithophel saw that his counsel was not followed, he saddled his ass, and arose, and gat him home to his house, to his city, and put his household in order, and hanged himself, and died, and was buried in the sepulchre of his father." While it has been suggested that it was Ahithophel's injured pride that drove him to suicide, it seems more likely that he realised that his days were numbered. As J. Baldwin points out, "By his delay, Absalom had forfeited the advantage, and the seasoned strategist Ahithophel knew that since David would now regain control, there was no longer any future for him. Ahithophel would face death for treason against the king. Calmly he accepted the situation, and resolved what he would do. The steps he took all contribute to the picture of a very calculating statesman, totally aware of all that is at stake, who follows to its bitter conclusion the path of logic and reason...it was a tragic end for an undoubtedly able man, who at one time had been an invaluable counsellor to David (2 Sam 16.23) but who had turned traitor.'

We must be sure we maintain complete loyalty to "great David's greater Son." Ahithophel forsook God's anointed king when the tide of popular opinion had swung against him in favour of Absalom. Judas betrayed "the Lord's Christ" when His enemies were plotting His death. But David remained king, and the Lord Jesus remains the "heir of all things" (Heb 1.2). The apparent success of God's enemies does not mean that He has lost the battle, and that we are only supporting a lost cause. We can remain loyal to the Lord Jesus with complete confidence, knowing "that at the name of Jesus every knee shall bow...and that every tongue should confess that Jesus Christ is Lord to the glory of God the Father" (Phil 2.10-11). Ahithophel made a tragic mistake. Let's make sure that **we** don't do the same when the future looks uncertain and the "going gets hard." It is always dangerous to reject divinely-appointed authority in whatever form, and this includes recognition of assembly elders. See 1 Thessalonians 5.12-13.

5) The Pursuit by Absalom (vv.24-26)
Once across the Jordan, David made for Mahanaim, which was Ish-bosheth's capital. Mahanaim was evidently a fortified city (see 18.24). David's escape effectively thwarted Ahithophel's plan of campaign, which was to strike when David was weary and disorganised. Although Absalom, who had been anointed king (19.10), wasn't far behind, David now had time to regroup and prepare for battle. Notice that Absalom appointed Amasa as his commander-in-chief. We will meet him again later. See 19.13, 20.4-12. Amasa was related to David. David had two sisters: Zeruiah, mother of Joab and Abishai, and Abigail, mother of Amasa (see 1 Chron 2.16). However, the father of Abigail was Ithra (otherwise known as Jether, 1 Chron 2.17), not Jesse, from which we can conclude that Abigail, was half-sister to David, and possibly this was the case with Zeruiah as well. Perhaps Absalom wanted to sow discord in David's family by placing Joab's cousin in command of his army. If so, he certainly succeeded, as we shall see.

6) The Provision for David (vv.27-29)
The hospitality of Shobi, Machir, and Barzillai must have been most welcome! They were deeply concerned about David and his men: "the people is hungry, and weary, and thirsty, in the wilderness" (v.29). The three men were quite diverse. For a start, one was a Gentile, and two were Jews, but they were in fellowship with each other!

i) Shobi. His ancestry is most interesting: "Shobi the son of Nahash of Rabbah of the children of Ammon. So Hanun (2 Sam 10.1) had a brother! But as J. Baldwin observes, "he must have been more like his loyal father than the ruthless Hanun, who succeeded to the Ammonite throne (2 Sam 10.1-4)." Ittai was a Philistine convert, and it seems that Shobi was an Ammonite convert! In view of the fact that we have no further information about him, it is unwise to speculate, but it is tempting to describe him as a man from a doomed city who identified himself with God's anointed king. Or, a man who was an alien "from the commonwealth of Israel", and a stranger "from the covenants of promise, having no hope, and without God in the world" who became a fellowcitizen "with the saints, and of the household of God" (Eph 2.12,19).

ii) Machir. "Machir the son of Ammiel of Lo-debar." Whilst we have heard of him before, this is the first time that we actually meet him. This was the man who was host to Mephibosheth before David brought him to Jerusalem. See 2 Samuel 9.4-5. "David now reaps a reward for his kindness to the crippled son of Jonathan" (F. Gardiner).

iii) Barzillai. "Barzillai the Gileadite of Rogelim." This is our first encounter with him, but not the last. See 19.31-32. He was "a very aged man, even fourscore years old: and he had provided the king of sustenance while he lay at Mahaniam; for he was a very great man." More about him later.

It is very beautiful to see three men from totally different backgrounds, and diverse in age, ministering to the king of Israel without any discord among them. The church at Antioch was like that. "Now there were in the church that was at Antioch certain prophets and teachers; as Barnabas, and Simeon that was called Niger, and Lucius of Cyrene, and Manaen, which had been brought up with Herod the tetrarch, and Saul" (Acts 13.1). The church was made up of all sorts of people. There were no religious distinctions ("Barnabas...Saul...Manaen"), there were no colour distinctions ("Niger" means "black"), there were no national divisions ("Lucius of Cyrene"), and there were no social divisions ("Manaen" was the foster-brother of Herod). What a mixed bunch! But they were all people who had "believed, and turned unto the Lord" (Acts 11.21). They all worked and prayed together in complete harmony, and they all "ministered to the Lord" (v.2). There should be no divisions in the local church.

These three men, all evidently well-to-do, ensured that David and his men could rest comfortably ("beds", which according to Keil & Delitzsch means "bedding"), wash properly ("basins" or "field kettles", Keil & Delitzsch), and eat well ("wheat, and barley, and flour, and parched corn, and beans, and lentiles, and parched pulse (dried vegetables), and honey, and butter, and cheese of kine"). Ziba had provided for David earlier (16.1), but his motives were suspect. There is no question of mixed motives here. As A. McShane observes, "encouragements in the darkest days of life are never wanting." God sometimes provides for His people from unexpected sources.

CHAPTER 18.1-33

"Thou art worth ten thousand of us"

David was no longer "weary and weak handed" (17.2). The success of Hushai's counsel at Jerusalem had given him time to cross the Jordan into comparative safety, and the provision of Shobi, Machir and Barzillai had renewed his strength for the coming battle with Absalom. David's ability to fight on this occasion can be attributed to the help of these men, not to mention Zadok, Abiathar, Jonathan, Ahimaaz, and the unnamed women. This reminds us that other believers are strengthened and helped in the spiritual battle through our fellowship with them. We must never think that our contribution is too small to be of any value.

This chapter can be divided in the following way: *(1)* The deployment of the army (vv.l-5); *(2)* The defeat of Israel (vv.6-8); *(3)* The death of Absalom (vv.9-18); *(4)* The despatch of the messengers (vv.19-32); *(5)* The distress of David (v.33).

1) The Deployment of the Army (vv.l-5)
"And David numbered the people that were with him, and set captains of thousands and captains of hundreds over them" (v.l). We should notice: *(A)* the appointment of commanders (v.2); *(B)* the appreciation of David (vv.3-4); *(C)* the anxiety for Absalom (v.5).

A) The appointment of commanders (v.2)
"And David sent forth a third part of the people under the hand of Joab, and a third part under the hand of Abishai the son Zeruiah, and a third part under the hand of Ittai the Gittite.'" It appears therefore that Joab had to share the command with his brother Abishai and Ittai the Gittite, but "as it turned out, Joab proved as independent and impetuous as ever (vv.9-16)' (J. Baldwin). There are at least three things to notice here:

a) David took the initiative. He took the battle to Absalom. We get the impression that David was on the offensive, not the defensive. It is often said that 'the best means of defence is attack.' This is very true in gospel work. We cannot expect success if we wait for people to make contact with us. We must make contact with them.

b) David was organised. He had a command structure, with three generals plus "captains of thousands and captains of hundreds." His soldiers were not left "to do their own thing." The injunction, "Let all things be done decently and in order ("by arrangement')" (1 Cor 14.40), refers particularly to procedure in assembly meetings, but it makes a sound principle for any aspect of the Lord's work.

c) David included Ittai. As we have already noticed, although Ittai was a "new convert", he was devoted to David (see 1 Sam 15.19-22). Now he has a position of immense responsibility in the battle. David obviously recognised his ability, and made sure that it was used.

B) The appreciation of David (vv.3-4)

David was ready to take overall command on the battlefield (v.2), but his men were too concerned for his welfare to allow this to happen. They knew that the objective of Absalom was to kill David. "Thou shalt not go forth: for if we flee away, they will not care for us ("attach no importance to this", Keil & Delitzsch); neither if half of us die, will they care for us: but now thou art worth ten thousand of us." (David had slain "his ten thousands", 1 Sam 18.7).Whilst they probably meant that David was worth ten thousand of them as far as Absalom was concerned, they obviously placed tremendous value on him themselves: "therefore now it is better that thou succour us out of the city." There are a number of lessons here:

a) We should value our heavenly Commander. He is "the chiefest among ten thousand" (Song 5.10). He is certainly "worth ten thousand of us!"

b) We should recognise the value of His unseen ministry. "For in that he himself hath suffered being tempted, he is able to succour them that are tempted" (Heb 2.18). He is unseen, but He is always there!

c) We should value our spiritual leaders. "And we beseech you. brethren, to know them which labour among you, and are over you in the Lord, and admonish you; and to esteem them very highly in love for their work's sake" (1 Thess 5.12-13).

d) We should recognise the value of unseen prayer on our behalf. Not all believers are in the "front line" of the battle, but we can all "succour them out of the city." Paul puts it like this: "We had the sentence of death in ourselves, that we should not trust in ourselves, but in God which raiseth the dead ...Ye also helping together by prayer for us" (2 Cor 1.9-11).

2 Samuel

C) The anxiety for Absalom (v.5)
Great stress is laid on David's final instructions to his three commanders: "Deal gently for my sake with the young man, even with Absalom. And all the people heard when the king gave all the captains charge concerning Absalom." He might not have said this if it was someone else's son. H. Mowvley sums up the two sides to this command as follows: "On the one hand it shows David's love and loyalty to one of his children and his readiness as a father, to forgive his rebellion. He could even overlook the fact that his son was out to be rid of him in order to fulfil his selfish ambition. On the other hand, we may see it as a weakness in David in that he was ready to put his own sentimental feelings for his family before the need of his nation for stability and prosperity. As often, in the character of David as drawn by this writer, we find a mixture of motives which is true to our human experience."

2) The Defeat of Israel (vv.6-8)
The precise location of "the wood of Ephraim" has been debated, and there is no need for us to enter the arena. The various arguments are set out by Kiel & Delitzsch. Absalom lost 20,000 men either directly, by "the sword", or indirectly, by "the wood." Keil & Delitzsch suggest that "the woody region was most likely full of ravines, precipices, and marshes, into which the flying foe was pursued, and where so many perished."

Perhaps the greatest tragedy lies in the words: "So the people went out into the field **against Israel**: and the battle was in the wood of Ephraim; where **the people of Israel** were slain before the servants of David. And there was a great slaughter that day of twenty thousand men." We are therefore reminded that this was a civil war. The hostility between Israel in the north and Judah in the south kept on surfacing (see, for example, 2 Sam.19.41-43; 20.1-2), and ultimately led to the terrible division between Israel and Judah after the death of Solomon. See 1 Kings 12.16-17 etc. It is equally tragic when God"s people today are so busy fighting each other that they have no time to engage the satanically led "principalities" and "powers." It happened at Corinth: "brother goeth to law with brother, and that before the unbelievers" (1 Cor 6.6). It happened in the churches of Galatia: "For all the law is fulfilled in one word, even in this; Thou shalt love thy neighbour as thyself. But if ye bite and devour one another, take heed that ye be not consumed one of another" (Gal 5.14-15). There are therefore some solemn lessons for us in v8: "For the battle was there scattered over the face of all the country: and the wood **devoured** more people that day than the sword **devoured**." As A.McShane observes, "self-destruction from internal strife can be more devastating than onslaughts by outside forces...internal strife and division is more harmful to an assembly than attacks of the enemy from the outside."

3) The Death of Absalom (vv.9-18)
It can be summed up like this: **(A)** hanged in an oak (vv.9-13); **(B)** executed by Joab (vv.14-16); **(C)** buried under stones (vv.17-18).

A) Hanged in an oak (vv.9-13)
a) The helplessness of Absalom (v.9). "And Absalom met the servants of David. And Absalom rode upon a mule, and the mule went under the thick boughs of a great oak, and his head caught hold of the oak..." Contrary to what we are usually told, the chapter does not say that Absalom was left hanging by his hair! According to F.Gardner (Ellicott"s Commentary) this "common idea...seems to have originated with Josephus." It would be tempting to say that Absalom's death was largely brought about by his personal beauty, but we mustn't base lessons on insecure foundations! One thing is clear: it was a humiliating end for Absalom. It might have been more satisfactory for him if he had died in battle at the head of his army, but David's men didn't even have to engage in a duel with him. He hung helplessly from a tree! So much for his pride. "Whosoever exalteth himself shall be abased" (Lk 14.11).

b) The faithfulness of the soldier (vv.10-13). "And a certain man saw it, and told Joab, and said, Behold, I saw Absalom hanged in an oak. And Joab said unto the man that told him, And, behold, thou sawest him, and why didst thou not smite him there to the ground? And I would have given thee ten shekels of silver, and a girdle." The "girdle" probably implied promotion. Compare 1 Sam.18.4. As J. Baldwin observes, "this man from the ranks is admirable in his resistance to bribery." "Though I should receive a thousand shekels of silver in mine hand, yet would I not put forth mine hand against the king's son: for in our hearing the king charged thee and Abishai and Ittai, saying, Beware that none touch the young man Absalom. Otherwise I should have wrought falsehood against mine own life: for there is no matter hid from the king, and thou thyself wouldest have set thyself against me."

There is a clear lesson here for us. This common soldier would not disobey the command of the king, even though this would have been approved by such a senior officer as Joab, and we must remain loyal to the word of God however great the pressure on us to abandon its teaching. Sometimes that pressure can be exerted by people who should know better, making it necessary to say, even in "Christian" circles, "we ought to obey God rather than men" (Acts 5.29). But Joab was unimpressed and, unlike the soldier, proceeded to take matters into his own hands. "Neither his former friendship with Absalom, nor his regard for David's wish, could stay the cruel hand of Joab" (A.McShane).

B) Executed by Joab (vv.14-16)
"And he took three darts ("staves", JND margin) in his hand, and thrust them through the heart of Absalom, while he was yet alive in the midst of the oak. And ten young men that bare Joab's armour compassed about and smote Absalom. and slew him." According to Keil & Delitzsch, the last clause of verse 14 belongs to what follows: "Still living (i.e. as he was still alive) in the midst of the terebinth, ten young men, Joab's armour bearers, surrounded him, and smote him to death."

This may seem surprising in view of the fact that a few years earlier Joab had engineered the return of Absalom from exile, but this had only led to rebellion against David. It seems therefore that Joab, "impatient with David's indulgence towards his son' (J. Baldwin), decided that it would be in the best interests of the country to end Absalom's life while he had the opportunity. The death of Absalom certainly brought the battle to an end: "And Joab blew the trumpet. and the people returned from pursuing after Israel: for Joab held back the people" (v.16).

C) Buried under stones vv.17-18)
The "very great heap of stones" ("a huge cairn of field stones", J. Baldwin) which marked Absalom's grave "in a great pit in the wood'", contrasts vividly with the monument he had erected to himself in "the king's dale." The pillar was intended to commemorate his reign, but the heap of stones, which would cease to be identifiable in a relatively short time, marked his ignominious end. He failed to learn the lesson that "God's way up is down.' "God resisteth the proud, and giveth grace to the humble" (1 Pet. 5.5). Absalom "**reared up** for himself a pillar", but he was buried **under** "a very great heap of stones." Absalom's words, "I have no son to keep my name in remembrance", appear to contradict 2 Sam. 14.27, but presumably he lost his three sons in their infancy. Let's remember that we will all leave some kind of monument behind us, either creditable or discreditable.

4) The Despatch of the Messengers (vv.19-32)
This section describes the way in which the news of victory was conveyed to David. The messengers were, in order of mention, Ahimaaz (v.19) and

Cushi (v.21). The passage commences with Joab at the battle-front, and concludes with David in the gate of Mahanaim. We can divide these verses as follows: **(A)** their departure (vv.19-23) and **(B)** their arrival (vv.24-32).

A) Their departure (vv.19-23)
We have already met Ahimaaz. but this is the first mention of Cushi who was, in all probability, a descendent of Cush (Gen 10.6) and therefore a foreigner.

a)   The desire of Ahimaaz (vv.19-20). "Let me now run, and bear the king tidings, how the Lord hath avenged him of his enemies." This was vetoed by Joab: "Thou shalt not bear tidings this day, but thou shalt bear tidings another day: but this day thou shalt bear no tidings, because the king's son is dead." Joab evidently realised that Ahimaaz would find it particularly difficult to tell David that Absalom was dead, and he was proved right. Ahimaaz, who knew the facts only too well, avoided a direct answer to David's anxious question. See v.29. We can therefore conclude that Joab wished to save Ahimaaz the embarrassment of arriving at Mahanaim without the will to tell David the bad news, reminding us that we should "consider one another" (Heb 10.24).

b)   The despatch of Cushi (v.21). "Go and tell the king what thou hast seen. And Cushi bowed himself unto Joab, and ran." J. Baldwin suggests that 'Joab chose a foreigner to take the message' because "for him it would be merely a duty, and his words would not be emotionally charged." Keil & Deltizsch suggest that Cushi was "a Moorish slave in the service of Joab."

c)   The determination of Ahimaaz (vv.22-23). "Then said Ahimaaz the son of Zadok yet again to Joab, But howsoever, let me, I pray thee, also run after Cushi. And Joab said. Wherefore wilt thou run, my son, seeing that thou hast no tidings ready?" or "seeing that there is no news suited [to thee]" (JND). Keil & Delitzsch render this as follows: "and there is no striking message for thee" with the explanation, "no message that strikes the mark, or affects anything." As we have already noticed, this proved to be the case (v.29). But Ahimaaz was not easily deterred, and having twisted Joab's arm "ran by way of the plain, and overran Cushi." We can applaud his zeal and energy, but he wasn't the man for the job.

B) Their arrival (vv.24-32)
Our attention is now transferred to Mahanaim where David "sat between the two gates." These were the inner and outer city gates, between which the elders of the city customarily sat. The watchman saw two men running towards the city, and David concluded that both men carried good news.

This is implied by the fact that they were running alone. "If he be alone, there is tidings in his mouth." A group of people running would have suggested a retreat!

a) The arrival of Ahimaaz (vv.27-30)
He was identified by the watchman before he reached the city, to which David said, "He is a good man, and cometh with good tidings." This was precisely what Joab wanted to avoid! He knew that the arrival of Ahimaaz would bolster David's hopes, only to see them crash when he discovered the truth. Ahimaaz was able to say "All is well" ("Peace!"), and "Blessed be the Lord thy God, which hath delivered up the men that lifted up their hand against my lord the king", but he could not bring himself to give a direct answer to the question, "Is the young man Absalom safe?" All he could say was, "When Joab sent the king's servant (referring to Cushi) and me thy servant, I saw a great tumult, but I knew not what it was." He knew very well that Absalom was dead (v.20). Ahimaaz was not able to give David the news he wanted, and was told, "Turn aside and stand here."

There are several important lessons in these verses. There are three "good men" in the Bible: Ahimaaz ("a good man...with good tidings"). Joseph of Arimathaea ("he was a good man, and a just", Lk 23.50), and Barnabas ("a good man, and full of the Holy Ghost and of faith", Acts 11.24). We should notice the following:

i) Ahimaaz was consistent. He was "a good man...with good tidings." The man and the message were not at variance. Timothy was told, "Take heed unto thyself and unto the doctrine" (1 Tim 4.16).

ii) Ahimaaz was reticent. He was unable to deliver the painful message. When confronted with a direct question, he was unable to give a direct answer. Ahimaaz gladly related the good news, but was reluctant to give the bad. Quite obviously, there are times when we should do all we can to avoid hurting people's feelings, but we must be faithful in conveying every aspect of the gospel. The Lord Jesus did this: "He that believeth on the Son hath everlasting life: and he that believeth not the Son shall not see life; but the wrath of God abideth on him" (Jn 3.36).

iii) Ahimaaz was dismissed. "Turn aside and stand here. And he turned aside, and stood still." The man who failed to give precise news was told to stand aside.

b) The arrival of Cushi (vv.31-32)
For the second time David asks the question, "Is the young man Absalom

safe?" Cushi answers "objectively and yet kindly" (J. Baldwin). He omits Absalom's name and avoids the word "dead", but his message is perfectly clear: "The enemies of my lord the king, and all that rise against thee to do thee hurt, be as that young man is." Cushi conveys the bad news in the gentlest way possible, and there is a lesson here for us all. It is worth noticing that both Ahimaaz and Cushi acknowledge that the Lord had given them victory (vv.19,28,31).

5) The Distress of David (v.33)
"And the king was much moved, and went up to the chamber over the gate, and wept: and as he went, thus he said, O my son Absalom, my son, my son, Absalom! Would God I had died for thee, O Absalom, my son, my son!" Absalom means "father of peace", but he brought David no peace at all. He died in disgrace, and this must have contributed to David's distress. Having made proper allowance for "all that a loving father goes through on the death of his son" (J. Baldwin), it remains that "David was criminally weak at this crisis in allowing the feelings of the father to completely outweigh the duties of the monarch" (F. Gardiner). He shed no tears over the death of twenty thousand of the Lord's people. As we shall see, Joab was obliged to rebuke him for failing to recognise the bravery of his army in saving him from Absalom. See 19.1-8. David's torment must have been partly due to his consciousness that his own moral failure had contributed to Absalom's downfall. The man who failed to exercise self-restraint "in the matter of Uriah the Hittite" forfeited his right to correct his "ambitious and spoiled son" (J. Baldwin), with terrible results. David had now paid "threefold", but even this was not the end. It was to be "fourfold" (2 Sam 12.6).

David would have died for his son: the Lord Jesus **did** die for us.

CHAPTER 19.1-23

"Why speak ye not a word of bringing the king back?"

News of victory "in the wood of Ephraim" was swamped by David's sorrow over the death of Absalom. When the messengers arrived, David's only question was, "Is the young man Absalom safe?" (18.29,32). He showed no interest whatsoever in the welfare of his three generals or in his loyal soldiers. Human emotions are very deep, and it would be quite wrong to censure David's grief out of hand, but he paid no regard to his responsibilities as king of Israel. Affairs of state were forgotten. He was completely consumed by his personal loss: "O my son, Absalom, my son, my son Absalom! Would God I had died for thee, O Absalom, my son, my son!" (18.33). He was more concerned for the son who would have killed him than he was for the brave men who would have died for him.

Chapter 19, which begins with David's continuing sorrow, can be divided into two parts: **(1)** David's reprimand by Joab (vv.1-8) and **(2)** David's return to Jerusalem (vv.9-43). The length of the chapter demands two studies, and this necessitates a rather arbitrary division of the verses. We will therefore address vv.1-23 now, and vv.24-43 in the next study.

1) David's Reprimand by Joab (vv.1-8)
In these verses we have **(A)** the inconsolable king (vv.1-4), and **(B)** the indignant general (vv.5-8).

A) The inconsolable king (vv.1-4)
"And it was told Joab, Behold the king weepeth and mourneth for Absalom." This could not have surprised Joab. He knew very well how much David loved his evil son. See ch.18.5. But David's sorrow had an adverse effect on morale: "The victory that day was turned into mourning unto all the people: for the people heard say that day how the king was grieved for his son. And the people gat them by stealth that day into the city, as people

being ashamed steal away when they flee in battle." There are some important lessons here:

i) We must not become so obsessed with our personal problems that we discourage others. Every right-minded Christian recognises the implications of Paul's illustration that "whether one member suffer, all the members suffer with it; or one member be honoured, all the members rejoice with it" (1 Cor 12.26). But unrelieved gloom and despondency can be depressing and discouraging for fellow-believers. Some people can be so immersed in their own problems and difficulties that they appear to forget God's goodness to them. This leads us to add that

ii) We must not become so obsessed with our personal problems that we forget to give God thanks. "In every thing give thanks; for this is the will of God in Christ Jesus concerning you" (1 Thess 5.18). Both Ahimaaz and Cushi gave glory to God for the victory (18.28,31), but not a word from David!

iii) We must not become so obsessed with our personal problems that we fail to appreciate others. David's victorious army returned to Mahanaim without a single word of appreciation for their valour in battle. Paul was so different. He could have been thoroughly depressed by his imprisonments, but he was thankful to God for those who helped him. He referred to his "bonds" when writing to the Philippians (1.7,13,14,16) but this didn't stop him thanking God for their "fellowship in the gospel from the first day until now" (1.5). He did not forget the kindness of Onesiphorus to him during his last imprisonment: "he oft refreshed me, and was not ashamed of my chain: but when he was in Rome, he sought me out very diligently, and found me" (2 Tim 1.16-17).

iv) We must not become so obsessed with our personal problems that we forget our responsibilities. For a short while, the nation was left leaderless. David isolated himself: "the king covered his face, and the king cried with a loud voice, O my son Absalom, O Absalom, my son, my son!" As J. Baldwin observes, "having covered his face, he could not see other people; and while he cried with a loud voice, he could not hear what anyone wanted to say to him. He wished to be quite alone."

"This is one of the dangers of sorrow: that in our grief for those who are gone we lose our interest in those who are living, and slacken our zeal in the work which is allotted to us. However great our bereavements, we may not drop our tasks until the Master calls us away." Dr J R.Miller (*Springs in the Valley*).

Paul put it like this: "We are troubled on every side, yet not distressed; we are perplexed, but not in despair; persecuted, but not forsaken; cast down, but not destroyed" (2 Cor 4.8-9).

B) The indignant general (vv.5-8)
Joab was brutally frank with David. H. Mowvley puts it like this: Joab "went to see David, to give him a piece of his mind. The time for sympathy had passed; what was needed was some straight talking and Joab was just the man to do it." He set out the implications of David's conduct as follows:

i) He had dishonoured the very people who had saved his life and the life of his family: "Thou hast shamed this day the faces of thy servants, which this day have saved thy life, and the lives of thy sons and of thy daughters, and the lives of thy wives, and the lives of thy concubines."

ii) He had reversed the commandment of God. Leviticus 19.18 stated, "thou shalt love thy neighbour as thyself", but David had turned this on its head: "thou lovest thine enemies, and hatest thy friends." His unabated sorrow implied that he loved Absalom, his enemy, and hated his friends who had delivered him from Absalom.

iii) He had disregarded the loyalty of his commanders and his men. "Thou hast declared this day, that thou regardest neither princes not servants."

iv) He had implied that he was willing to sacrifice his loyal supporters so that Absalom could live. "For this day I perceive, that if Absalom had lived, and we all had died this day, then it had pleased thee well." He thought more of treacherous Absalom than he did about his faithful followers.

Joab certainly did not "beat about the bush!" While it is unlikely that Joab believed that David had deliberately acted in this way, he makes it very clear that this was the impression gained by the onlooker. But more than that, the situation was so serious that David was in danger of losing the support of his men. "Now therefore arise, go forth, and speak comfortably unto thy servants: for I swear by the Lord, if thou go not forth, there will not tarry one with thee this night: and that will be worse unto thee than all the evil that befell thee from thy youth until now." The overall lesson is clear: obsession with ourselves will affect **us**, as well as other people. We cannot do without the fellowship of God's people. What impressions do people have of us? Do they see us as people who are so self-centred that we have no time for anybody else? Generally speaking, people can only stand so much, and tend to withdraw their fellowship. The sorrows and difficulties of life are very real, but in them all we should still "consider one another to provoke unto love and good works" (Heb 10.24).

We must remember too that these lessons are most important for all who lead the Lord's people. The words "speak comfortably" mean "speak to the heart." Compare 2 Chronicles 30.22. An isolated leader is a contradiction in terms. Good leadership involves motivation and encouragement. Elders cannot expect the whole-hearted support of the assembly if they never express their gratitude or give encouragement to God's people.

David did respond to Joab's admonition. "Then the king arose, and sat in the gate." What followed was presumably a belated victory parade. It marked the total rout of Absalom's army. There was no enemy left to fight: "And **all** the people came before the king: **for** Israel (the tribes who had followed Absalom) had fled **every man** to his tent."

The section ends with David sitting in the gate of Mahanaim reviewing his army (and probably pondering some "unfinished business" in connection with Joab: see v.13), but he was still in exile. The balance of the chapter describes his return to Jerusalem.

2) David's Return to Jerusalem (vv.9-43)
We can divide this section of the chapter as follows: **(A)** the agitation for his return (vv.9-15); **(B)** the people awaiting his return (vv.16-30); **(C)** the people accompanying his return (vv.31-40); **(D)** the animosity at his return (vv.41-43). It is worth noticing that David did not immediately reclaim the throne, just as he never actively sought the throne in the first place. He wanted to return under the right conditions. David had no desire to enforce his reign: far better to have willing subjects!

A) The agitation for his return (vv.9-15)
It is rather surprising to discover that it was the recently-defeated "tribes of Israel" who first mentioned the matter! F. Gardiner (Ellicott's Commentary) makes the point that "Judah was naturally particularly slow in returning to

2 Samuel

its allegiance. It had shown especial ingratitude to David and had formed the cradle and centre of the rebellion."

i) Israel's initiative (vv.9-10)

"And all the people were at strife throughout all the tribes of Israel, saying, The king saved us out of the hand of our enemies, and he delivered us out of the hand of the Philistines; and now he is fled out of the land for Absalom. And Absalom, whom we anointed over us, is dead in battle. Now therefore why speak ye not a word of bringing the king back?" It really seems quite unbelievable! There is no hint of sorrow over their dreadful mistake in following Absalom in the first place. David had been anointed by Samuel at God's command (1 Sam 16.12), but Israel had anointed Absalom. It is disastrous to set aside men of God's choice in favour of men who are "flavour of the month." That mistake cost them twenty thousand men! There is no suggestion of an apology to David for treating him so despicably after he had proved to be such an able king. J. Baldwin expresses it rather well. "There appears to be political naivety in the inference that a new king can be anointed and followed as an experiment; if it fails the *status quo* can be restored!" (This still happens. It is called democracy!)

We must not treat the Lord like that! The New Testament reminds us that the Lord Jesus "gave himself for our sins, that he might deliver us from this present evil world" (Gal 1.4) but that it is possible to turn our backs on Him in favour of false teaching: "I marvel that ye are so soon removed from him that called you into the grace of Christ unto another gospel" (Gal 1.6). Israel appeared to think that all they had to do was ask, and David would return. The experiment with Absalom was just a hiccup. They forgot that there were thousands of grieving mothers, wives and children in the land. Yes, the Lord does restore (Ps 23.3), but backsliding comes with a terrible price tag.

ii) Judah's invitation (vv.11-15)

Israel's initiative in seeking David's return prompted him to ask the elders of Judah why they were "the last to bring the king back to his house" (vv.11-12). After all, David was "anointed "king over the house of Judah seven years before he was anointed "king over Israel." See 2 Samuel 5.5. The message was routed via Zadok and Abiathar, whose priestly authority would be readily recognised by the tribal elders. David could rightly say of the men of Judah, "Ye are my brethren, ye are my bones and my flesh" (v.12), although Israel made the same claim. See 2 Samuel 5.1. Judah was the royal tribe, of whom Jacob had said, "The sceptre shall not depart from Judah, nor a lawgiver from between his feet, until Shiloh come; and unto him shall the gathering of the people be" (Gen 49.10). But this privileged tribe seemed slow to grasp the greatest of its blessings – the presence of the king! The expression "ye are my bones and my flesh" emphasises Judah's identification with David, just as it emphasises the identification of Eve with Adam (Gen 2.23) and the church with Christ (Eph 5.30). Bearing in mind our relationship with the Lord Jesus, with all its unique privileges and blessings, are **we** slow to give Him the place of honour in our lives? Do **we** keep Him at a distance in the same way that the men of Judah left David at Mahanaim?

According to J. Baldwin, David was unwise to ignore the desire of the northern tribes in favour of Judah, and missed an opportunity to "unify the kingdom by rising above tribal factions and loyalties." The appointment of Amasa (Absalom's general, 2 Sam 17.25) in place of Joab (v.13) could have been an "olive branch" to the tribes who had supported Absalom. It seems more likely, however, that the demotion of Joab in favour of Amasa (both men were David's cousins) was David's way of repaying Joab for disobeying his orders in killing Absalom. It was to prove a disastrous appointment for Amasa. See 2 Samuel 20.4-12. Once again, David was swayed by personal feelings rather than statesmanship. As A.McShane points out, "the man who had served under Absalom as commander in chief, and should have been put to death for his treason, is appointed to the post formerly held by the one who had delivered the king from death." It reminds us that our personal feelings should not be allowed to cloud our better judgment.

The appeal of David to the tribe of Judah resulted in his unanimous recall to the throne. "And he bowed the heart of all the men of Judah, even as the heart of one man; so that they sent this word unto the king, Return thou, and all thy servants" (v.14). At first glance, this seems a very happy ending to David's exile, but only Judah was present. "So the king returned, and came to Jordan. And **Judah** came to Gilgal, to go to meet the king, to conduct the king over Jordan" (v.15). This created friction in the nation (19.41-43) and resulted in another rebellion (20.1). There are at least three lessons here:

a) The central place of the king. "So **the king** returned, and came to Jordan. And Judah came to Gilgal, to go to meet **the king**, to conduct **the king** over Jordan" This reminds us that "in all things" the Lord Jesus must have "the pre-eminence" (Col 1.18).

b) The unity of Judah. They had the "heart of one man." There was not one dissentient voice amongst them. They were "perfectly joined together in the same mind and in the same judgment" (1 Cor 1.10). Paul's desire for the Philippians was that "whether I come and see you, or else be absent, I may hear of your affairs, that ye stand fast in one spirit, with one mind striving together for the faith of the gospel" (Phil 1.27).

c) The danger of a party spirit. Leaders cannot afford to have favourites, and assemblies cannot afford cliques. There was "envying, and strife, and divisions" at Corinth: "one saith, I am of Paul; and another, I am of Apollos" (1 Cor 3.3-4). Elders are to "take heed…to **all** the flock" (Acts 20.28).

B) The people awaiting his return (vv.16-30)
We now renew our acquaintance with Shimei and Mephibosheth. "And Shimei… came down" (vv.16-23); "And Mephibosheth…came down" (vv.24-30).

i) Shimei (vv.16-23)
"Political changes made all the difference to the allegiances of Shimei, who had insulted David only a short time before on his outward journey" (2 Sam 16.5-8) (J. Baldwin). It reminds us of the proverb: "don't tread on people's heads as you climb the ladder because they will kick you down as you descend!" There can be no doubt that Shimei feared for his life, and was anxious to prove his loyalty to David. He "hasted and came down with the men of Judah to meet king David" (v.16)." Perhaps he felt that his case could be strengthened by the presence of a thousand fellow-tribesmen to greet the king ("look at the people I've influenced on your behalf") or perhaps he just felt that there was safety in numbers!

Ziba was there too (v.17), complete with his "fifteen sons and twenty servants" (9.10). Perhaps he wanted to pledge his loyalty to David in view of the fact that Mephibosheth wasn't far away (v.24) and "truth will out!" Both Shimei and Ziba crossed the Jordan to meet David, and Shimei "fell down before the king as he was (just) crossing over the Jordan" (JND) by the ferry boat. We must notice **(a)** his plea (vv.19-20) and **(b)** his preservation (vv.21-23).

a) His plea (vv.19-20). He asks for clemency on the ground of his confession of guilt ("thy servant doth know that I have sinned") and on the ground of his changed allegiance ("I am come first this day of all the house of Joseph, to go down to meet my lord the king"). It all sounds good, but we have to question Shimei's sincerity. He was a "fair weather friend." It was all very well to called David "my lord" (v.19) and "my lord the king" (vv.19,20) when he was returning in triumph, but he had called David a "man of Belial" when he was fleeing for his life (16.7). David's servants and Ittai called David "my lord the king" **in his rejection** (15.15, 21). Are we faithful to our Lord in **His** rejection? It is easy to be a Christian when there's no possibility of reprisals!

b) His preservation (vv.21-23). Abishai was not impressed by Shimei's plea. "Shall not Shimei be put to death for this, because he cursed the Lord's anointed?" Abishai had not changed one bit! See 16.9. Compare 1 Samuel 26.8. There are two sides to David's answer.

In the first place, he did not wish to mar his return by "settling old scores." The "sons of Zeruiah" were only too fond of killing people. Perhaps David was thinking of the murder of Abner (David used similar language in 2 Samuel 3.39), or possibly of the death of Absalom. In both cases Joab and Abiathar had acted against David's wishes, but not now. "What have I to do with you, ye sons of Zeruiah, that ye should this day be adversaries unto me? Shall there any man be put to death this day in Israel? For do not I know that I am this day **king over Israel?**" This was no time for revenge! Perhaps, however, David was resorting to political expediency. Shimei was a Benjamite "of the house of Saul" (16.5) and his execution might have sent shock waves through the other tribes.

In the second case, David's clemency towards Shimei would have been most laudable if he really had forgiven him. But had he? When David was on his death-bed he remembered the bitter hatred of Shimei, and charged Solomon to bring "his hoar head…down to the grave with blood" (2 Kings 2.8-9), even though he had sworn on oath that Shimei would not die (v.23). Quite clearly, David never trusted Shimei again.

ii) Mephibosheth (vv.24-30)
"And Mephibosheth the son of Saul came down to meet the king, and had neither dressed his feet, nor trimmed his beard, nor washed his clothes, from the day the king departed until the day he came again in peace."

Chapter 19.24-43

"Yea, let him take all"

In the first of our two studies in 2 Samuel 19 we noticed that the chapter can be divided into two main sections: **(1)** David's reprimand by Joab (vv.1-8) and **(2)** David's return to Jerusalem (vv.9-43).

1) David's Reprimand by Joab (vv.1-8)
As we have seen, these verses deal with **(A)** the inconsolable king (vv.1-4), and **(B)** the indignant general (vv.5-8).

2) David's Return to Jerusalem (vv.9-43)
We have already noticed that this section of the chapter can be divided in the following way: **(A)** the agitation for his return (vv.9-15); **(B)** the people awaiting his return (vv.16-30); **(C)** the people accompanying his return (vv.31-40); **(D)** the animosity at his return (vv.41-43).

A) The agitation for his return (vv.9-15)
Although it was the recently-defeated "tribes of Israel" who first mentioned David's return, he made no attempt to re-cross the Jordan until Judah replied to his question, "Why are ye the last to bring the king back to his house?" (v.11). Once they said, "Return thou, and all thy servants", David crossed the river by "a ferry boat" (v.18) to be met by Shimei and Mephibosheth. This brings us to:

B) The people awaiting his return (vv.16-30)
"And Shimei...came down" (vv.16-23); "And Mephibosheth...came down" (vv.24-30).

i) Shimei (vv.16-23)
We have already noted that Shimei's plea for mercy would have fallen on deaf ears if it had been addressed to Abishai, but David spared his life, although not indefinitely (2 Kings 2.8-9).

ii) Mephibosheth (vv.24-30)

According to Ziba, Mephibosheth had looked on David's exile as an opportunity to gain the throne: "To day shall the house of Israel restore me the kingdom of my father" (2 Sam 16.3). It looked an unlikely story at the time, and now the true facts emerge. David had evidently been a little premature in saying to Ziba, "Behold, thine are all that pertained unto Mephibosheth" (2 Sam 16.4). We must notice:

a) His appearance v.24. "And Mephibosheth the son of Saul came down to meet the king, and had neither dressed his feet, nor trimmed his beard, nor washed his clothes, from the day the king departed until the day he came again in peace." This certainly didn't look much like the man described by Ziba! His appearance suggested someone in deep mourning. Compare Ezekiel 24.17. While it would be quite wrong to suggest that we should follow Mephibosheth's example and neglect our appearance (the mind boggles!), we should be people who are more concerned about the interests of our absent Lord than we are about our own affairs. There is a personal cost involved. Nobody could say that Mephibosheth was having a jolly good time in David's absence! His heart was with David in exile, "from the **day** the king departed until the **day** he came again in peace." What kind of impression do we create? Shouldn't people be able to see our loyalty to Christ in His absence? Shouldn't people know that we are waiting for the Lord's return? Mephibosheth refrained from 'normal' behaviour, and Christians should be people who "love not the world, neither the things that are in the world" (1 Jn 2.15).

b) His explanation vv.25-27. As they stand in the AV, the words "when he came to Jerusalem to meet the king" refer to an interview which took place when David arrived home. However, this has been rendered as follows: "And as soon as Jerusalem came to meet the king' (JND) meaning 'Now when Jerusalem (i.e. the inhabitants of the capital) came to meet the king" (Keil & Delitzsch). Technicalities apart, Mephibosheth explains that he had been completely misrepresented by Ziba. "My lord, O king, my servant deceived me...and he hath slandered thy servant unto my Lord the king." Paul experienced this too: "as we be slanderously reported, and as some affirm that we say" (Rom 3.8). So did the Lord Jesus: see, for example Luke 23.2-5, "We found this fellow perverting the nation, and forbidding to give tribute to Caesar...He stirreth up the people, teaching through all Jewry, beginning from Galilee to this place." Sadly, people will resort to anything in attempting to discredit God's people, and undermine their testimony. Ziba had slandered David for personal advantage, but there was no thought of this in the heart of Mephibosheth. We should notice too that although Mephibosheth stated the facts, he did so without bitter recrimination against Ziba.

c) His assurance (v.27) "My lord the king is as an angel of God: do therefore what is good in thine eyes." By describing David as "an angel of God" Mephibosheth expressed his confidence in David. He would be able to reach the right conclusion about Ziba's deception and act accordingly. This is the second occasion on which David is described in this way. See 2 Samuel 14.17, "The word of my lord the king shall now be comfortable: for as an angel of God, so is my lord the king to discern good and bad." This reminds us that we can confidently commit our affairs to the Lord. Read 1 Corinthians 4.3-5. Note the words, "he that judgeth me is the Lord." He is "the righteous judge" (1 Tim.4.8).

d) His submission v.28. Mephibosheth was content to leave everything in David's hands. He deserved nothing: "For all of my father's house were but dead men before my lord the king: yet didst thou set thy servant among them that did eat at thine own table. What right therefore have I yet to cry any more unto the king?" Compare 2 Samuel 9.8. Mephibosheth never forgot the grace of David, and we should never forget "the exceeding riches of his (God's) grace toward us through Christ Jesus" (Eph. 2.7). Mephibosheth did not attempt to assert his "rights" because he didn't have any! We can all say with Paul, "by the grace of God I am what I am" (1 Cor 15.10). None of us have any right to complain to God! We live in a world where people "trumpet" their rights, but conveniently forget their duties! Do notice the repeated expression "My lord, O king...my lord the king...my lord the king" (vv.26-28).

e) His rejoicing vv.29-30. Do we detect a little peevishness in David's reply: "Why speakest thou any more of thy matters? I have said, Thou and Ziba divide the land?" This seems to be David's way of admitting that he had made a mistake in assigning everything to Ziba in the first place (16.4). "David retracted the hasty decree in 16.4 so as to modify the wrong that he had done to Mephibosheth, but he had not courage enough to retract it altogether" (Keil & Delitzsch). But Mephibosheth soars above it all: "Yea, let him take all, forasmuch as my lord the king is come again in peace unto his own house." Here was the crowning evidence that Mephibosheth had been maligned by Ziba! It was everything to Mephibosheth that the king had returned. His presence at David's return was not motivated by any thought of reward. His own interests were of secondary importance. Is it everything to us that the King is coming back?!

Before we turn our attention to Barzillai, look back over 2 Samuel and piece together the references to "my lord the king." You'll find them in 3.21; 9.11; 14.17; 15.15; 15.21; 19.20; 19.27-28; 19.30. Now there's a profitable little study! Look at it in New Testament terms: "And Thomas answered and said unto him, My Lord and my God" (Jn 20.28).

C) The people accompanying his return, vv.31-40
"And **Barzillai** the Gileadite came down from Rogelim, and went over Jordan with the king, to conduct him over Jordan...then the king went on to Gilgal, and **Chimham** went on with him" (vv.31,40). We have met Barzillai before (17.27-29), but this is the first and last time we meet Chimham. But our brief acquaintance with him will yield some important lessons. These will emerge as we consider Barzillai, and we must now consider *(i)* his loyalty (v.31); *(ii)* his longevity (v.32); *(iii)* his liberality (v.32); *(iv)* his lowliness (vv.33-37a); *(v)* his longing (vv.37b-40).

i) His loyalty (v.31)
Unlike Shimei, Barzillai was no "fair weather friend." He was consistent in his allegiance to David. He had supported David in his enforced exile: now he witnesses his return in triumph. David was not unmindful of Barzillai's loyalty: "come thou over with me, and I will feed thee with me in Jerusalem" (v.33). Barzillai had fed David in the obscurity of Mahanaim, and now David offers him a place at his own dining-table in the capital city! Faithfulness to Christ in His rejection will be wonderfully rewarded. One day He will say, "Come thou over with me, and I will feed thee with me in heaven!" This is how Paul put it: "For I reckon that the sufferings of this present time are not worthy to be compared with the glory which shall be revealed in us" (Rom 8.18).

The loyalty of Barzillai reminds us of the loyalty of Onesiphorus to Paul in similar circumstances: "This thou knowest, that all they which are in Asia be turned away from me...The Lord give mercy to the household of Onesiphorus; for he oft refreshed me, and was not ashamed of my chain" (2 Tim 1.15-16).

ii) His longevity (v.32)
"Now Barzillai was a very aged man, even fourscore years old." He didn't anticipate many more years: "How long have I to live, that I should go up

with the king to Jerusalem?...I am this day fourscore years old..." (vv.34-35). It was this same old man who had helped David very shortly before at Mahanaim. He beautifully illustrates Psalm 92.12-14: "The righteous shall flourish like the palm tree: he shall grow like a cedar in Lebanon. Those that be planted in the house of the Lord shall flourish in the courts of our God. They shall still bring forth fruit in old age; they shall be fat and flourishing." His taste and his hearing weren't too good (v.35), but he was in good spiritual health! Old men and women have an honoured place in scripture. Caleb was older than Barzillai, and he was undiminished in spiritual **and** physical vigour! "I am this day fourscore and five years old. As yet I am as strong this day as I was in the day when Moses sent me: as my strength was then, even so is my strength now, for war, both to go out, and to come in. Now therefore give me this mountain..." (Josh 14.1-12). Moses was even older. He was "an hundred and twenty years old when he died: his eye was not dim, nor his natural force abated" (Deut 34.7). His life's work commenced at eighty! Early in the New Testament we meet Simeon and Anna. Simeon was evidently an old man. He was happy to die once "he had seen the Lord's Christ" (Lk 1.25-29). Anna was at the very least eighty-four years old, but in all probability she was well over one hundred (Lk 1.36-37). Both of them spoke about the Lord Jesus. See Luke 1.33, 38. Now there's "fruit in old age!" We ought to value older brothers and sisters in Christ, and thank God for their godliness.

iii) His liberality (v.32)
"He had provided the king of sustenance while he lay at Mahanaim; for he was a very great man." (Unlike Mephibosheth who had nothing, (v.28). Barzillai was "a very aged man" and "a very great man." See 17.27-29). We could say that he had some excellent spiritual daughters in "Mary called Magdalene... Joanna...Susanna, and many others, which ministered unto him (the Lord Jesus) of their substance" (Lk 8.3). They ministered to Him in His death as well. See, for example (Lk 23.55 - 24.1). The devotion of these godly women is a lesson to us all. We too can 'minister' to the Lord. See Acts 13.2, where the word "ministered" *(leitourgeo)* refers to priestly service. Compare Hebrews 10.11.

But we must not forget our financial responsibilities. Barzillai was evidently a wealthy man, but it is not how much a man has but how he uses it that is important. In this connection, it is interesting to notice how the apostle John prayed for Gaius: "Beloved, I wish above all things that thou mayest prosper and be in health, even as thy soul prospereth" (3 Jn v.2). It isn't often that we hear people praying that the Lord will prosper His people in financial and material terms! But John knew that Gaius was a good steward of his material possessions ("Beloved, **thou doest faithfully** whatsoever thou doest to the brethren, and to strangers" v.5), and prayed that he might have the financial ability and the necessary health to continue this good work.

At the other end of the financial scale, the poverty-stricken believers in Macedonia "abounded unto the riches of their liberality" (2 Cor 8.2). This statement is equally true of the "certain poor widow" (Mk 12.41-44). In his commentary on Mark's Gospel, Harold St.John observes that "the arithmetic of heaven differs from that of earth". She "cast more in, than all they which have cast into the treasury." The Lord Jesus was not concerned with the value of the gift in itself, but with its value to the widow. She gave all that she possessed, "for all they did cast in of their abundance: but she of her want did cast in all that she had, even all her living." Whether we are like Barzillai, or like the poor widow, or more likely, somewhere in between, may the Lord help us to meet our responsibilities in connection with the Lord's servants and the Lord's work.

iv) His lowliness (vv.33-37a)
Barzillai did not 'jump at the opportunity' to move from the "backwoods" of Mahanaim to the very heart of David's kingdom. In the first place, he didn't want to be a burden to David (v.35), and in the second he didn't feel worthy of such an honour (v.36). He had no desire to end his days in "a blaze of glory." He didn't want to make a name for himself. There is something rather beautiful about his request: "Let thy servant, I pray thee, turn back again, that I may die in mine own city, and be buried by the grave of my father and of my mother" (v.37). It reminds us of the "great woman" of Shunem. When offered a high honour in the land she simply replied, "I dwell among mine own people" (2 Kings 4.13). Whatever our age, we all ought to say "How long have I to live?" (v.34) and make sure that we spend our remaining time on earth in the interests of the Lord Jesus Christ.

Barzillai expressed the sentiments of many older people: 'I don't want to be a burden to anybody.' He was completely unselfish. Surely, too, we all share his feeling of unworthiness:

> Oh, what am I, that I should be
> The object of God's wondrous grace?
> That He should send His son to me,
> That I might see Him face to face?
>   J L Harding

v) His longing (vv.37b-40)

"But behold thy servant Chimham; let him go over with my lord the king; and do to him what shall seem good to thee. And the king answered, Chimham shall go over with me, and I will do to him that which will seem good unto thee: and whatsoever thou shalt require of me, that will I do for thee." According to Josephus, the Jewish historian, Chimham was Barzillai's son and this suggestion is supported by 1 Kings 2.7, where David gives instructions to Solomon: "But shew kindness unto the sons of Barzillai the Gileadite, and let them that be of those that eat at thy table: for so they came to me when I fled because of Absalom thy brother." Jeremiah 41.17 refers to "the habitation of Chimham, which is by Bethlehem", from which "it is supposed that David conveyed to Chimham a house upon his own paternal estate" (F. Gardiner).

Barzillai was obviously concerned about the future welfare of Chimham, and wanted the best possible prospects for him. Peter was deeply concerned about this as well: "I will not be negligent to put you always in remembrance of these things, though ye know them, and be established in the present truth. Yea, I think it meet, as long as I am in this tabernacle, to stir you up by putting you in remembrance; knowing that shortly (like Barzillai) I must put off this my tabernacle, even as our Lord Jesus Christ hath shewed me. Moreover I will endeavour that ye may be able after my decease to have these things always in remembrance" (2 Pet 1.12-15).

> 'Old man', a fellow pilgrim cried,
> 'Why build you a bridge at eventide?'
> And the builder raised his old grey head,
> 'Good friend, on the path I have come', he said,
> 'A youth is following in the twilight dim.
> You see, I am building a bridge for him.'

Paul put it like this: "And the things that thou hast heard of me among many witnesses, the same commit thou to faithful men, who shall be able to teach others also" (2 Tim 2.2). In business, "management succession" is an important issue. Future spiritual leadership should be a matter of deep concern to assembly elders.

In accordance with Barzillai's wishes "the king kissed Barzillai, and blessed him; and he returned to his own place. Then the king went on to Gilgal, and Chimham went on with him." As A. Mc Shane observes: "It ought to be the aim of all the aged and useful brethren to produce men who can fill the gaps that will be left by their passing" and, we add, to produce men who will enjoy the presence and blessing of "great David's greater Son."

D) *The animosity at his return (vv.41-43)*
David had been escorted over the Jordan by "all the people of Judah...and also half the people of Israel" (v.40) and this was deeply resented by the other northern tribes. It does not take a great deal of discernment to see here the seeds of the terrible division between north (Israel) and south (Judah) that took place after the death of Solomon. At the height of his reign, David "reigned over all Israel (all twelve tribes); and...executed judgment and justice unto all his people" (8.15). But now tempers rose. Judah insisted that they had every right to conduct the king over Jordan and repudiated the idea that there had been any favouritism or material inducement involved (v.42). Israel's counter-argument was their greater numerical strength, and the fact that the first suggestion to bring back the king had come from them (v.43, referring to v.10). The phrase "men of Judah" occurs four times in vv.40-43, and they certainly didn't know that "a soft answer turneth away wrath" (Prov.15.1): "the words of the men of Judah were fiercer than the words of the men of Israel" (v.43).

In all, it is a most unhappy picture. The "men of Israel" who had followed Absalom now wanted to share the honour of bringing David back from exile! We might have expected them to have kept a low profile! On the other hand, David might have exercised a little more diplomacy in the interests of national unity, and called for all the tribes to welcome him back. As it stood, both sides justified their stance, and neither side was willing to show the least humility. In the circumstances, Paul would have said, "Let your moderation (gentleness, yieldingness, or sweet reasonableness) be known unto all men" (Phil 4.5). It was an explosive situation, and "the self-appointed leader of the disaffected tribes, Sheba, the son of Bichri, took advantage of the discontent, and declared independence for Israel under his own leadership" (J. Baldwin). See 20.1-2.

No wonder the Psalmist said, "behold, how good and how pleasant it is for brethren to dwell together in unity" (Ps 133.1). We must all "walk worthy of the vocation wherewith ye are called, with all lowliness and meekness, with longsuffering, forbearing one another in love; endeavouring to keep the unity of the Spirit in the bond of peace" (Eph 4.1-3). See also Romans 12.10 and Philippians 2.3.

CHAPTER 20.1-26

"Then cried a wise woman out of the city"

As we have seen, the triumphant return of David from exile was marred by dissension between Judah in the south and the remaining tribes of Israel to the north. The concluding verses of Chapter 19 do not make pleasant reading. It has been said that "every silver lining has a dark cloud!" Discontent amongst God's people is the breeding ground for division, and in this chapter Sheba the son of Bichri took advantage of the situation to lead another rebellion against David. The chapter can be divided as follows: **(1)** the rebellion of Sheba (vv.1-2); **(2)** the return to Jerusalem (v.3) **(3)** the murder of Amasa (vv.4-13); **(4)** the siege of Abel (vv.14-22); **(5)** the officers of David (vv.23-26).

(1) The Rebellion of Sheba (vv.1-2)
"And there happened to be there a man of Belial, whose name was Sheba, the son of Bichri, a Benjamite: and he blew a trumpet and said, We have no part in David, neither have we inheritance in the son of Jesse: every man to his tents, O Israel." We should note the following:

a) The description of Sheba (v.1)
He is described as "a man of Belial…a Benjamite." As we have seen before, the word "Belial" means "worthless." It is used, for example, of the sons of Eli (1 Sam 2.12), Nabal (1 Sam 25.17, 25), and the two men employed by Jezebel to discredit Naboth (1 Kings 21.10). It occurs in 2 Corinthians 6.15 where it is used of Satan. We are to "follow after the things that make for peace, and things wherewith one may edify another" (Rom 14.19), and "mark them which cause divisions and offences contrary to the doctrine which ye have learned; and avoid them" (Rom 16 17). Dividing God's people is more than "worthless": it is satanic. Sheba was a Benjamite, the tribe of Saul, which reminds us that old hopes and aspirations die hard. Did Sheba want to re-establish Saul's kingdom?

b) The declaration by Sheba (v.1)

He does not describe David as "the Lord's anointed" (19.21), but as "the son of Jesse." As A. McShane points out, "It would not have helped his cause had he reminded the people that David was "the Lord's anointed." People who cause divisions in assemblies carefully avoid any reference to the God-given authority of the elders. See Acts 20.28. The cry, "We have no part in David, neither have we inheritance in the son of Jesse: every men to his tents, O Israel" (which reminds us of Luke 19.14), was repeated by the ten tribes almost fifty years later. See 1 Kings 12.16. The tongue of Sheba was certainly "full of deadly poison" (James 3.8).

c) The division by Sheba (v.2)

It was a division between "every man of Israel" and the "men of Judah." The speed at which this happened shows very clearly that there had been no true repentance over the rebellion under Absalom. It was a quick change of allegiance on the part of the northern tribes: the men of Israel had described David as "near of kin to us" and "our king" (19.42-43), but now because they hadn't got their own way, they "went up from after David, and followed Sheba the son of Bichri." But "the men of Judah clave unto their king, from Jordan even to Jerusalem", which evidently means that, unlike the other tribes, they did not desert him as he made his way to Jerusalem. Do we "cleave to the Lord?" Barnabas "exhorted them all (the Christians at Antioch) that with purpose of heart they would cleave unto the Lord" (Acts 11.23).

2) The Return to Jerusalem (v.3)

"Then David came to his house at Jerusalem; and the king took the ten women his concubines, whom he had left to keep the house, and put them in ward, and fed them, but went not in unto them. So they were shut up unto the day of their death, living in widowhood." All we can say is that David had been told what would happen to these women (12.11-12), but did nothing to protect them (15.16), with fearful results (16.21-22). Isn't this further evidence of the repercussions of David's sin? We must never forget that other people are affected by our sin and disobedience. On a wider front, this was another result of abandoning God's will in relation to marriage: "Therefore shall a man leave his father and his mother, and shall cleave unto his wife (not "wives"): and they shall be one flesh" (Gen 2.24). The expression "one flesh" contains no room whatsoever for polygamy or concubinage.

3) The Murder of Amasa (vv.4-13)

Following the death of Absalom, David had vowed to replace Joab by Amasa

2 Samuel

as his commander-in-chief. "Say ye to Amasa, Art thou not of my bone, and of my flesh? God do so to me, and more also, if thou be not captain of the host before me continually in the room of Joab" (19.13). This had a tragic outcome. This is not surprising. David did not ask the Lord for guidance. Compare 21.1. In fact, the only reference to the Lord in this chapter is made by the "wise woman" (v.19).

a) The directions to Amasa (vv.4-5)
"Then said the king to Amasa, Assemble me the men of Judah within three days, and be thou here present. So Amasa went to assemble the men of Judah." Joab who with all his faults was nevertheless a well-tried general with undoubted skill on the battle-field, was effectively demoted. It is somewhat ironic that amongst his victories was the defeat of Amasa, who was Absalom's commander-in-chief (17.25), and this could hardly have given much confidence to the men of Judah. It certainly enraged Joab, who could not tolerate any rivals. This reminds us that great care should be taken in making assembly appointments. Timothy was told, "Lay hands on no man suddenly" (1 Tim 5.22). It is inadvisable to assign responsibilities to people who do not have the confidence of their fellow-believers, and who show no particular aptitude for the task in question.

b) The delay of Amasa (vv.5-6)
"But he tarried longer than the set time which he had appointed him. And David said to Abishai, Now shall Sheba the son Bichri do us more harm than did Absalom: take thou thy lord's servants, and pursue after him, lest he get him fenced cities, and escape us." Amasa's first assignment as commander of the army revealed his shortcomings. His failure to appear within the "set time" with the army filled David with alarm, since any delay would give Sheba the opportunity to consolidate his position by capturing fortified cities in the north. Let's apply this in two ways:

i) In assembly life situations can arise which demand immediate action. These are highlighted by the words, "Know ye not that a little leaven leaveneth the whole lump? (1 Cor 5.6; Gal 5.9). In the first case it is moral evil, and in the second it is doctrinal error. They must be dealt with immediately. If not, they will spread. To delay is disastrous.

ii) In our personal lives things can take place which also demand immediate action. For example, we have to ensure that unclean thoughts or practices are not allowed to take root in our minds and lives. "Let not sin therefore reign in our mortal body, that ye should obey it in the lusts thereof" (Rom 6.12).

Notice in passing that David asked Abishai, not Joab, to lead the expedition against Sheba. Joab was certainly there, and it wasn't long before he made his presence felt, but David was evidently doing all in his power to exclude him from leadership.

c) The death of Amasa (vv.7-13)
The expedition reaches "the great stone which is in Gibeon (some ten miles north-west of Jerusalem") and Amasa reappears to take command. But not for long. It was all too much for Joab: "And Joab's garment that he had put on was girded unto him, and upon it a girdle with a sword fastened upon his loins in the sheath thereof; and as he went forth it fell out." Precisely what happened next is not easy to determine. Did he pick up the sword, and use it on the unsuspecting Amasa? Or did he have another sword underneath his cloak? One thing is clear, Joab was quite experienced in killing people in cold blood. He had done exactly the same about thirty years before: "And when Abner was returned to Hebron, Joab took him aside in the gate to speak with him quietly, and smote him there under the fifth rib, that he died..." (3.27). Like Abner before him, Amasa suspected nothing: "And Joab said unto Amasa, Art thou in health my brother? And Joab took Amasa by the beard with the right hand to kiss him. But Amasa took no heed to the sword that was in Joab's hand: so he smote him therewith in the fifth rib, and shed out his bowels to the ground, and struck him not again; and he died."

Perhaps Solomon was thinking of Amasa when he wrote: "He that hateth dissembleth with his lips, and layeth up deceit within him; when he speaketh fair, believe him not: for there are seven abominations in his heart" (Prov 26.25). Joab kissed and then murdered Amasa. Judas Iscariot kissed the Lord Jesus, and in so doing betrayed Him (Lk 22.47-48). Whilst the Lord Jesus was not surprised by the hypocrisy of Judas, false friendship isn't always easy to detect at first as far as we are concerned. But let's make sure that *we* are not in the business of deceiving other people. David speaks about "a double heart" (Ps 12.2).

As J. Baldwin observes, "The pursuing army was aghast at the sight of general Amasa's gruesome body; everyone halted in order to weigh up what had happened and how to proceed, but Joab's man on duty made sure that all the people got the message: Joab was in control of the king's army, though all unbeknown to the king! ("He that favoureth Joab, and he that is for David, let him go after Joab", v.11). Once the corpse was removed, there was no obstacle to prevent the total army's pursuit of Sheba under Joab's leadership. Abishai disappears from the record, unable to hold his own once Joab had asserted his authority."

But this was not the end of the matter. After the execution of Sheba, Joab "returned to Jerusalem unto the king", and "was over all the host of Israel" (vv.22-23). But on his deathbed, David gave Solomon the following instructions: "Moreover thou knowest also what Joab the son of Zeruiah did to me, and what he did to the two captains of the hosts of Israel, unto Abner the son of Ner, and unto Amasa the son of Jether, whom he slew, and shed the blood of war in peace, and put the blood of war upon his girdle that was about his loins...Do therefore according to thy wisdom, and let not his hoar head go down to the grave in peace" (1 Kings 2.5-6). Later, Solomon told Benaiah to "fall upon him (Joab), and bury him; that thou mayest take away the innocent blood, which Joab shed, from me, and from the house of my father. And the Lord shall return his blood upon his own head, who fell upon two men more righteous and better than he, and slew them with the sword, my father David not knowing thereof, to wit, Abner the son of Ner, captain of the host of Israel, and Amasa the son of Jether, captain of the host of Judah" (2 Kings 2.31-34). We must never forget the oft-quoted text: "Be not deceived; God is not mocked: for whatsoever a man soweth, that shall he also reap" (Gal 6.7).

4) The Siege of Abel (vv.14-22)
Abel or Abel-beth-Maachah (1 Kings 15.20; 2 Kings 15.29) lay at the extreme north of the land, near the city of Dan. It means "meadow of the house of Maacah" and may be connected in some way to Maachah, Absalom's mother (2 Sam 3.3). She certainly came from that direction.

a) The war against the city (vv.14-15)
It looks as though the people who originally supported Sheba ("every man of Israel", v.2) made no attempt to stop Joab, and probably joined the expedition. "And he went through all the tribes of Israel unto Abel, and to Beth-maachah, and all the Berites: and they were gathered together, and went also after him." This is not surprising. Joab's reputation was enough to frighten anyone into submission! Joab employed the usual siege tactics. The "bank against the city" refers to a siege mound that enabled the

attackers to approach the city wall by a gentle gradient and pound it with battering rams. The "bank" was built in the "trench" or "ditch" (not the same word as 1 Samuel 17.20 etc) which was part of the city fortifications.

It is worth observing that Abel was under siege because of a man who refused to recognise "the Lord's anointed." People who refuse to bow to the authority of Christ in their lives bring trouble wherever they go. See Luke 19.41-44.

b) The wisdom of the woman (vv.16-19)
"Then cried a wise woman out of the city, Hear, hear; say, I pray you unto Joab, Come near hither, that I may speak with thee. And when he was come near unto her, the woman said, Art thou Joab? And he answered, I am he. Then she said unto him, Hear the words of thine handmaid. And he answered, I do hear." This is the second "wise woman" in 2 Samuel. Compare 14.2. (We shouldn't forget the "poor wise man" who "by his wisdom delivered the city", Eccl 9.13-15). This reminds us that wisdom is not the sole possession of men. The assembly that ignores its sisters makes a serious mistake. We should notice the "meek and quiet spirit" (1 Pet 3.4) of the "wise women" (she made no attempt to harangue Joab), together with her humility ("thine handmaid"). She made three main points:

i) The wisdom of the city.
"They were wont to speak in old time, saying, They shall surely ask counsel at Abel: and so they ended the matter" (v.18). Evidently, Abel had been celebrated for the wisdom of its inhabitants, and the "wise woman" therefore makes the point that the voice of the city should be heard. Joab could therefore expect a wise answer, not an intemperate response. Paul refers to "the wisdom of the wise...the wisdom of this world...the wisdom of men" (1 Cor 1.19,20; 2.5), but spiritual wisdom is entirely different. It is acquired in the Lord's presence. This is illustrated in Deuteronomy 17.8-13 where a matter too difficult for local settlement was to be brought to the "place which the Lord thy God shall choose" and decided by "the priest that standeth to minister there before the Lord thy God." We are told that "the priest's lips should keep knowledge, and they should seek the law at his mouth: for he is the messenger of the Lord of hosts" (Mal 2.7). Wisdom and prayer are indissolubly linked: "If any of you lack wisdom, let him ask of God, that giveth to all men liberally, and upbraideth not, and it shall be given him" (James 1.5). Spiritual wisdom can only be acquired through communion with God over His word. Notice references to wisdom in Colossians: 1.9, 1.28, 3.16, 4.5.

ii) The peaceful disposition of the city. The "wise woman" spoke in the name of the city in saying "I am one of them that are peaceable and faithful in Israel." The city did not have a reputation for belligerence and warfare. Wisdom and peace go together: "But the wisdom that is from above is first pure, then peaceable, gentle, and easy to be intreated, full of mercy and good fruits, without partiality, and without hypocrisy" (Jas 3.17).

iii) The threat to the city. "Thou seekest to destroy a city and a mother in Israel: why wilt thou swallow up the inheritance of the Lord?" Quite clearly Joab who, unlike the "wise woman", showed no spiritual appreciation whatever of the Lord's people, had not given any reason for the attack. Although the guidelines in Deuteronomy 20 refer to an attack on a foreign city, it is worth noticing that the first move was to "proclaim peace unto it" (v.10). But Joab hadn't even taken into consideration the reputation of Abel. The city was "a mother in Israel", which suggests that it was a mother-figure to the surrounding villages, and "the inheritance of the Lord." The "wise woman" makes it very clear that Joab should not treat the Lord's people in this way. God's people are "to consider one another to provoke unto love and to good works" (Heb 10.24).

c) The withdrawal from the city (vv.20-22)
Having ascertained from Joab why the city was under siege, and how it could be lifted, the "woman went unto all the people in her wisdom." She had identified the precise problem, and was able to report that it could be solved satisfactorily with a minimum of casualties. People like that are invaluable. So often problems arise and wholesale damage results because they are not dealt with properly. The process of "battering" (v.15) is allowed to continue without any intervention. Notice how Paul dealt with the various factions at Corinth (1 Cor 1.11-12) and the warring sisters at Philippi (Phil 4.2).

Once the inhabitants of the city had "cut off the head of Sheba the son of Bichri, and cast it out to Joab", the army "returned from the city, every man to his tent. And Joab returned to Jerusalem unto the king." Once again, Joab returned victorious after saving the kingdom. His capability and confidence was beyond doubt. But he had murdered a man in the process. David could hardly discipline Joab, for he too had murdered a man in cold blood. See 2 Samuel 12.9. Sin brings terrible complications, doesn't it? Notice that the chapter begins with Sheba blowing a trumpet (v.1) and ends with Joab blowing a trumpet (v.22). Galatians 6.7 again!

5) The Officers of David (vv.23-26)

These verses should be compared with 2 Samuel 8.16-18. At that time, David was at the height of his reign. Now, having re-established his authority over the kingdom after some tumultuous events, we have a second list of his ministers of state.

i) Joab (v.23). He was "over all the host of Israel." Having successfully disposed of all rivals (including Amasa), he presided as the unchallenged commander-in-chief. But we look in vain for him amongst David's "mighty men" (23.8).

ii) Benaiah (v.23). He remained over "the Cherethites and over the Pelethites." As we noted in ch. 8.18 they were evidently David's bodyguard. It seems ironical that Benaiah should follow Joab here. He executed Joab, and replaced him! See 2 Kings 2.28-35.

iii) Adoram (v.24). He was a new minister of state with a new post. "And Adoram was over the tribute." He is evidently the same person as Adoniram (1 Kings 4.6). He is called Adoram again in 1 Kings 12.18, and Hadoram in 2 Chron 10.18. He served David, Solomon and Rehoboam (at the beginning of whose reign he was stoned to death by Israel), and must therefore have received his appointment at quite a young age! Since the word "tribute" means "tributary labourers" (Keil & Delitzsch, supported by Gesenius), he had the unenviable task of gathering "forced labourers for public works" (A. McShane). This appears to have involved Israelites at times (e.g. 1 Kings 5.13-14) and foreigners taken captive in war (e.g.1 Kings 9.20-22). Adoram died when he attempted to "raise the tribute" in Israel (1 Kings 12.18).

iv) Jehoshaphat (v.24). He was still in office, and went on to serve Solomon as well (1 Kings 4.3). He was the kings "remembrancer." A very important job!

v) Sheva (v.25). He had evidently replaced Seraiah as David's "Secretary of State." The office work must continue!

vi) Zadok and Abiathar (v.25). Zadok remained in office, but Ahimelech had been replaced by Abiathar. But Abiathar's days as priest were numbered. He backed Adonijah (1 Kings 1.7), and was relieved of his office by Solomon (1 Kings 26-27). It seems from 1 Kings 2.35 that Abiathar was regarded as the senior of the two priests.

vii) Ira (v.26). "And Ira also the Jairite was a chief ruler *(cohen)* about David." He was a new appointment, and replaced David's sons who are called "chief rulers" *(cohen)* in 8.18. There are no prizes for guessing why they were replaced! Two of them were dead anyway! Ira was certainly not "a personal priest alongside Zadok and Abiathar" as H. Mowvley suggests, but a confidential adviser. The word *cohen* is translated "friend" in 1 Kings 4.5.

CHAPTER 21.1-22

"God was intreated for the land"

The last four chapters of 2 Samuel are a kind of epilogue or appendix and cover different periods in the life of David. The six parts in the section form a concentric pattern as follows:

1) A disaster during his reign (21.1-14)
2) A role of honour during his reign (21.15-22)
3) A Psalm during his reign (22.1-51)
3) A Psalm at the end of his reign (23.1-7)
2) A role of honour at the end of his reign (23.8-39)
1) A disaster at the end of his reign (24.1-25)

The section commences with a legacy from the past, and ends with a legacy for the future. David inherited a problem caused by Saul (21.4), and made provision for Solomon by purchasing Araunah's threshing-floor (24.24) which became the site on which the temple was built (2 Chron 3.1). It is worth noticing that both episodes end similarly: "God was intreated for the land" (21.14): "the Lord was intreated for the land" (24.25).

2 Samuel 21 clearly divides into two parts: **(1)** Avenging the Gibeonites (vv.1-14); **(2)** Slaying the giants (vv.15-22).

1) Avenging the Gibeonites (vv.1-14)
"Then there was a famine in the days of David three years, year after year." While it is not possible to fix the exact time, it does seem that the three-year famine took place within the first ten years of David's reign over all Israel (5.1-5). While A. McShane suggests that "it is unlikely that the famine would be long delayed after the death of Saul, otherwise the people would have been at a loss to know why the evil committed by their king had been passed over for so long", it must have taken place after David's mercy to

2 Samuel

Mephibosheth (9.1-13) since David spared him from death (21.7). We can look at these verses as follows: *(a)* the enquiry (v.1a); *(b)* the explanation (v.1b); *(c)* the expiation (vv.2-9); *(d)* the entombment (vv.10-14)

a) The enquiry (v.1a)
David realised that something was seriously wrong and "enquired of the Lord." We tend to regard famines as natural disasters, but in Old Testament times they were evidence of divine displeasure. See, for example, 1 Kings 8.35: "When heaven is shut up, and there is no rain, because they have sinned against thee"; Psalm 105.16, "Moreover he called for a famine upon the land: he brake the whole staff of bread"; Jeremiah 24.10, "And I will send the sword, the famine, and the pestilence, among them." It is noteworthy that whilst David "enquired of the Lord", nothing similar is said in Ruth 1.1

There is another kind of famine. The Psalmist calls it "leanness" of soul (Ps 106.15). Gaius certainly did not suffer from it! His soul prospered! (3 Jn v.2). He was "nourished up in the words of faith and of good doctrine" (1 Tim 4.6). Loss of appetite for God's word, and for fellowship and communion with Him, are a signal that something is desperately wrong.

If we have lost "the joy of the Lord" (Neh 8.10) we must follow David's example and "enquire of the Lord" to ascertain the cause. If assembly life has become barren and there seems to be little or no "fruit of the Spirit", then we must follow David's example again in this way. It is worth noticing that God deliberately brought famine conditions upon His people when they failed to give Him first place. Read Haggai 1.9-11 carefully. "Leanness" of soul is a "wake-up call" from God. Tragically, the church at Laodicea just didn't realise that they were stricken by spiritual famine. See Revelation 3.17.

b) The explanation (v.1b)
"And the Lord answered, It is for Saul, and for his bloody house, because he slew the Gibeonites." Further information follows: "Saul sought to slay them in his zeal to the children of Israel and Judah" (v.2). He is described as "the man that consumed us, and that devised against us that we should be destroyed from remaining in any of the coasts of Israel" (v.5). Saul's crime against the Gibeonites was equally a crime against God. He had offended the Lord. This is something we must never forget. While other people may suffer from our wrong-doing, sin is chiefly an offence against God.

We do not know **when** Saul committed this crime. The withholding of this information is significant since it reminds us that while events may not be recorded in history they **are** recorded in heaven. God knew exactly when it happened! Doesn't this remind us that "neither is there any creature that is not manifest in his sight: but all things are naked and opened unto the eyes of him with whom we have to do?" (Heb 4.13).

Saul had violated the covenant made by Joshua and Israel with the Gibeonites some four hundred years previously. See Joshua 9. While the Gibeonites had taken Joshua and the princes of Israel "for a ride", the covenant could not be dissolved "because the princes of the congregation had sworn unto them **by the Lord God of Israel"** (v.18). (Do remember that they were "taken for a ride" because they "asked not counsel at the mouth of the Lord", v.14). Let's say two things here:

i) The passage of time does not mean that we are free to alter our mind. In this case, four hundred years had passed, but God expected His people to maintain the national commitment made in His name. He expects the same from us as well. Centuries have passed since God's word was written. But it remains the unalterable word of God. Are **we** committed to it?

ii) The supposed interests of God's people do not mean that we can alter our mind. In this case, Saul thought that it was in the best interests of Israel and Judah to eliminate the Gibeonites. He was certainly not the last man to think in this way. There are plenty of people about today who think that God's people can be better served by overriding the original teaching of God's word in favour of something more in keeping with modern trends. Saul's "zeal to the children of Israel and Judah" did not compensate in any way for his disobedience.

These verses emphasise the serious consequences of a broken covenant, reminding us that we cannot expect to "play fast and loose" with the word of God, and escape unscathed. Disobedience brings solemn consequences.

c) The expiation (vv.2-9)
"Wherefore David said unto the Gibeonites, What shall I do for you? and wherewith shall I make the atonement (*kaphar*: the covering of the sin committed against them: its removal from sight), that ye may bless the inheritance of the Lord?" This is followed by the Gibeonites" request (vv.4-6a), and David's response (vv.6b-9). David began well by "enquiring of the

Lord" (v.1), but we are not told that he asked for further help. Sometimes we ask for the Lord's guidance, and then proceed without further reference to Him.

i) The request (vv.4-6a). "We will have no silver nor gold of Saul, nor of his house; neither for us shalt thou kill any man in Israel…The man that consumed us, and that devised against us that we should be destroyed from remaining in any of the coasts of Israel, let seven men of his sons be delivered unto us, and we will hang them up unto the Lord in Gibeah of Saul, whom the Lord did choose." The Gibeonites evidently appealed to Numbers 35.31-33: "Moreover ye shall take no satisfaction (i.e. "no silver or gold") for the life of a murderer, which is guilty of death: but he shall surely be put to death…So ye shall not pollute the land wherein ye are: for blood it defileth the land: and the land cannot be cleansed of the blood that is shed therein, but by the blood of him that shed it." Doesn't this remind us that "without shedding of blood is no remission" (Heb 9.22) and that we have "not been redeemed with corruptible things, as silver and gold…but with the precious blood of Christ" (1 Pet 1.18-19). Notice the words, "Gibeah of Saul, whom the Lord did choose." This emphasises his responsibility. Saul abused his particular privileges by overriding the covenant with the Gibeonites.

This raises an important question. Given that "the land cannot be cleansed of the blood that is shed therein, but by the blood of him that shed it", how can the death of the "seven men of his sons" be reconciled with the fact that "the fathers shall not be put to death for the children, neither shall the children be put to death for the fathers: every man shall be put to death for his own sin" (Deut 24.16). Amaziah certainly obeyed this clear command: "He slew his servants which had slain the king his father. But the children of the murderers he slew not: according unto that which is written in the book of the law of Moses…The father shall not be put to death for the children, nor the children be put to death for the fathers; but every man shall be put to death for his own sin" (2 Kings 14.5-6). The answer to this difficult problem may lie with the role played by the "seven men of his sons."

ii) The response (vv.6b-9). "And the king said, I will give them. It is important to notice that the Lord did say in answer to David's enquiry: It is for Saul, **and for his bloody house…**"(v.1). We know that Rizpah was Saul's concubine (2 Sam 3.7) so that Armoni and Mephibosheth (not to be confused with

Jonathan's son) were his direct sons. Not "sons" in the sense of grandchildren or descendants. They **could** therefore have been old enough to be implicated in the slaughter of the Gibeonites. The "five sons of Michal the daughter of Saul" (they were actually the sons of Merab) **could** fall into the same category, but it does have to be said that they were evidently younger than the two sons of Rizpah. The answer to the difficulty may lie in this direction, although the suggestion is not confirmed by any known commentators.

It should be noted that Michal, Saul's daughter had no children of her own (2 Sam 6.23), but since we are told that the five sons were "brought up for Adriel the son of Barzillai the Meholathite" we can assume that his wife Merab (1 Sam 18.19), Michal's sister, was either dead or incapacitated. They are therefore called "the five sons of Michal." Bearing in mind, however, that the Hebrew means "borne to" (JND) as opposed to "brought up" (AV), the passage could be read as follows: "and the five sons [of the sister of] Michal the daughter of Saul, whom she had borne to Adriel" (JND). The statement by Keil & Delitzsch that "the name *Michal*, which stands in the text, is founded upon an error of memory or a copyist's mistake" is highly dangerous and should be regarded with suspicion.

Mephibosheth, the son of Jonathan was spared (v. 7). Had he been included with the seven "sons", David would have become guilty of the same crime as Saul. He would have broken an oath. "But the king spared Mephibosheth, the son of Jonathan the son of Saul, because of the Lord's oath that was between them, between David and Jonathan the son of Saul." We must beware of inconsistency!

David "delivered them (the 'seven sons') into the hands of the Gibeonites, and they hanged them in the hill before the Lord: and they fell all seven together, and were put to death in the days of harvest, in the first days, in the beginning of barley harvest." (The reference to "barley harvest" evidently refers to the time of year, rather than the existence of a harvest to reap). It was fitting that they should be "hanged...in the hill", referring to "Gibeah of Saul" (v.6), since Gibeah was Saul's home (1 Sam 10.26). The fact that they were "hanged...before the Lord" emphasises that the crime against the Gibeonites was sin against God. The public display of their bodies (the word "hanged" means "to fasten to a stake") emphasises that justice was seen to be done. As F. Gardiner observes, "the sin had been outrageous; its punishment must be conspicuous." It was regarded as a national sin: hence the famine. This is why Deuteronomy 21.22-23 did not apply in this case.

2 Samuel

d) The entombment (vv.10-14)
According to Keil & Delitzsch, barley harvest took place "about the middle of Nisan, our April." These commentators suggest that Rizpah "took sackcloth (the coarse hairy cloth that was worn as mourning), and spread it for her upon the rock" as a bed. However, F. Gardiner *(Ellicott's Commentary)* suggests that "she spread the sackcloth as a tent to form a rough shelter during the long watch." The "long watch" lasted until it began to rain as the sign that God's anger had been appeased. It is noteworthy that Rizpah said nothing. It was "a time to keep silence" (Eccl 3.7).

David respected Saul as "the Lord's anointed" (1 Sam 26.9) during his life and continued to do so after his death. Touched by the devotion of Rizpah to her sons by Saul, he arranged for the bones of Saul and Jonathan to be exhumed at Jabesh-gilead (1 Sam 31.11-13) and reburied, with the bones of his seven descendants who had been put to death, in "the sepulchre of Kish his (Saul's) father" at Zelah in Benjamin. It can be said of David that he was not "overcome of evil", but overcame "evil with good" (Rom 12.21).

2) Slaying the Giants (vv.15-22)
Four incidents are recorded here, of which all except the first appear again, with differences of detail, in 1 Chronicles 20.4-8, which commence as follows: "and it came to pass after this", that is, after the final defeat of the Ammonites (vv.1-3), which is also described in 2 Samuel 12.26-31. The four giants all belonged to the same family as Goliath. "These four were born to the giant in Gath, and fell by the hand of David, and by the hand of his servants" (v.22). It has been suggested that *rapha* (meaning "giant") was actually a family name so that we could read: "These four were born to Raphah in Gath." We are not told why these four cases are cited. Possibly they were regarded, like Goliath, as the Philistine champions, and therefore their death at the hands of David and his men represented total victory over the Philistines. The passage covers a series of engagements: "after this...there was again a battle...there was yet a battle" (vv.18,19,20).

a) Ishbi-benob (vv.15-17)
He was killed by **Abishai**. "Moreover the Philistines had yet war again with Israel; and David went down, and his servants with him, and fought against the Philistines: and David waxed faint." We should notice three things in these verses:

i) The age of David. He "waxed faint", which suggests that he was no

longer in "the prime of life." But this did not blunt his enthusiasm. David did not "take early retirement" and make for the coast! He was still willing to engage the enemy in warfare. There are many servants of God, brothers and sisters, who "wax faint" but remain in "the front line" of the spiritual battle.

ii) The aim of Ishbi-benob. "And Ishbi-benob, which was of the sons of the giant, the weight of whose spear weighed three hundred shekels of brass in weight (said to be about eight pounds: half the weight of Goliath's spear, 1 Sam 17.7), he being girded with a new sword (or 'new armour'; see JND), thought to have slain David" (v.16). Ishbi-benob evidently intended to tackle David with an old weapon, but in new armour! The enemy has always got something new to wear! Perhaps a new evolutionary theory, or a modern interpretation of the Bible. The incident also reminds us that spiritual leaders are "right in the firing line." No wonder Paul told the Ephesian elders to "take heed...**unto yourselves**, and to all the flock" (Acts 20.28).

iii) The aid of Abishai. "But Abishai the son of Zeruiah succoured him (helped or aided him) and smote the Philistine, and killed him." Now there's a nice touch. Abishai, David's nephew, was obviously a younger man, and it is always encouraging to see younger men helping older men. This resulted in a general concern for David's welfare. "Then the men of David sware unto him, saying, Thou shalt go no more out with us to battle, that thou quench not the light of Israel." (Compare 1 Kings 11.36). They obviously valued him immensely, and this is confirmed, for different reasons, in 2 Samuel 18.3, "But now thou art worth ten thousand of us: therefore now it is better that thou succour us out of the city." David had become the "light of Israel" because the Lord was his light: "For thou art my lamp, O Lord: and the Lord will lighten my darkness" (22.29), or as it appears in Psalm 18.28, "For thou wilt light my candle: the Lord my God will enlighten my darkness." The enemy will always attempt to extinguish the light. The "light of Israel" certainly guided others, as we shall see next. Paul said, "Be ye followers of me, even as I also am of Christ" (1 Cor 11.1).

b) Saph (v.18)
He was killed by **Sibbechai.** "And it came to pass after this, that there was again a battle with the Philistines at Gob (Gezer: possibly in or near Philistine territory): then Sibbechai the Hushathite slew Saph, which was one of the sons of the giant." Saph is called Sippai in 1 Chronicles 20.4. According to 1 Chronicles 27.11, Sibbechai was "the leader of the eighth division of the

army" (Keil & Delitzsch). Sibbecai (a slightly different spelling, but the same man) is mentioned in 1 Chronicles 11.29, and we are told that he is known as "Mebunnai the Hushathite" in 2 Samuel 23.27. He was one of David's "mighty men." We know a great deal about Abishai, but comparatively little about Sibbechai. But his exploit is recorded. God is aware of our service for him. The fact that we may be quite obscure people does not mean that we cannot be "mighty men" for God! Remember the "others" in Hebrews 11.35-38.

c) Lahmi-Goliath's brother (v.19)
He was killed by **Elhanan.** "And there was again a battle in Gob with the Philistines, where Elnathan the son of Jaare-oregim (meaning "forest of the weavers"), slew the brother of Goliath the Gittite, the staff of whose spear was like a weaver's beam." Compare this with 1 Chronicles 20.5: "And there was war again with the Philistines; and Elhanan the son of Jair slew Lahmi the brother of Goliath the Gittite, whose spear staff was like a weaver's beam." These verses have been thoroughly debated. Some have concluded that there were two Goliaths, and others that Elhanan is another name for David! But as Keil and Delitzsch observe, "there is nothing at all strange in the reference to a brother of Goliath, who was also a powerful giant, and carried a spear like Goliath." This must have been a tremendous encouragement to David. One of his men confronted and defeated Goliath's brother! David could no longer "run through a troop" and leap "over a wall", but here was someone who could repeat his victory in the valley of Elah. There is nothing more satisfying to older men than the sight of young men doing exploits for God (Dan 11.32).

d) Sixdigit (v.20)
He was killed by **Jonathan.** "And there was yet another battle in Gath (in Philistine territory), where was a man of great stature, that had on every hand six fingers, and on every foot six toes, four and twenty in number; and he also was born to the giant. And when he defied Israel, Jonathan the son of Shimeah the brother of David slew him." (Can you improve on "Sixdigits?"). Jonathan was David's nephew. Shimeah is elsewhere called Shammah (1 Sam 16.9,17.13). Jonathan's brother was Jonadab (2 Sam 13.3,32) and he is described as "a very subtil man." He was certainly not a good friend to Amnon (2 Sam 13.3). But his brother Jonathan was made of different stuff. Brothers can be "as different as chalk and cheese." Jonadab caused uncle David a great deal of distress, but Jonathan caused him a great deal of joy. After all, he followed in his uncle's footsteps! The New Testament

tells us to "obey them that have the rule over you, and submit yourselves: for they watch for your souls, as they that must give account, that they may do it (the work) with joy (as in the case of Jonathan), and not with grief (as in the case of Jonadab): for that is unprofitable for you" (Heb 13.17).

The closing statement, "these four were born to the giant in Gath, and fell by the hand of David, and by the hand of his servants", includes David because although he was no longer in the "front line", he remained the guide and inspiration of his people. We may not always be conspicuous in our service, but our prayerful ministry and encouragement is vital.

CHAPTER 22.1-28

"And David spake unto the Lord the words of this song"

David's song of thanksgiving in this chapter also occurs as Psalm 18, and the differences between them are "due doubtless to revisions by David himself in preparing the Psalm for the chief musician for use in the public services" (A.G. Clarke).

INTRODUCTION (v.1)

The introduction is virtually the same as the heading to Psalm 18: "And David spake unto the Lord the words of this song in the day that the Lord had delivered him out of the hand of all his enemies, and out of the hand of Saul" (v.1). It is generally suggested that the song was composed shortly after the battle of Gilboa (1 Sam 31), but its heading and structure suggest a later date. In this connection it is noteworthy that similar words occur in 2 Samuel 7.1, "And it came to pass, when the king sat in his house, and the Lord had given him rest round about from all his enemies..." As A. McShane observes, "the song was David's expression of appreciation for his deliverance from his enemies in general, and from Saul in particular." Since the previous chapter refers to both Saul and the Philistines, David's song is in exactly the right place! It clearly divides into two sections.

i) David's thanksgiving to God for **delivering** him from his enemies (vv.2-28). It is noticeable that David does not refer here to any attempt on his part to destroy them. Bearing in mind that the Lord delivered David from the murderous intentions of Saul, and that David never lifted a finger against him, it does seem that this section of the song refers to that particular time in David's life. He was delivered "out of the hand of Saul."

ii) David's thanksgiving to God for enabling him to **destroy** his enemies (vv.29-51). This speaks for itself. David pursued and consumed his

Chapter 22A

adversaries to the extent that "I beat them as small as the dust of the earth, I did stamp them as the mire of the street" (v.43). These were external enemies, principally the Philistines (2 Sam 5.17-25). He was delivered "out of the hand of **all** his enemies."

The length of the song demands two studies, and we will follow the division suggested above:

1) David's Deliverance from his Enemies (vv.2-28)
This part of his song can be divided into four parts **(a)** David's deliverer (vv.2-4); **(b)** David's distress (vv.5-7); **(c)** David's deliverance (vv.8-20); **(d)** David's integrity (vv.21-28).

a) David's deliverer (vv.2-4)
"The Lord is my rock, and my fortress, and my deliverer; the God of my rock; in him will I trust: he is my shield, and the horn of my salvation, my high tower, and my refuge, my saviour; thou savest me from violence. I will call on the Lord, who is worthy to be praised: so shall I be saved from mine enemies." It is worth noticing that in Psalm 18 David's thanksgiving is prefaced by the words "I will love thee, O Lord, my strength" (v.1). That was his spontaneous reaction as he revised the manuscript for the chief musician. Compare Psalm 116.1, "I love the Lord, because he hath heard my voice and my supplications."

The opening section of the song is a veritable gold mine. The Lord was everything to David: "*my* rock...*my* fortress...*my* deliverer...*my* rock...*my* shield...*my* salvation...*my* high tower...*my* refuge...*my* saviour." J. Baldwin calls this "a torrent of metaphors" which "proclaims to the world that David has found his God to be a rock of ages, utterly dependable in all kinds of dangerous situations, infinitely resourceful in delivering His servant from death." We can think about this in terms of the past, the present, and the future.

i) The past. It does seem that in all probability David is recalling here particular occasions on which God had delivered him. Rocks and strongholds (fortresses) figure prominently in the story of his persecution by Saul. The word **"rock"** occurs twice in our English version (in v.2 and v.3), but the Hebrew words are different.

The first word is *sela* (v.2) and it refers to an elevated rock or a cliff. It occurs in 1 Samuel 23.25, "David...came down into a **rock**." Notice that David called the place "Sela-ham-mahlekoth" (the rock of the separations or divisions).

The second word is *sur* (v.3) and it refers to a sharp rock. It is used in 1 Samuel 24.2, "Saul...went to seek David and his men upon the **rocks** of the wild goats." The word "fortress" is *metsudah*: it occurs in 1 Samuel 22.4, "they dwelt with him all the while that David was in the **hold**", and 1 Samuel 24.22, "David and his men gat them up unto the **hold**." (The word reflects in the name "Masada", Herod's well-known fortress by the Dead Sea). Perhaps David was thinking of these incidents at this point in the song, and therefore used the same words.

David gladly acknowledges that his past preservation did not lie merely in rocks and strongholds, but in the Lord Himself. He proved that "the name of the Lord is a strong tower: the righteous runneth into it, and is safe" (Prov 18.10). In the millennium, "a man shall be as an hiding place from the wind, and a covert from the tempest; as rivers of water in a dry place, as the shadow of a great rock *(sela)* in a weary land" (Is 32.2). The "man" is "the man Christ Jesus" (1 Tim 2.5).

ii) The present. We should notice that David does not say, 'The Lord **was** my rock, and my fortress, and my deliverer", but "The Lord **is** my rock, and my fortress, and my deliverer." The Lord who had delivered David in the past had not changed. In New Testament language, He is "the same yesterday, and to day, and for ever" (Heb 13.8). Paul put it like this: "But we had the sentence of death in ourselves, that we should not trust in ourselves, but in God which raiseth the dead: who delivered us from so great a death, and doth deliver: in whom we trust that he will yet deliver us" (2 Cor 1.9-10).

iii) The future. "In him will I trust (v.3)...I will call on the Lord, who is worthy to be praised: so shall I be saved from mine enemies (v4)." Whilst David wrote the song "in the day that the Lord had delivered him out of the hand of all his enemies" (v.1), he had no illusions about the future. There would be more enemies! That would mean continuing faith and more prayer! He was confident that the Lord who had never failed him in the past could be completely trusted for help and deliverance in the future. Whilst David was a powerful king with "mighty men", he placed his entire confidence in the Lord. He is "worthy to be praised."

b) David's distress (vv.5-7)

"When the waves of death encompassed me about, the floods of ungodly men made me afraid; the sorrows of hell compassed me about; the snares of death prevented me: in my distress I called upon the Lord, and cried to my God: and he did hear my voice out of his temple, and my cry did enter into his ears." We must notice:

i) The crisis. David went in fear of his life for something like seven years, but there was one particular occasion on which capture and death seemed inevitable. "And Saul went on this side of the mountain, and David and his men on that side of the mountain: and David made haste to get away for fear of Saul; for Saul and his men compassed David and his men round about to take them" (1 Sam 23.26). David is possibly referring to this occasion here. It is worth pointing out that the words "sorrows of hell" (v.6) should not be regarded as divine judgment. David is not referring to the destination described in Luke 16.23, but to death in a general sense. The word *sheol* is often translated "grave" (e.g. Isaiah 38.10).

ii) The cry. In another Psalm, David wrote: "The eyes of the Lord are upon the righteous, and his ears are open to their cry." (34.12). We mustn't miss the personal relationship here: "I called upon the Lord, and cried to *my* God." This is why his prayer was heard. "The Lord rewarded me according to my righteousness...for I have kept the ways of the Lord, and have not wickedly departed from *my* God" (vv.21-22). As J. Baldwin notes, the words, "he did hear *my* voice" and "*my* cry did enter into his ears", mean that God distinguishes "the individual's need amid all the cries that reach His ears." The "temple" (v.7) is "the sanctuary in the heavens, the dwelling place, the palace of Jehovah, as in Psalm 11.4" (J. Flanigan, commenting on Psalm 18.6).

We should pause now and remember that the Lord Jesus cried "My God, my God, why hast thou forsaken me?" (Ps 22.1) He had every right to say "My God", but He was forsaken. We know why this took place. God "made him to be sin for us, who knew no sin; that we might be made the righteousness of God in him" (2 Cor 5.21). But we should add that "when he had offered up prayers and supplications with strong crying and tears unto him that was able to save him from death (out of death)" he "was heard in that he feared (because of his piety)" (Heb 5.7). He was not saved from dying, but He was saved "out of death" by resurrection.

2 Samuel

c) David's deliverance (vv.8-20)

The vivid imagery in this section is reminiscent of the phenomena accompanying God's presence at Sinai (Ex 19.16-20). Compare "the earth shook and trembled" (v.8) with the whole mount quaked greatly" (Ex 19.18). Compare "there went up a smoke out of his nostrils" (v.9) with "mount Sinai was altogether on a smoke" (Ex 19.18). Compare "fire out of his mouth devoured" (v.9) with "the Lord descended upon it in fire" (Ex 19.18). Compare "He bowed the heavens also, and came down" (v.10) with "And the Lord came down upon mount Sinai" (Ex 19.20). Compare "the most High uttered his voice" (v.14) with "God answered him by a voice" (Ex 19.19).

As far as we are aware, David's deliverance was not accompanied by the audible, visible and tangible evidences of God's presence at Sinai, but He was present in mighty power to save His servant. The language used here suggests a violent storm. The "smoke" (v.9) suggests a thundercloud; the "fire out of His mouth" (v.9) suggests sheet lightning; the "dark waters, and thick clouds of the skies" suggest rain-clouds. It is a poetical picture of Gods' wrath. "Then the earth shook and trembled; the foundations of heaven moved and shook, because he was **wroth**" (v.8). The suggestion that David is using figurative language here is supported by v.17, "he drew me out of many waters", referring to deliverance from "the waves of death" and "the floods of ungodly men" (v.5). We should notice God's intense anger against those that ill-treat His people. He cares deeply about His children. "He that toucheth you toucheth the apple of his eye" (Zech 2.8).

i) His power. "Then the earth shook and trembled; the foundations of heaven moved and shook, because he was wroth" (v.8). Nothing can impede His will. He moves heaven and earth to defend and deliver His people.

ii) His anger. "There went up a smoke out of his nostrils, and fire out of his mouth devoured: coals were kindled by it" (v.9). Fire is an emblem of judgment. Compare Psalm 21. 9, "Thou shalt make them as a fiery oven in the time of thine anger: the Lord shall swallow them up in his wrath, and the fire shall devour them." Smoke is also used as an emblem of judgment in Deuteronomy 29.20: "The Lord will not spare him, but then the anger of the Lord and his jealousy shall smoke against that man." According to Keil & Delitzsch, "the figurative idea is that of snorting or violent breathing, which indicates the rising of wrath. Smoke is followed by fire…"

iii) His imminence. "He bowed the heavens also, and came down; and darkness was under his feet" (v.10). "As in a storm the dark clouds seem to lower and almost touch the earth, so had God stooped in His wrath to deal with His enemies" (J.Flanigan).

iv) His mobility. "And he rode upon a cherub, and did fly: and he was seen upon the wings of the wind" (v.11). The cherubim form the Lord's chariot. See Ezekiel 1 which describes the body (vv.9-14), the wheels (vv.15-21), the purity (vv.22-25), the throne (vv.26) and the Occupant (vv.27-28) of the chariot. Note that the "living creatures (the cherubim: see Ezekiel 10.1) ran and returned as the appearance of a flash of lightning" (v.14).

v) His invisibility. "And he made darkness pavilions round about him, dark waters, and thick clouds of the skies" (v.12). "God in His wrath withdraws His face from man. He envelopes Himself in clouds" (Keil & Delitzsch). He is unseen to natural eyes, although one day "every eye shall see him" (Rev 1.7).

vi) His judgment. "Through the brightness before him were the coals of fire kindled. The Lord thundered from heaven, and the most High uttered his voice. And he sent out arrows, and scattered them; lightning, and discomfited them" (vv.13-15). The "arrows" evidently refer to hail. See the parallel passage in Psalm 18.12-14, and compare Revelation 8.7.

vii) His deliverance. "And the channels of the sea appeared, the foundations of the world were discovered, at the rebuking of the Lord, at the blast of the breath of his nostrils. He sent from above, he took me; he drew me out of many waters (possibly alluding to the rescue of Moses from the Nile); he delivered me from my strong enemy, and from them that hated me; for they were too strong for me. They prevented me in the day of my calamity: but the Lord was my stay. He brought me forth also into a large place: he delivered me, because he delighted in me" (vv.16-20). Having been threatened by "the **floods** of ungodly men" (v.5), David testified to divine deliverance: "He drew me out of **many waters**. He delivered me from my strong enemy, and from them which hated me: for they were too strong for **me**" (vv.16-17). Through this experience David was faced with his own inadequacy and proved his own words: "God is our refuge and strength, a very present help in trouble" (Psalm 46. 1). We all need to realise our own weakness and limitations, and trust implicitly in the Lord.

"Tis what I know of Thee, my Lord and God,
That fills my soul with peace, my lips with song;
Thou art my health, my joy, my staff and rod;
Leaning on Thee in weakness I am strong.

The Lord answered David's prayer: "**I called** upon the Lord, and **cried** to my God: and **he did hear** my voice" (v.7). It was divine deliverance: "**He** sent from above, **he** took me; **he** drew me out of many waters; **he** delivered me….**he** brought me forth also into a large place: **he** delivered me…" (vv.17-20). "Salvation is of the Lord!" (Jonah 2.9). He is well able to answer the prayers of His people. David found himself in "distress", that is, in a narrow, straitened position (v.7). J. Baldwin calls it "straits" or "tight corners." But now he is in "a large place" (v.20). There seemed no way out in vv.5-6, but now he is no longer hemmed in by enemies and enjoys perfect liberty.

The language here is strikingly reminiscent of events at the Red Sea. The words, "the Lord caused the sea to go back by a strong east wind all that night" (Ex 14.21-22), are converted into poetic language here: "Then the channels (beds) of waters were seen, and the foundations of the world were discovered (uncovered) at thy rebuke, O Lord, at the blast of the breath of thy nostrils" (v.15). Israel certainly seemed to be "in distress" in Exodus ch.14. Moses told the Lord that Pharaoh would say "they are entangled in the land, the wilderness hath shut them in" (v.3). But after their deliverance Israel sang, "Thou shalt bring them in, and plant them in the mountain of thine inheritance" (Ex 15.17). That could certainly be described as "a large place!" Israel could rightly say, "He delivered me from my strong enemy, and from them that hated me: for they were too strong for me" (v.18). Pharaoh pursued Israel with "six hundred chosen chariots, and all the chariots of Egypt, and captains over every one of them" (Ex 14.7).

d) David's integrity (vv.21-28)
The closing section of this part of the song expands the words, "he delivered me, because he delighted in me" (v.20). There are two paragraphs *(i)* David speaks personally (vv.21-25); *(ii)* David speaks generally (vv.26-28).

i) David speaks personally (vv.21-25). The paragraph begins and ends with reference to David's "righteousness" and "cleanness": "The Lord rewarded me according to my righteousness: according to the cleanness of my hands hath he recompensed me (v.21)…Therefore the Lord hath recompensed me according to my righteousness: according to my cleanness in his eyesight" (v.25). We must not think that David is taking credit for his deliverance. As Keil & Delitzsch observe, "the "righteousness" and "cleanness of hands", i.e. the innocence, which David attributed to himself were not perfect righteousness or holiness before God, but the righteousness of his endeavours and deeds as contrasted with the unrighteousness and wickedness of his adversaries and pursuers, and consisted in the fact that he endeavoured earnestly and sincerely to walk in the ways of God and to keep the divine commandments." In particular, he had refused to kill Saul, and waited for the Lord to vindicate him (1 Sam 26.8-11). His deliverance from all his enemies was proof that he had acted rightly. See Psalm 66. 18-19, "If I regard iniquity in my heart, the Lord will not hear me: but verily God hath heard me; he hath attended to the voice of my prayer." Although surrounded by enemies (vv.3-5), David was amongst those who "commit their souls in well-doing to a faithful Creator" (1 Pet 4. 19 JND).

David's words, "my righteousness" and the "cleanness of my hands" are explained in vv.22-24. Notice three positives and three negatives in these verses. The positives are put first: "I have kept the ways of the Lord...all his judgments were before me...I was also upright before him." The negatives follow: "I...have not wickedly departed from my God...I did not depart from them...have kept myself from mine iniquity." Compare Psalm 45.7: "Thou lovest righteousness, and hatest wickedness..." Love for God's will and God's word is the best bulwark against sin.

ii) David speaks generally (vv.26-28). This paragraph illustrates Gal 6. 7-8, "Be not deceived: God is not mocked: for whatsoever a man soweth, that shall he also reap." Notice the law of sowing and reaping here: "With the merciful thou wilt shew thyself merciful, and with the upright man thou wilt shew thyself upright. With the pure thou wilt shew thyself pure; and with the froward ("perverse", JND) thou wilt shew thyself unsavoury ("contrary", JND)." This reminds us of the words of Azariah to Asa: "The Lord is with you, while ye be with him" (2 Chron 15.1-2). Whilst it seems that David wrote this song before his moral aberration in 2 Samuel 11 (remember that 2 Samuel chs.21-24 are an appendix and cover various periods in his reign), he lived to prove the accuracy of all these statements, including the last: "with the froward thou wilt shew thyself unsavoury."

The paragraph ends with a contrast between the humble and the haughty. "And the afflicted people thou wilt save: but thine eyes are upon the haughty, that thou mayest bring them down" (v.28). The expression "the afflicted" is used to describe "the pious and depressed in the nation" and "haughty" describes "the godless rich and mighty in the nation" (Keil & Delitzsch). Peter reminds us that "God resisteth the proud, and giveth grace to the humble" (1 Pet 5.5). "Though the Lord be high, yet he hath respect unto the lowly: but the proud he knoweth afar off" (Ps 138.6).

On the basis of our present life-style, do we have the moral right to count on God's help? The principle remains: "Draw nigh to God, and he will draw nigh to you. Cleanse your hands, ye sinners; and purify your hearts, ye double minded" (Jas 4.8). Only then can we say, "the Lord will lighten my darkness. For by thee I have run through a troop; by my God have I leaped over a wall" (vv.29-30).

CHAPTER 22.29-51

"And David spake unto the Lord the words of this song"

We have already noticed that David's song of thanksgiving in this chapter also occurs as Psalm 18, and that the introduction (v.1) is virtually the same as the superscript to the psalm. There is an interesting correspondence between the introduction and 2 Samuel 7.1, "And it came to pass, when the king sat in his house, and the Lord had given him rest round about from all his enemies", but David's victories in 2 Samuel 8 could well form the background to the song. We read twice here that "the Lord preserved David whithersoever he went" (vv.6,14). We have also noticed that the song divides into two sections:

i) David's thanksgiving to God for ***delivering*** him from his enemies (vv.2-28). In this case, he is evidently referring to ***internal*** enemies. It is noticeable that David does not refer here to any attempt on his part to destroy them, which was certainly true in the case of Saul. See 1 Samuel 24.1-7 and 1 Samuel 26.1-11. He left the matter with God, who delivered him "out of the hand of **Saul**." As we have seen, this could have particular reference to 1 Samuel 23.24-29.

ii) David's thanksgiving to God for enabling him to ***destroy*** his enemies (vv.29-51). In this case David is evidently referring to ***external*** enemies. This section is quite different. David is on the warpath: "I have pursued mine enemies and destroyed them" (v.38)…I have consumed them, and wounded them, that they could not arise (v.39)…Thou hast also given me the necks of mine enemies (v.41)…I beat them as small as the dust of the earth, I did stamp them as the mire of the street" (v.43). David certainly didn't do this to Saul and his men! He refers now to national enemies, principally the Philistines (2 Sam 5.17-25). He was delivered "out of the hand of **all** his enemies."

In view of the length of the song, with its two clear divisions, we divided our study as follows:

1) David's Deliverance from his Enemies (vv.2-28)
We have already considered this under four paragraph headings: *(a)* David's deliverer (vv.2-4); *(b)* David's distress (vv.5-7); *(c)* David's deliverance (vv.8-20); *(d)* David's integrity (vv.21-28). This brings us to:

2) David's Destruction of his Enemies (vv.29-51)
We can also consider this section under four headings: *(a)* The perfection of the Lord (vv.29-32); *(b)* The provision by the Lord (vv.33-37); *(c)* The power from the Lord (vv.38-46); *(d)* The praise to the Lord (vv.47-51).

We should notice the connection with the previous verses which culminate with the words, "And the afflicted people thou wilt save: but thine eyes are upon the haughty, that thou mayest bring them down" (v.28). David proved the veracity of these words. He belonged to the "afflicted people" but the Lord had saved him! Now he speaks about his salvation (vv.29-37), together with the way in which his haughty enemies had been defeated (vv.38-46).

a) The perfection of the Lord (vv.29-32)
The words, "As for God, his way is perfect" (v.31), lie at the centre of this paragraph. The word perfect *(tamin)* means "whole" or "complete" (Young's Analytical Concordance), and we should notice the following:

i) The perfection of God's help (vv.29-30).
"For thou art my lamp, O Lord: and the Lord will lighten (enlighteneth), JND) my darkness. For by thee I have run through a troop: by my God have I leaped over a wall." Keil & Delitzsch suggest that "darkness" refers to the way in which the Lord "had lifted him out of a condition of depression and contempt into one of glory and honour." David certainly had his "black" moments. See, for example, 1 Samuel 27.1. Paul knew something about this as well. See, for example, 1 Corinthians 2.3, Philippians 2.27. The present tense ("enlighteneth") also expresses David's confidence for the future. He was assured of the Lord's ongoing help. David takes no credit for his achievements: "**thou** art my lamp, O Lord...for **by thee** I have run through a troop: **by my God** have I leaped over a wall." The "troop" suggests superior forces (compare 1 Samuel 30.8), and the "wall" great obstacles. Remember:

> Got any valleys you think are uncrossable?
> Got any mountains you can't tunnel through?
> God specialises in things thought impossible:
> He can do what none other can do.

Or, in Bible language, "I know both how to be abased, and I know how to abound: every where and in all things I am instructed both to be full and to be hungry, both to abound and to suffer need. I can do all things through Christ which strengtheneth me" (Phil 4.12-14).

ii) The perfection of God's ways (v.31). Solomon said that "there is **a way** which seemeth right unto a man, but the end thereof are the ways of the death" (Prov 14.12), "But as for God, **his way** is perfect." He never makes a mistake. We may not always understand what He does and why He does it, but we can rest with absolute confidence in the fact that "He hath done all things well" (Mk 7.37). We do have to remember that "My thoughts are not your thoughts, neither are your ways **my ways**, saith the Lord. For as the heavens are higher than the earth, so are **my ways** higher than your ways, and my thoughts than your thoughts" (Is 55.8-9). Having surveyed God's purpose for Israel, Paul exclaims: "O the depth of the riches both of the wisdom and knowledge of God! how unsearchable are his judgments, and **his ways** past finding out!" (Rom 11.33).

We must apply this to ourselves practically, and say that "his way", as revealed in the scriptures, cannot be bettered. What He wants us to do, and how He wants us to do it, must be perfect. Paul calls this "that good, and acceptable, and perfect, will of God" (Rom 12.2). Our prayer should be, "Teach me **thy way**, O Lord" (Ps 27.11).

iii) The perfection of God's word (v.31). "The word of the Lord is tried." The word "tried" refers to the process of refining. There is no dross in the word of God. "The words of the Lord are pure words: as silver tried in a furnace of earth, purified seven times" (Ps 12.6). Peter refers to the "sincere milk of the word" (1 Pet 2.2). "Sincere" means "guileless" or "pure" (W.E.Vine).

iv) The perfection of God's strength (vv.31-32). "He is a buckler (shield) to all those that trust in him. **For** who is God, save the Lord? and who is a rock, save our God?" Do notice the personal note here: "to **all** those that trust in him." We can trust Him absolutely. Just think about His three titles here. In the first place He is "God" (*"El"*, the "Mighty One"); in the second He is "the Lord" *("Jehovah"*, emphasising His eternity); in the third He is "our God" *("Elohim"*, a plural word reminding us that He is the triune God).

b) The provision by the Lord (vv.33-37)
These verses remind us of 2 Corinthians 3.5-6, "Not that we are sufficient

of ourselves to think anything as of ourselves; but our sufficiency is of God: who also hath made us able ministers of the new testament." Notice how the Lord had provided for David: "**God** is my strength and power: and **he** maketh my way perfect. **He** maketh my feet like hinds' feet, and setteth me upon my high places. **He** teacheth my hands to war; so that a bow of steel is broken by mine arms. **Thou** hast also given me the shield of **thy** salvation: and **thy** gentleness hath made me great. **Thou** hast enlarged my steps under me; so that my feet did not slip." This reminds us that "his divine power hath given unto us all things that pertain to life and godliness" (2 Pet 1.3). It also reminds us that we are to be "strong in **the Lord**, and in the power of **his** might" and "put on the whole armour of **God**" (Eph 6.10-11).

The passage is rich material for meditation and preaching. **Strength** ("God is my strength and power"); **stability** ("He maketh my feet like hinds' feet"); **salvation** ("Thou hast also given me the shield of thy salvation"); **safety** ("Thou hast enlarged my steps under me; so that my feet did not slip"). You should have no difficulty in constructing a fine sermon from these verses! Here are a few comments on them:

i) "God is my strength and power: and he maketh my way perfect" (v.33). We cannot miss the connection with v.31: "As for God, his way is perfect *(tamin)*": now, "he maketh my way perfect *(tamin)*." The word is sometimes rendered "upright." God's great desire is to reproduce His own character in His people.

ii) "He maketh my feet like hinds' feet: and setteth me upon my high places" (v.34). Compare Deuteronomy 32.13 and Habakkuk 3.19. The "high places" refer to David's elevated position as king of Israel. His throne was stable.

iii) "He teacheth my hands to war; so that a bow of steel is broken by mine arms" (v.35). We must remember that "the weapons of our warfare are not carnal, but mighty through God to the pulling down of strongholds" (2 Cor 10.4). This is best illustrated by the way in which Jericho was conquered. We need to handle our weapons correctly. We are engaged in a war! See Ephesians 6.12. Steel as we know it today did not exist when the Authorised Version was published, but the word was obviously in use in connection with metallurgy. It refers to "brass" or, better "copper" or "bronze."

iv) "Thou hast given me the shield of thy salvation: and thy gentleness hath made me great" (v.36). J. Flanigan calls this a "strangely beautiful expression". Where would any of us be if God had not dealt with us in this way? In David's own words, "He hath not dealt with us after our sins; nor rewarded us according to our iniquities" (Ps 103.10). The Lord Jesus was characterised by gentleness: "He shall not strive, nor cry; neither shall any man hear his voice in the streets. A bruised reed shall he not break, and smoking flax shall he not quench" (Mt 12.18-20).

He combines strength (v.35) and gentleness (v.36), and this is beautifully described in Isaiah 40.10-11, "Behold, the Lord God will come with **strong hand**, and his arm shall rule for him…He shall feed his flock like a shepherd: he shall gather the lambs with his arm, and carry them in his bosom, and shall **gently** lead those that are with young".

v) "Thou hast enlarged my steps under me; so that my feet ("ankles", JND) did not slip" (v.37). Keil & Delitzsch explain this as follows: "God made his steps broad…provided the walker with a broad space for free motion, removing obstructions and stumbling-blocks out of the way." In our own words, "the Lord enabled David to keep his balance!" Listen to David again: "Thou hast delivered my soul from death: wilt thou not deliver my feet from falling, that I may walk before God in the light of the living?" (Ps 57.13). Solomon put it like this: "When thou goest, thy steps shall not be straitened; and when thou runnest, thou shalt not stumble" (Prov 4.12). Compare Jude v.24: "Now unto him that is able to keep you from falling, and to present you faultless before the presence of his glory with exceeding joy."

David had been equipped by the Lord in this way for warfare against his enemies, and we now join him in his military campaigns. Having equipped His servant, God remained by his side in the conflict. So:

c) The power from the Lord (vv.38-46)
David is careful to acknowledge that he was "strong in the Lord, and in the power of his might" (Eph 6.10). The enemy had been utterly routed. While David refers to himself, "*I* have pursued mine enemies, and destroyed them (v38)…*I* have consumed them, and wounded them" (v.39), he takes no personal credit for victory: "***thou*** hast girded me with strength to battle (v.40)…***Thou*** hast given me the necks of mine enemies" (v.41). Paul puts it as follows: "in all these things we are more than conquerors through **him**

that loved us" (Rom 8.37). God has not changed. He can enable us to overcome. But do we "call on the Lord, who is worthy to be praised?" Only then can we say, "so shall I be saved from my enemies" (v.4). Perhaps we are not even aware of enemy activity. It's terrible to think that we could be defeated without even knowing it! We should notice the correspondence between this passage and Ephesians 6: the "darkness" (v.29) reminds us of "the rulers of the darkness of this world"; "the word of the Lord" (v.31) reminds us of "the sword of the Spirit, which is the word of God"; "feet" (v.34) remind us of "feet shod with the preparation of the gospel of peace"; "shield" (v.36) reminds us of "the shield of faith"; "girded" (v.40) reminds us of "loins girt about with truth."

If we are correct in assuming that David originally wrote the song either when "he sat in his house, and the Lord had given him rest round about from all his enemies" (2 Sam 7.1) or after his four campaigns described in 2 Samuel 8, then "mine enemies (v.38)...them that rose up against me (v.40)...them that hate me" (v.41) were particularly the Philistines. David "smote the Philistines from Geba until thou come to Gazer (2 Sam 5.25), and "smote the Philistines, and subdued them" (2 Sam 8.1). During the first of the two battles described in 2 Samuel 5, the Philistines "left their images, and David and his men burned them" (2 Sam 5.21) and he could be referring to this saying, "They looked, but there was none to save; even unto the Lord, but he answered them not" (v.42).

In recalling his triumphs over external enemies, David also mentions the Lord's help in establishing him as king over Israel itself. "Thou also hast delivered me from the strivings of my people, thou hast kept me to be head of the heathen: a people which I knew not shall serve me. Strangers shall submit themselves unto me: as soon as they hear, they shall be obedient unto me. Strangers shall fade away, and they shall be afraid out of their close places" (vv.44-46). We must therefore notice

i) "My people" (v.44). "Thou also hast delivered me from the strivings of **my people**." This evidently refers to the years described in 2 Samuel 3.1, "Now there was long war between the house of Saul and the house of David." This period included the murder of Abner by Joab, and the murder of Ish-bosheth by Baanah and Rechab.

ii) Other people (v.44). "Thou hast kept me to be head of the heathen: **a people** which I knew not shall serve me." These verses (vv.44-46) have been translated as follows: "Thou hast kept me to be head of the nations: A people I knew not doth serve me: strangers come cringing unto me: at the hearing of the ear, they obey me. Strangers have faded away, and they come trembling forth from their closed (fortified) places" JND.

David was therefore both king of Israel and "head of the heathen!" This points us to "Great David's greater Son" who will be acknowledged as "King of Israel" (John 1.49) and "King of nations" (Jer 10.7). See Psalm 2: "Yet have I set my king upon my holy hill of **Zion** (v6)...Ask of me, and I shall give thee the **heathen** for thine inheritance, and the uttermost parts of the earth for thy possession" (v.8).

All this causes David to conclude his song with praise to God for His goodness and faithfulness to him:

d) The praise to the Lord (vv.47-51)
We should notice four strands in David's thanksgiving to the Lord for His delivering power:

i) He is the living God. "The Lord liveth; and blessed be my rock; and exalted be the God (*Elohim*, plural) of the rock of my salvation" (v.47). Or, "Jehovah liveth; and blessed be my rock; and exalted be the God, the rock of my salvation" (JND). The word "rock" (*sur*) occurs several times in Deuteronomy 32 where it is used as a divine title: "Of the Rock that begat thee thou art unmindful, and hast forgotten the God that formed thee...For their rock is not as our Rock" (vv.18,31). The word "rock" suggests strength and security, and that can only be true because He is the living God. Like the Thessalonians, we "serve the living and true God", and are identified with Him in three ways: we are **the children of the living God"** (Rom 9.26); we have "**the Spirit of the living God"** (2 Cor 3.3); we (the local assembly) are "**the temple of the living God"** (2 Cor 6.16).

ii) He is the intervening God. "It is God *(El)* that avengeth me, and that bringeth down the people (plural, "peoples", referring to the Gentile nations)) under me, and that bringeth me forth from mine enemies: thou also hast lifted me up on high above them that rose up against me: thou hast delivered me from the violent man" (vv.48-49). The "violent man" could refer to Saul. As J. Baldwin observes, "one specific answer to prayer can bring home the fact that the Lord lives...David had countless occasions to which he could point, and which he summarises now."

iii) He is the praiseworthy God. "Therefore will I give thanks unto thee, O Lord, among the heathen, and I will sing praises unto thy name" (v.50). Notice where David expresses his thanks to God: it is "among the heathen." It is very easy to confess Him when we gather with fellow-believers, but do we confess Him before unsaved people?

This verse is cited by Paul in Romans 15.8-9, "Now I say that Jesus Christ was a minister of the circumcision for the truth of God, to confirm the promises made unto the fathers: and that the Gentiles might glorify God for his mercy; as it is written, For this cause will I confess to thee among the Gentiles, and sing unto thy name". The quotation is the first of four prophetical passages cited to show that Christ would bring blessing to both Jew and Gentile.

iv) He is the faithful God. "He is the tower of salvation for his king: and sheweth mercy to his anointed, unto David, and to his seed for evermore" (v.51). David refers here to the promises made to him in 2 Samuel 7.16, "And thine house and thy kingdom shall be established for ever before thee: thy throne shall be established for ever." The singular collective noun ("his seed") points forward to Christ. Compare Genesis 22.18 and Galatians 3.16. The Lord Jesus will fulfil all the promises made to David: "He shall be great, and shall be called the Son of the Highest: and the Lord God shall give unto him the throne of his father David: and he shall reign over the house of Jacob for ever; and of his kingdom there shall be no end" (Lk 1.32-33).

The way in which this "song" ends is similar to the conclusion of other songs of praise. "Sing ye to the Lord, for he hath triumphed gloriously; the horse and his rider hath he thrown into the sea" (Ex 15.21). "The adversaries of the Lord shall be broken to pieces; out of heaven shall he thunder upon them: the Lord shall judge the ends of the earth; and he shall give strength unto his king, and exalt the horn of his anointed" (1 Sam 2.10). "He hath holpen his servant Israel, in remembrance of his mercy; as he spake to our fathers, to Abraham, and to his seed for ever" (Lk 1.54-55).

CHAPTER 23.1-7

"The last words of David"

This chapter clearly divides into two sections **(1)** "the last words of David" (vv.1-7) and **(2)** "the names of the mighty men whom David had" (vv.8-39). In this study we will deal with the first of these. So:

1) David's Last Words (vv.1-7)
We have already noticed that the last four chapters of 2 Samuel form a kind of epilogue or appendix and cover different periods in the life of David. The six parts in the section form a concentric pattern:

a) A disaster during his reign (21.1-14)
b) A role of honour during his reign (21.15-22)
c) A Psalm during his reign (22.1-51)
c) A Psalm at the end of his reign (23.1-7)
b) A role of honour at the end of his reign (23.8-39)
a) A disaster at the end of his reign (24.1-25)

The two psalms that lie at the centre of this arrangement are not there by accident. Although written at different times, there is a clear connection between "the words of this song, in the day that the Lord delivered him out of the hand of all his enemies" (22.1) and "the last words of David" (23.1). In the first Psalm, David praises the Lord for delivering him from all his enemies, and concludes by anticipating the fulfilment of God's promises to him. "He…sheweth mercy to his anointed, unto David, and his seed for evermore" (22.51). The dark and difficult years that followed its composition did not make David doubt the promises of God, and his "last words" look forward to the reign of a Ruler who will fulfil "the everlasting covenant, ordered in all things, and sure" (23.5). Scholars have pointed out that the word "said" (*naan*, 23.1) is used particularly of divine utterances and only of human beings when they claim divine inspiration (F. Gardiner, *Ellicott's*

Commentary). David is speaking as a prophet, and this is expressly stated in vv.2-3.

Although these are not David's "last words" in the strictest sense, they are his final composition. Like the "last words" of Jacob (Gen ch 49) and Moses (Deut ch 33), David's "last words" are significant and important. They can be divided as follows. *(A)* David's calling (v.1); *(B)* David's inspiration (vv.2-3a); *(C)* David's message (vv.3b-4); *(D)* David's house (v.5); *(E)* David's enemies (vv.6-7). These verses are often compared with Numbers 24.15-17. This is another of the few passages in which the word "said" *(naan)* occurs.

A) David's calling (v.1)
He was sure of his calling! "David the son of Jesse said, and the man who was raised up on high, the anointed of the God of Jacob, and the sweet psalmist of Israel, said..." David tells us four things about himself. He was:

i) "The son of Jesse." This emphasises his humble origins. David never forgot that he "sprang from a lowly family, and was raised in the little village of Bethlehem" (A McShane). The Lord Jesus was born in "Bethlehem Ephratah...little among the thousands of Judah" (Mic 5.2). He too was "the son of Jesse." See Isaiah 11.1, "And there shall come forth a rod out of the stem of Jesse, and a Branch shall grow out of his roots." We should never forget that "before honour is humility" (Prov 15.33). The Lord Jesus, who had every right to honour, nevertheless "humbled himself...wherefore God also hath highly exalted him" (Phil 2.8-9). Paul urged the Corinthians to remember their "calling". God delights to use the humblest and most unlikely material so that "no flesh should glory in his presence". Read 1 Corinthians 1.26-29. Hannah put it like this. "He raiseth up the poor out of the dust, and lifteth up the beggar from the dunghill, to set them among princes, and to make them inherit the throne of glory" (1 Sam 2.8). This follows.

ii) "The man (*geber*, meaning 'mighty man,)...raised up on high." **Not**, "the man that raised himself up on high!" Listen to Asaph. "The Lord...chose David also his servant, and took him from the sheepfolds: from following the ewes great with young he brought him to feed Jacob his people, and Israel his inheritance" (Ps 78.70-71). This is the man who said, "**thou** hast kept me to be head of the heathen: a people which I knew not shall serve me. Strangers shall submit themselves unto me. as soon as they hear, they shall be obedient unto me" (2 Sam 22.44-45). David was "head of the heathen" as well as the king of Israel. But he set us a good example in ascribing praise to the Lord for his exaltation. Compare 1 Corinthians 4.7, "What hast thou that thou didst not receive? Now if thou didst receive it, why dost thou glory, as if thou hadst not received it?" This was addressed to a church that came "behind in no gift" (1 Cor 1.7) but had evidently forgotten that "in every thing" they were "enriched **by him**, in all utterance, and in all knowledge" (v.5). We must never become "big heads" with matching feet!

iii) "The anointed of the God of Jacob." **Not**, "the anointed of the God of Israel!" Once again, David is speaking with great humility. The God "who had blessed Jacob in spite of his unworthiness, had honoured him in spite of his nothingness" (A McShane). Perhaps David was thinking of his own chequered career here. How much we all owe to the grace of God, both before and after conversion. The Psalmist said, "Happy is he that hath the God of Jacob for his help, whose hope is in the Lord his God" (Ps 146.5).

iv) "The sweet psalmist of Israel." It is interesting to notice that David does not describe himself as "the great warrior of Israel!" A. McShane suggests that this illustrates the saying that "the pen is mightier than the sword" since "the day came when his warfare was over…but his writings will remain for ever". The early Christians certainly sang some of his compositions (they must be included in Ephesians 5.19; Colossians 3.16), and so do we! How about Psalm 23. David was not only Israel's anointed king: as "the composer of Israel's songs of praise, he promoted the spiritual edification of that kingdom" (Keil & Delitzsch).

As we have seen, David is looking back over his life, and ascribing all praise to God for the way in which He had used and blessed him. Perhaps we should take the opportunity to do the same, and thank God for all His mercy and grace. Paul speaks for us all in saying, "by the grace of God I am what I am" (1 Cor 15.10).

B) David's inspiration (vv.2-3a)

"The Spirit of the Lord spake by me, and his word was in my tongue. The God of Israel said, the Rock of Israel spake to me." David claimed the same authority as the prophets who said, "Thus saith the Lord". We should notice

(i) that God spoke through him. "The Spirit of the Lord **spake by me**, and his word was in my tongue".

2 Samuel

(ii) that God spoke to him. "The God of Israel said, the Rock of Israel ***spake to me***." Whilst David is referring here particularly to what follows (vv.3b-4), it is important to notice how the New Testament confirms the inspiration of David's psalms. "For David himself said by the **Holy Ghost,** The Lord said to my Lord, Sit thou on my right hand, till I make thine enemies thy footstool" (Mk 12.36); "Men and brethren, this scripture must needs have been fulfilled which the **Holy Ghost** by the mouth of David spake before concerning Judas…for it is written in the book of Psalms, Let his habitation be desolate, and let no man dwell therein" (Acts 1.16-20).

We must remember, of course, that ***"All*** scripture is given by inspiration of God" (2 Tim 3.16). The word rendered "inspiration" *(theopneustos)* comes from *"theo"*, meaning "God", and *"pneo"*, meaning "to blow" or "to breathe", hence the expression, "God-breathed." The word emphasises the **source** of Scripture, rather than the **channel** by which we have received it. It describes "breathing out", rather than "breathing in." The Scriptures are ***still*** "warm with the breath of God." We prove this every time we open our Bibles.

The divine titles in these verses should be noticed. "The Spirit of the Lord…The God of Israel…the Rock of Israel". The word "Rock" is a divine title. "he is the **Rock**, his work is perfect…he forsook God which made him, and lightly esteemed the **Rock** of his salvation…Of the **Rock** that begat thee thou art unmindful…How should one chase a thousand, and to put ten thousand to flight, except their **Rock** had sold them, and the Lord had shut them up? For their rock is not as our **Rock**" (Deut 32.4,15,18, 30,31). It is used in the New Testament of the Lord Jesus. "they drank of that spiritual **Rock** that followed them: and that **Rock** was Christ" (1 Cor 10.4); "the stone which the builders rejected, the same is become the head of the corner, and a stone of stumbling, and a rock of offence" (1 Pet 2.8). In fact the Lord Jesus uses the title of Himself (Mt 16.18). These verses therefore clearly refer to the Godhead, and this should heighten our reverence for the Scriptures. It is the word of the triune God.

C) David's message (vv.3b-4)
"He that ruleth over men must be just, ruling in the fear of God: and he shall be as the light of the morning, when the sun riseth, even a morning without clouds; as the tender grass springing out of the earth by clear shining after rain." We should notice.

i) How a man must rule. He must be "just" in relation to men and "ruling in the fear of God" in relation to God. Alas, his own son failed after an illustrious start, let alone many of the kings that followed. Even David himself had failed on both counts. But the final occupant of David's throne (Is 9.7) will establish the kingdom "with judgment and with justice, from henceforth even for ever". He will "reign in righteousness" (Is 32. 1), and "in the fear of the Lord" (Is 11.3). There are important lessons here for assembly elders. Their leadership must be characterised by integrity and righteousness. "A bishop ("overseer" JND) must be blameless (irreproachable JND)" (1 Tim 3.2). But this is far more than observing a strict code of conduct. The "fear of God" describes an attitude of heart and mind that shrinks from causing Him grief and displeasure. It is sadly possibly for Christian leaders to say the right thing, but not be right themselves. Hence the injunctions "Take heed therefore unto **yourselves**, and to all the flock" (Acts 20.28), and "Take heed unto **thyself**, and unto the doctrine" (1 Tim 4.16).

ii) How his rule will have effect. "He shall be as the light of the morning, when the sun riseth, a morning without clouds; when the tender grass springeth out of the earth, through clear shining after rain" (RV). J. Baldwin puts it nicely. "Such a ruler, says the Lord, is to be compared with three lovely experiences common to mankind everywhere: the early morning, when light dawns, the warmth of the sun on a cloudless morning, and rain that enables the grass to sprout even after long drought. All three elements are necessary for the healthy growth of plants, without which all life would cease; and for society the righteous ruler has an equally vital part to play". "Great David's greater Son" will reign in this way. David glimpses the coming kingdom here! "The Sun of righteousness" will "arise with healing in his wings" (Mal 4.2), and "He shall come down like rain upon the mown grass; as showers that water the earth" (Ps 72.6). Once again, there are important lessons here for assembly elders. As every gardener knows (only too well!), grass quickly responds to sun and rain. It is good "growing weather." The Lord's people need spiritual light, warmth, and refreshment in order to grow. It is the work of elders to stimulate and encourage the spiritual growth of the assembly.

D) David's house (v.5)
"Although my house be not so with God; yet hath he made with me an everlasting covenant, ordered in all things, and sure: for this is all my salvation, and all my desire, although he make it not to grow". As F. Gardiner observes, "this verse is extremely difficult and admits of two interpretations". As it stands in the English versions, it means that "David recognised how far he and his house had failed to realise the ideal description set forth: yet since God's promise is

sure, this must be realised in his posterity". It contrasts the unworthiness of his family with the faithfulness of God. The alternative rendering does seem to fit the context better, and has much to commend it. "Is not my house thus with God? For he hath made with me an everlasting covenant, ordered in all, and sure. For all my salvation and all my desire, shall he not cause it to spring forth?" It does seem that David is pondering the prophecy of Nathan here (2 Sam 7.16) and expressing his complete confidence in the promise of God. The word "grow" *(tsamach)* is rendered "bud" in Psalm 132.17, "There will I make the horn of David to bud *(tsamach)*". Notice the absolute certainty of the covenant with David: it is "everlasting...ordered...sure."

E) David's enemies (vv.6-7)

"But the sons of Belial shall be all of them as thorns thrust away, because they cannot be taken with hands: but the man that shall touch them must be fenced with iron and the staff of a spear; and they shall be utterly burned with fire in the same place". See JND: "And the man that will touch them provideth himself with iron and the staff of a spear", reminding us that the Lord Jesus will "break them with a rod of iron" (Ps 2. 9). We should notice.

i) Their character. We have met "the sons of Belial (meaning "worthless") before See 1 Sam 1.16; 2.12; 10.27. They are likened to thorn bushes which were not only useless but dangerous, choking good growth. See Genesis 3.18; Matthew 13.7, 22.

ii) Their control. "They are to be dealt with as thorns too prickly to be handled with bare hands, needing to be destroyed" (H. Mowvley). "Many were the painful memories which David had of the cruelty of those whom he sought to control. Some of them he allowed to be near him, and at times dealt with them too leniently" (A. McShane).

iii) Their condemnation. "Utterly burned with fire." As A. McShane points out, "the figure of thorns being burned illustrates the end of the wicked, and is common to both Old and New Testaments". See Isaiah 33.12; Hebrews 6.8. This anticipates the time when "The Son of man shall send forth his angels, and they shall gather out of his kingdom all things that offend, and them which do iniquity; and shall cast them into a furnace of fire: there shall be wailing and gnashing of teeth" (Mt 13.41-42).

The last words of David therefore assure us that the ungodly will not triumph. It describes the righteousness of divine rule, and the destiny of the wicked.

CHAPTER 23.8-39

"The names of the mighty men"

As we have already seen, this chapter divides into two sections **(1)** "the last words of David" (vv.1-7) and **(2)** "the names of the mighty men whom David had" (vv.8-39).

1) David's Last Words (vv.1-7)
These verses contain David's final composition, rather than his "last words" in the strictest sense. David looks back and reflects on the way in which the Lord has used and blessed him, and looks forward to the reign of the Lord Jesus, the "root and the offspring of David" (Rev 22.16), who would "be just, ruling in the fear of God" and whose reign would be "as the light of the morning, when the sun riseth, even a morning without clouds; as the tender grass springing out of the earth by clear shining after rain" (vv.3-4). We have already noticed that in David's "last words" he refers to **(a)** his calling (v.1); **(b)** his inspiration (vv.2-3a); **(c)** his message (vv.3b-4); **(d)** his house (v.5); **(e)** his enemies (vv.6-7).

2) David's Mighty Men (vv.8-39)
"These be the names of the mighty men whom David had...." This section should be read in connection with 1 Chronicles chs.11-12. 1 Chronicles ch.11 runs parallel to 2 Samuel 23.8-39, and lists David's mighty men who "strengthened themselves with him in his kingdom, and with all Israel, to make him king, according to the word of the Lord concerning Israel" (v.10). 1 Chronicles 12 gives us lists of mighty men in connection with David's residence at Ziklag (vv.1-22) and his coronation at Hebron (vv.23-40). While individual names occur, particularly in vv.1-22, various groups of people are singled out for particular comment, particularly in vv.23-40. There's plenty of material here for careful study. See the *addendum*. Returning now to 2 Samuel 23.8-39, it is important to make some general points:

2 Samuel

A) David's organisation
David's army was not a disorganised rabble. He had a command structure. *(i)* Although not mentioned here by name (perhaps the omission is significant), Joab was commander-in-chief. See 2 Samuel 24.2, 1 Chronicles 11.6. *(ii)* The army was divided into twelve detachments, each of which served for one month in the year, and these were commanded by twelve of the men named in 2 Samuel ch.23 and 1 Chronicles 10.10-47. See 1 Chronicles 27.1-15. There are thirty-six names in 2 Samuel ch.23, and possibly Joab must be added to make the "thirty and seven in all" mentioned in v.39. The fact that Joab is not mentioned could relate to the way in which he assassinated Abner, something most grievous to David (2 Sam 3.32-34). Do *we* give the King grief?

This reminds us that "God is not the author of confusion, but of peace, as in all churches of the saints" (1 Cor 14.33). The assembly should be a place where everything should be done "decently and in order" (1 Cor 14.40) and where the Lord's people function in harmony with each other (Rom 12.4-8; 1 Cor 12.4-31). This is illustrated throughout the Old Testament. See, for example, the instructions for pitching camp (Num ch.2) and moving camp (Num ch.10).

B) David's appreciation
David did not claim all honours for himself. Not all his mighty men achieved the same heights, but each was valued for his achievements. "David was too good a leader not to appreciate the achievements of his followers" (A. McShane). Whilst the passage reminds us that leaders amongst God's people should appreciate the support and help of their fellow-believers, we must *all* acknowledge our indebtedness to each other. Remember that even "God is not unrighteous to forget your work and labour of love, which ye have shewed toward his name, in that ye have ministered to the saints, and do minister" (Heb 6.10).

C) David's inspiration
A. McShane puts it nicely: "The shepherd boy who faced the giant single-handed made a headline which others could copy". A good leader inspires his men. Eleazar was "one of the three mighty men with David" (v.9). "Three of the thirty chief went down, and came to David" (v.13). The same three men "brake through the host of the Philistines, and drew water out of the well of Bethlehem...and brought it to David" (v.16). Courage is contagious: so is fear! We should notice that we have men here who were associated

with David after his anointing and before his enthronement. They shared his glory as they had shared his rejection. See 1 Timothy 2.12. It should also be noted that some names are only mentioned here. Their exploits for David are recorded, and nothing else, reminding us that we have:

> Only one life, 'twill soon be past:
> Only what's done for Christ will last.

David's "mighty men" fall into three categories: **(A)** "the first three" (vv.8-12); **(B)** "the three of the thirty" (vv.13-23); **(C)** the rest of "the thirty" (vv.24-39).

A) "The first three" (vv.8-12)
They are known by this description in v.19. In 1 Chronicles 11 they are also called "the three mighties" (v.12). Adino (v.8), Eleazar (v.9) and Shammah (v.11) are distinguished by what they accomplished **alone.** They are evidently named in order of precedence. The incidents obviously occurred in David's earlier years when the Philistines were an active threat.

i) **Adino**. "The Tachmonite that sat in the seat, chief among the captains; the same was Adino the Eznite: he lift up his spear against eight hundred, whom he slew at one time" (v.8). He is called, "Jashobeam, an Hachmonite, the chief of the captains" in 1 Chronicles 11.11. As "the chief among the captains" he was in charge of the first detachment (1 Chron 27.2).

ii) **Eleazar.** "And after him was Eleazar the son of Dodo the Ahohite, one of the three mighty men with David, when they defied the Philistines that were gathered there to battle, and the men of Israel were gone away (fled): he arose, and smote the Philistines until his hand was weary, and his hand clave (see Gen 2.24) to the sword: and the Lord wrought a great victory that day; and the people returned after him only to spoil" (vv.9-10). This happened at Pas-dammin (perhaps the same as Ephes-dammin, 1 Sam 17.1). Eleazar and David stood alone in "a parcel of ground full of barley" when everybody else had "fled from before the Philistines" (1 Chron 11.13-14). Do notice that Eleazar's hand "clave to the sword". Our hands should do the same: see Ephesians 6.17. He just didn't give up: he "smote the Philistines until his hand was weary." He was "stedfast" and "unmoveable" (1 Cor 15.58). During the conflict with Amalek, "Moses' hands were heavy", but with the help of Aaron and Hur "his hands were steady until the going down of the sun" (Ex 17.12). The two passages emphasise the necessity for steadfastness in prayer and in our use of God's word. We should notice that had there been no offensive against the enemy, there would have been no spoil!

iii) Shammah. "And after him was Shammah the son of Agee the Hararite. And the Philistines were gathered together into a troop, where was a piece of ground full of lentiles: and the people fled from the Philistines. But he stood in the midst of the ground, and defended it: and the Lord wrought a great victory" (vv.11-12). Shammah is not mentioned in 1 Chronicles 11, and some commentators (including Keil & Delitzsch) explain this by saying that three lines have been omitted through the wandering eye of a copyist. This does not seem to be a very helpful explanation. What ***is*** helpful is the fact that "the Lord wrought a great victory" (also v.10). Notice too that the Philistines evidently wanted the lentils, just as they wanted the barley (1 Chron 11.13). It is very important to ensure that the enemy doesn't rob us of our food. Shammah ensured the security of the food supply. We have to "earnestly contend for the faith" (Jude v.3), and be like Paul who could say "I have kept the faith" (2 Tim 4.7). The word "keep" means to keep by guarding (*tereo*). Paul had watched over "the faith", preserved "the faith", kept "the faith" against all attacks.

We must note again that these three men stood alone. We are wonderfully brave people when we're in a crowd, but what happens when we face opposition and difficulty alone? Well, like Adino, Eleazar and Shammah we can count on the presence and help of the Lord himself. Just like Paul: "At my first answer no man stood with me, but all men forsook me...Notwithstanding the Lord stood with me, and strengthened me..." (2 Tim 4.17). It can also be said that these men, and others, reflected the prowess of the king himself, which is not surprising. After all, he trained them! How much do ***we*** reflect the character and actions of the King?

B) "The three of the thirty" (vv.13-23)
The "first three" acted alone, but the second "three" acted together in vv.13-17. They "brake through the host of the Philistines, and drew water out of the well of Bethlehem, that was by the gate, and took it, and brought it to David" (v.16). Do notice that they didn't do this on David's instructions; they did it out of their devotion to him, and without regard for their own lives. Shouldn't we be looking for opportunities to serve one another, rather than waiting to be told? And shouldn't we take those opportunities, not just when it suits us or when there's not any risk involved, even though it means

sacrifice on our part? David recognised that only the Lord was worthy of such devotion. "Be it far from me, O Lord, that I should do this: is not this the blood of the men that went in jeopardy of their lives? Therefore he would not drink it" (v.17). Only the Lord "was worthy to receive such a costly portion, for in one sense it was as sacred as blood, having been obtained at the risk of three lives" (A. McShane). Compare Judges 5.18, "Zebulun and Naphtali were a people that jeoparded their lives unto the death in the high places of the field", and Acts 15.26, "Our beloved Barnabas and Paul, men that have hazarded their lives for the name of our Lord Jesus Christ".

The fact that "these three mighty men" (we are not given the name of the third man here, but it appears to have been "Ismaiah the Gibeonite", 1 Chronicles 12.4) acted together does not mean that they were not brave men in their own right.

i) Abishai. "And Abishai, the brother of Joab, the son of Zeruiah, was chief among three. And he lifted up his spear against three hundred, and slew them, and had the name among three. Was he not most honourable of three? Therefore he was their captain: howbeit he attained not unto the first three" (vv.18-19). See also 2 Samuel 21.16-17.

ii) Benaiah. He "had done many acts" (v.20). He had "a name among the three mighties" (1 Chron 11.24). Three of his "acts" are specified. Here are some suggestions for development. **(a)** Benaiah "slew two lionlike men of Moab" (v.20). Moab with its complacency (Jer 48.11), scorn (Jer 48.27) and pride (Jer 48.29) is a picture of "the flesh" (sinful human nature), of which Paul says, "For I know that in me (that is, in my flesh) dwelleth no good thing" (Rom 7.18). **(b)** Benaiah "went down also and slew a lion in the midst of a pit in time of snow" (v.20). No prizes for interpreting this: see 1 Peter 5.8. The Lord Jesus "went down...and slew a lion": "through death" He destroyed "him that had the power of death, that is, the devil" (Heb 2.14). Confronting the lion was extremely dangerous for Benaiah. In all probability it had been driven out of the hills by hunger. Just imagine facing a lion in a confined space! But think of the danger that faced the Lord Jesus. **(c)** Benaiah "slew an Egyptian (v.21). A big fellow too (1 Chron 11.23), with much better equipment (2 Sam 23.21). So, in figure, Benaiah defeated the world which once held us captive and from which the Lord Jesus has delivered us (Gal 1.4). We all ought to be like Benaiah, and triumph over our great spiritual enemies pictured here. For his bravery, Benaiah was placed over David's personal bodyguard. See 2 Samuel 8.18. It has been said that a bodyguard stops the bullet!

2 Samuel

We should add that Benaiah, who slew a lion, was a follower of David, who slew a lion and a bear (1 Sam 17.34-35), and not only that: both Benaiah and David slew giants. Benaiah slew a giant Egyptian, and David slew a giant Philistine. If you like, David was seen in Benaiah. Need we say more?

C) The rest of "the thirty" (vv.24-39)
Others might not have been so distinguished but their names are all recorded, reminding us that God does not overlook any of His people. As J. Baldwin points out, the list of "the thirty" illustrates "the ability of David to hold the allegiance of men from very different backgrounds". As might be expected, a number of his closest supporters came from the hill country of Judah, but other districts are mentioned, and so are several foreigners (vv.34,37,39). Notice "Eliam the son of Ahithophel the Gilonite" (v.34). See 2 Samuel 15.12, 31. He evidently remained faithful to David. It was not a question of "like father, like son!". It is significant that Uriah the Hittite is mentioned last. (v.39). God does not want us to forget the solemn lessons connected with the early death of this honourable man. The chapter ends on a sobering note.

Are our names on God's roll of honour?
Addendum
As noted in the introduction, 1 Chronicles 12 gives us lists of the men who joined David at Ziklag (vv.1-22) and who attended his coronation at Hebron (vv.23-40). Read 1 Samuel 27 and 2 Samuel 5 in this connection. Although individuals are named in the chapter, there is a particular emphasis on groups of people. The whole chapter is devoted to **warfare.** Here are some suggestions for further study.

1) Some general expressions
a) "Helpers of the **war**" (v.1). This emphasises that it wasn't a case of "going it alone." No man did it all himself: he was "a helper" in an overall enterprise.
b) "Men of **war**" (vv.8,38). This emphasises the outstanding characteristic of these men: they were fighters.
c) "Ready armed to the **war**" (vv.23-24). This emphasises, as stated, their readiness for battle.
d) "Mighty men of valour for the **war**" (v.25). This emphasises, as stated, their bravery.
e) "Expert in **war**" (vv.33,36). This emphasises that they were seasoned warriors, and you don't become one of those without experience. "Expert in war" in v.36 evidently has the same meaning as "keeping rank' (v.33) see JND.

f) "All instruments (weapons) of **war**" (vv.33,37). This emphasises that they were equipped and well-armed.

2) *Some particular expressions*
a) "Armed with bows, and could use both the right hand and the left in hurling stones and shooting arrows out of a bow" (v.2). Paul speaks about "the armour of righteousness on the right hand and on the left" (2 Cor 6.7). These men were strong all round!
b) "Men of war fit for the battle, that could handle shield and buckler" (v.8). The "buckler" was a small shield. So they were good at defence.
c) "Whose faces were like the faces of lions, and were as swift as the roes (gazelles) upon the mountains" (v.8). The former indicates that they meant business: they were no "soft touch!" The lion is known for his strength: see 2 Samuel 1.23. The latter indicates their mobility: they were both quick and sure-footed.
d) "Then the Spirit came upon Amasai, who was chief of the captains, and he said, Thine are we, David, and on thy side, thou son of Jesse: peace, peace be unto thee, and peace be to thine helpers; for thy God helpeth thee. Then David received them, and made them captains of the band" (v.18). David was only interested in committed men with genuine motives.
e) "For at that time day by day there came to David to help him, until it was a great host, like the host of God" (v.22). So help kept on coming. God's help is like that: it comes day by day.
f) "Men that had understanding of the times, to know what Israel ought to do" (v.32). That is, men with the ability to use discernment: men who could assess a situation, and give good advice. It's therefore not surprising that "all their brethren were at their command." Who wouldn't follow men like that?!
g) "Fifty thousand which could keep rank" (v.33). See also v.38, "keeping rank in battle array"(JND). The reason why they could "keep rank" is because "they were not of double heart" (v.33). "Keeping rank without double heart" (JND). See James 1.8, "A double minded man is unstable in all his ways."
h) "Not of double heart" (v.33). There was no heart trouble amongst David's men. They had "a perfect heart" (v.38), and "one heart to make David king" (v.38).

Plenty to think about here!

CHAPTER 24.1-25

"I have done very foolishly"

The books of Samuel commence and conclude with sacrifice (1 Sam 1.3; 2 Sam 24.25), but whilst 2 Samuel ends with an altar on one of the most significant sites in the Bible, the events leading to the purchase of the site make solemn reading. It is sobering to remember that the tragedy took place right at the end of David's life. Old age does not bring immunity from failure. Just think about Solomon! "It came to pass, when Solomon was **old,** that his wives turned away his heart after other gods" (1 Kings 11.4).

The chapter, which must be read in conjunction with 1 Chronicles 21.1-30, can be analysed in the following way: *(1)* The census by David (vv.1-9); *(2)* The choice by David (vv.10-17); *(3)* The cost to David (vv.18-25): or, if you want an alternative, numbering the people, choosing the judgment, and building the altar.

1) THE CENSUS BY DAVID, vv.1-9
At least three things should be noticed here *(a)* The anger of the Lord (vv.1-2); *(b)* The objection of Joab (v.3); *(c)* The insistence of David (vv.4-9).

a) The anger of the Lord, vv.1-2
"And again the anger of the Lord was kindled against Israel, and he moved David against them to say, Go, number Israel and Judah. For the king said to Joab the captain of the host, which was with him, Go now through all the tribes of Israel, from Dan even to Beer-sheba, and number ye the people, that I may know the number of the people". It is usually suggested, with good reason, that this was not a general census, but an assessment of David's military strength. This is confirmed by the expression "eight hundred thousand valiant men that drew the sword" (v.9). See also 1 Chron 21.5). Bearing in mind that chapters 21-24 form an appendix to the book, the words "and **again** the anger of the Lord was kindled against Israel" evidently

refer to His anger in connection with the death of the Gibeonites (21.1-14). In both cases, as we shall see, the entire nation suffered. Compare 21.14 ("And after that God was intreated for the land") and 24.25 ("So the Lord was intreated for the land, and the plague was stayed from Israel").

i) The reason for the Lord's anger. It was "kindled against **Israel**". Not, in the first case, against David personally. Whilst various suggestions have been made, no specific explanation is given. Keil & Delitzsch admit as much, but add, "we may seek for it generally in the rebellions of Absalom and Sheba against the divinely established government of David". This is an attractive explanation, but it is dangerous to make assumptions without solid facts. Other commentators suggest that "the anger of the Lord was kindled against Israel" because a census was taken without collecting the atonement money required in Exodus 30.11-16 ("When thou takest the sum of the children of Israel after their number, then shall they give every man a ransom for his soul unto the Lord, when thou numberest them; that there be no plague among them, when thou numberest them", v.12), but there is not the slightest hint here that this was the reason. In any case, the Lord's anger was expressed ***before*** the census was taken.

There seems to be far more mileage in the suggestion that the nation had become proud and self-confident. Once again, this is not specifically stated, but Joab certainly thought that it was true of David himself (see v.3), and it certainly seems possible that this was shared by Israel. A. McShane is well worth quoting here: "Once man takes the glory to himself, then the Lord has to show him his helplessness and nothingness. The devil fell by pride, and he knows that the most successful way to bring any testimony to ruins is to fill it with inflated thoughts about itself. The inseparable link between those who rule and those under rule, which is manifested in this passage, may seem to us somewhat confounding, for on the one hand it was David's sin, yet, on the other the people had also sinned. Pride is infectious and can readily spread." This does appear to be the best of the available suggestions. Pride heads the list of the seven things that the Lord hates (Prov 6.16). A. McShane adds: "Possibly there is more danger from pride in old-age than in youthful days. Looking back on the successes of life, and the changes for the better which have been made, can easily tempt one to feel a sense of importance."

ii) The occasion of the Lord's anger. "He moved David against them to say, Go, number Israel and Judah". It is now most important to consult the parallel passage: "And Satan stood up against Israel, and provoked David to number Israel" (1 Chron 21.1). This does not mean that the words, "he moved David against them", refer to Satan. It was the Lord Himself who "moved David against them." This does not mean either that 2 Samuel 24 and 1 Chronicles 21 are in contention. Both statements are absolutely correct. God was the **ultimate** cause in prompting David to number Israel, but Satan was the **instrumental** cause. In other words, God used Satan's animosity against Israel to deal with their sin. This is exactly what happened in the case of Job. Elihu pointed out that God acts to "withdraw man from his purpose, and hide pride from man" (Job 33.17) and it is striking to notice that once Satan had served God's purpose (Job 1-2), we hear no more of him in the rest of the book. In the same way, God allowed "the messenger of Satan" to "buffet" Paul, in order that he should not be "exalted above measure through the abundance of the revelations" (2 Cor 12.7). Satan appeared to have gained a major victory in preventing Paul from revisiting Thessalonica (1 Thess 2.18), but this only resulted in two wonderful New Testament letters! God knew exactly what He was doing in allowing Satan to attack Paul's health (2 Cor 12.7), and hinder his movements (1 Thess 2.18).

To sum up: God allowed Satan to appeal to David's pride in his achievements in order to judge Israel's sin. It is very important to remember that judgment did not fall on Israel because of David's sin, although he was guilty, but because of their own sin.

We cannot let this pass without noticing Satan's animosity against Israel: "And Satan stood up against Israel" (1 Chron 21.1). Satan hates Israel for the simple reason that they are God's people. The Scriptures make this very clear. See, for example, Zechariah 3.1, "And he shewed me Joshua the high priest standing before the angel of the Lord, and Satan standing at his right hand to resist him"; Revelation 12.13-17 "And when the dragon saw that he was cast unto the earth, he persecuted the woman which brought forth the man child…And the dragon was wroth with the woman, and went to make war with the remnant of her seed, which keep the commandments of God, and have the testimony of Jesus Christ". We should not be surprised at the level of anti-semitism in the world today. It will increase.

b) The objection of Joab (v.3)
"And Joab said unto the king, Now the Lord thy God add unto the people,

how many soever they be, an hundredfold, and that the eyes of my lord the king may see it; but why doth my lord the king **delight** in this thing?" That's a pretty good indication of David's pride! Compare 1 Chronicles 16.3, "The Lord make his people an hundred times so many more as they be: but, my lord the king, are they not all my lord's servants? Why then doth my lord require this thing? why should he be a cause of trespass to Israel?" There is an interesting comment on this in 1 Chronicles 27.23, "But David took not the number of them from twenty years old and under: because the Lord had said he would increase Israel like to the stars of the heavens". As A. McShane observes, "Had he forgotten his own words, 'There is no king saved by the multitude of a host' (Ps 3.16), and that in most of his exploits he was delivered in spite of being outnumbered by his opponents?" What was a "delight" to David was "abominable" to Joab (1 Chron 21.16).

There was nothing wrong in taking a census, always provided that it was taken at God's command. See, for example, Numbers 1.1-2, 3.16, 26.1-2. In this particular case, the motive was entirely wrong and Joab remonstrated with David, but to no avail. There are important lessons for us here. They are well expressed in Jeremiah 9.23-24, "Thus saith the Lord, Let not the wise man glory in his wisdom, neither let the mighty man glory in his might, let not the rich man glory in his riches: but let him that glorieth glory in this, that he understandeth and knoweth me, that I am the Lord which exercise lovingkindness, judgment, and righteousness in the earth: for in these things I delight, saith the Lord". Paul cites this passage in 1 Corinthians 1.31 in warning the church against spiritual pride. An assembly which becomes proud of its history, or its numbers, or its teaching, or its orthodoxy, is "riding for a fall". "He that glorieth, let him glory in the Lord".

c) The insistence of David (vv.4-9)
"Notwithstanding the king's word prevailed against Joab, and against the captains of the host. And Joab and the captains of the host went out from the presence of the king, to number the people of Israel" (v.4).

i) The places. Joab and his colleagues travelled **eastwards** ("over Jordan"): Gad and Gilead are mentioned (vv.5-6). They then turned **northwards** and travelled as far as Dan-jaan, which was probably the extreme north-eastern boundary of David's kingdom, and on to Zidon (Sidon) which was probably the extreme north-western boundary (v.6). Tahtim-hodshi gives the translators a headache, and we must leave it there! They then turned **southwards**, and travelled via Tyre and "all the cities of the Hivites, and of the Canaanites" to "the south of Judah, even to Beer-sheba" (v.7). According to Keil & Delitzsch, "all the cities of the Hivites, and of the Canaanites" refers to the "towns in the tribes of Naphtali, Zebulun, and Issachar...in which the Canaanites had not been exterminated by the Israelites, but had been only made tributary". This all took "nine months and twenty days" (v.8).

ii) The totals. "And Joab gave up the sum of the number of the people unto the king: and there were in Israel eight hundred thousand valiant men that drew the sword; and the men of Judah were five hundred thousand men" (v.9). Now we have a problem. According to 1 Chronicles 21.5, "And all they of Israel were a thousand thousand and an hundred thousand men that drew sword: and Judah was four hundred threescore and ten thousand men that drew sword". As F. Gardiner (Ellicott's Commentary) rightly observes, "there is no reason to suppose any corruption of the text in either case." This is very important: it is all too easy to assume that the text has been corrupted when we can't understand what it means! Quite obviously, the two sets of figures include or exclude different groups of people. Joab undertook the work unwillingly, and performed it imperfectly. According to 1 Chronicles 21.6, he refused altogether to number Levi and Benjamin; and according to 1 Chronicles 27.24, he "began to number, but he finished not", and no official record was made of the result: "neither was the number put in the account of the chronicles of king David". In the case of Israel, the number given in 1 Chronicles 21 exceeds the number given in 2 Samuel 24 by 300,000. Possibly therefore the total of 1,100,000 includes an estimate of the omitted tribes of Levi and Benjamin, although it is unlikely that Levi would be included in any case. On the other hand, it has been suggested that the figure of 1,100,000 could have included the regular army of 288,000, comprising twelve divisions of 24,000 each. See 1 Chronicles 27.1-15. This still leaves a difference of 12,000. Possibly this represents people from Sidon, Tyre and "the cities of the Hivites, and of the Canaanites" (vv.6-7). J. Baldwin suggests that since David included these cities as part of his empire, he therefore expected them to provide soldiers for his army. In the case of Judah, the number given in 2 Samuel 24 exceeds the number given in 1 Chronicles 21 by 30,000, and it is difficult to give a satisfactory explanation of this difference, although 2 Samuel 24.9 does not actually say that they "drew the sword". Perhaps 30,000 of them were not fighting men. We do not have all the relevant facts, but we do know that God's word is not self-contradictory.

2) The Choice by David (vv.10-17)

This part of the chapter, in which David has to choose one of three alternative methods of judgment (vv.12-13), begins and ends with confession: "I have sinned greatly…I have done very foolishly" (v.10); "I have sinned, and I have done wickedly" (v.17). The intervening verses deal with the choice of judgment (vv.11-14), the course of judgment (v.15) and the conclusion of judgment (v.16).

a) The confession of sin (v.10)

"And David's heart smote him after that he had numbered the people. And David said unto the Lord, I have sinned greatly in that I have done: and now, I beseech thee, O Lord, take away the iniquity of thy servant; for I have done very foolishly". For the second time we read that "David's heart smote him." Compare 1 Samuel 24.5. Do notice that David's conscience was awakened without the need for outside intervention, and that he immediately confessed his sin to God. There was no need for Nathan to visit him on this occasion. Compare 2 Samuel 11.1-14. This is very important. Sin in our lives must be dealt with immediately, including the sin of pride. Failure to confess sin will impair our fellowship with God. David knew this from bitter experience: "When I kept silence, my bones waxed old through my roaring all the day long. For day and night thy hand was heavy upon me: my moisture is turned into the drought of summer. Selah. I acknowledged my sin unto thee, and mine iniquity have I not hid. I said, I will confess my transgressions unto the Lord; and thou forgavest the iniquity of my sin. Selah" (Ps 32.3-5). We can now understand why the Psalm commences with the words, "Blessed is he whose transgression is forgiven, whose sin is covered" (v.1). The lesson is so clear: we must confess our sins and failures to God immediately, knowing that "if we confess our sins, he is faithful and just to forgive us our sins, and to cleanse us from all unrighteousness" (1 Jn 1.9). See also Proverbs 28.13, "He that covereth his sins shall not prosper: but whoso confesseth and forsaketh them shall have mercy." However, in this case, David's confession and prayer was not the end of the matter.

b) The choice of judgment (vv.11-14)

Things happened rapidly. "For when David was up in the morning ('And when David arose in the morning', JND), the word of the Lord came unto the prophet Gad, David's seer, saying, Go and say unto David, Thus saith the Lord, I offer thee three things; choose thee one of them that I may do it unto thee" (vv.11-12). We last met Gad in 1 Samuel 22.5 when he advised David to leave the cave of Adullam during his fugitive years. Gad was one of three historians who covered the life of David (1 Chron 29.29). He is called "the king's seer" in 2 Chronicles 29.25. (Do read the whole verse: it is most illuminating). The very fact that David was allowed to choose the form of judgment reflects God's mercy, and this flows through the chapter.

David did not express any resentment over the message. He evidently accepted the fact that judgment must come. We must remember that forgiveness is not always an escape route from divine judgment. The eternal security of the believer is never in question. The Lord Jesus said, "He that heareth my word, and believeth on him that sent me, hath everlasting life, and shall **not** come into condemnation (judgment); but **is** passed from death unto life" (Jn 5.24). But this does not mean that there are no consequences if we sin. David was forgiven after confessing his sin against Uriah, but he did not escape the consequences. They followed him to his deathbed (2 Kings 1.5). As we have seen, David was evidently very proud of his military strength ("why doth my lord the king **delight** in this thing?" v.3), and placed his confidence there rather than in the Lord. It also seems that the nation was guilty in the same way: "the anger of the Lord was kindled against **Israel"** (v.1). The Lord therefore determined to punish the pride of David and the nation by reducing their number either by famine, war, or pestilence. It is worth noticing "thy land" (v.13). The very land in which David delighted for the wrong reasons would be overtaken by tragedy.

In his dilemma, David chose the last of the three alternatives: ("seven years of famine", "three months" flight from his enemies, or "three days' pestilence", v.13) with the explanation: "let us fall now into the hand of the Lord; for his mercies are great: and let me not fall into the hand of man" (v.14). He had great confidence in the "hand of man" before (v.3). Whilst his decision involved the shortest period of time, this did not necessarily mean the least possible degree of judgment. David knew that he could depend "on the Lord's mercy, which he had learnt to trust (Ps 40.11), as opposed to man's humanity, which he had reason to distrust" (J. Baldwin). As we shall see, David was not mistaken (v.16). Keil & Delitzsch point out that although it is not easy to see how David's decision applied to famine, he was probably thinking of the fact that famine creates "dependence upon those who are still in possession of the means of life".

c) The course of judgment (v.15)
"So the Lord sent a pestilence upon Israel from the morning (presumably the morning of Gad's visit, v.11) even to the time appointed: and there died

of the people from Dan (in the north) to Beer-sheba (in the south) seventy thousand men". At first glance, the words "even to the time appointed" do seem to suggest the entire period of the "three days' pestilence." But there is a very strong suggestion this was not the case, which brings us to:

d) The conclusion of judgment (v.16)

"And when the angel stretched out his hand upon Jerusalem to destroy it, the Lord repented him of the evil, and said to the angel that destroyed the people, It is enough: stay now thine hand" (v.16). Keil & Delitzsch conclude on grammatical grounds that "the time appointed" refers to the evening sacrifice on the first of the three days. Whether or not this was the case, and we have to leave the technical arguments to the experts, it does seem that in His wrath, God remembered mercy. See Habakkuk 3.2. David was right in saying "his mercies are great" (v.14). We can **all** say, "It is of the Lord's mercies that we are not consumed, because his compassions fail not. They are new every morning: great is thy faithfulness" (Lam 3.22-23). Was "the angel that destroyed the people" also employed as "the destroyer" in Egypt? (Ex 12.23). We can only conclude that God must judge sin wherever it occurs: even amongst His people. As we shall see, the angel was standing over mount Moriah when he was commanded to sheath his sword (1 Chron 21.16). The actual place is called here "the threshingplace of Araunah the Jebusite." Presumably, David was in Jerusalem at the time and saw the angel approaching over mount Moriah.

e) Confession of sin (v.17)

"And David spake unto the Lord when he saw the angel that smote the people, and said, Lo, I have sinned, and I have done wickedly: but these sheep, what have they done? let thine hand, I pray thee, be against me, and against my father's house." Further details are given in 1 Chronicles 21.16-17. The angel was evidently visible, and this ensured that everybody realised that this was not a natural plague. Whilst divine judgment had not fallen on Israel solely because of David's sin, he assumed full responsibility for the welfare of his people. He never lost his shepherd heart. See 1 Samuel 16.11, Psalm 78.70-72. It is all too easy to blame other people when things go wrong. Nehemiah (Neh 1.6-7) and Daniel (Dan 9.4-6,20) certainly didn't disassociate themselves from Israel's sin. There is an interesting correspondence between David and Paul here-see Romans 9.1-3.

3) The Cost to David (vv.18-25)

Divine judgment on Israel was met by an altar (vv.21,25), and we should notice at least three things here: *(a)* the obedience of David (vv.18-19); *(b)* the purchase of the threshingfloor (vv.20-24); *(c)* the site of the altar (v.25).

a) The obedience of David (vv.18-19)
"And Gad came that day to David, and said unto him, Go up, rear an altar unto the Lord in the threshingfloor of Araunah the Jebusite. And David, according to the saying of Gad, went up as the Lord commanded. " "The saying of Gad" was nothing less than the commandment of the Lord." Compare 1 Corinthians 14.37: "If any man think himself to be a prophet, or spiritual, let him acknowledge that the things that I write unto you are the commandments of the Lord." On the other hand, we must beware of people who teach "for doctrines the commandments of men" (Mt 15.9). David "went up as the Lord commanded." We cannot stress too frequently that the secret of spiritual progress is simple obedience to God's word: "Hath the Lord as great delight in burnt-offerings and sacrifices, as in obeying the voice of the Lord? Behold, to obey is better than sacrifice, and to hearken than the fat of rams" (1 Sam 15.22).

b) The purchase of the threshingfloor (vv.20-24)
J. Baldwin describes Araunah (he is called Ornan in 1 Chronicles 21.15) as "evidently one of the well-known landowners remaining in the vicinity of Jerusalem after David's capture of the city". Araunah was in a difficult bargaining position. The deal had to be struck as quickly as possible. It was a question of life or death (v.21). He was also obviously negotiating with the king! Although he offered for nothing all that David requested and more, there can be little doubt that he did not expect to be taken at his word. His approach is usually compared with the bargaining stance of Ephron the Hittite (see Gen 23.7-17), who casually mentioned the sum he expected (v.15) despite the fact that he had originally offered the site to Abraham for nothing (v.11). David's words are memorable: "Nay; but I will surely buy it of thee at a price ("for the *full* price", 1 Chronicles 21.24).neither will I offer burnt-offerings unto the Lord my God of that which doth cost me nothing" (v.24). This is still a valid principle. God values the sacrificial stewardship of His people. The Macedonian believers are a case in point (2 Cor 8.1-5). The Lord Jesus paid the "full price" in meeting God's wrath against sin.

Do beware of commentators who say that because David paid "fifty shekels of silver" (v24), but according to 1 Chronicles 21.25 he paid 'six hundred shekels of gold', no other course is left, therefore, than to assume that the number must be corrupt in one of the texts". Shame on Keil & Delitzsch who are generally so helpful! C. I .Scofield gives the correct answer here: "2 Samuel 24 records the price of the **threshingfloor** (Heb. *goren*); 1 Chronicles 21.25 of the **place** (Heb. *magom*, literally "home" as in 1 Sam 2.20) or area on which afterward the great temple, with its spacious courts, was built (2 Chron 3.1). David gave fifty shekels of silver for the *goren*; six hundred shekels of gold for the *magom*."

c) The site of the altar (v.25)

"Just as the altar and sacrifice stayed the hand of judgment, so the only resort for failing saints today is to return in true repentance to the Cross, and value afresh the one sacrifice for sin" (A. McShane). The chapter demonstrates that "God resisteth the proud, but giveth grace unto the humble" (Jas 4.6).

In our introduction, we called it "one of the most significant sites in the Bible". Araunah's threshingfloor stood on mount Moriah. "Then Solomon began to build the house of the Lord at Jerusalem in mount Moriah, where the Lord appeared unto David his father, in the place that David had prepared in the threshingfloor of Ornan the Jebusite" (2 Chron 3.1). So the site was the place where a son was offered (Genesis 22.2), where judgment was averted (2 Samuel 24.25): further details are given in 1 Chronicles 21.26-28) and where praise and worship were offered to the Lord (2 Chronicles 5.11-14).

Need we say more?

244